Shelby Foote

THE CIVIL WAR

A NARRATIVE

Shelby Foote

THE CIVIL WAR

A NARRATIVE

1

★ ★ ★

SECESSION TO FORT HENRY

40th Anniversary Edition

BY SHELBY FOOTE
AND THE EDITORS OF TIME-LIFE BOOKS,
ALEXANDRIA, VIRGINIA

All these were honoured in their generations,
and were the glory of their times.

There be of them,
that have left a name behind them,
that their praises might be reported.

And some there be, which have no memorial;
who are perished, as though they had never been;
and are become as though they had never been born;
and their children after them.

But these were merciful men,
whose righteousness hath not been forgotten.

With their seed shall continually remain
a good inheritance,
and their children are within the covenant.

Their seed standeth fast,
and their children for their sakes.

Their seed shall remain for ever,
and their glory shall not be blotted out.

Their bodies are buried in peace;
but their name liveth for evermore.

— ECCLESIASTICUS XLIV

Contents

★ ★ ★

★

Introduction

★ ★ ★ **A**ll this — companioned now, for the first time, with colored maps and a host of period photographs and drawings — began in the spring of 1954 when I received a letter from Bennett Cerf, proprietor of Random House, asking if I'd be interested in writing "A Short History of the Civil War." The single volume he had in mind was intended to be one in a sequence of works on American history. A similar series was enjoying enviable success at the time. Moreover, the vaunted Civil War Centennial already was glimmering on the horizon, beckoning publishers and literary agents and authors all across what one of that war's leading generals called "the fair, broad, abounding land."

I had just moved to Memphis from my lifelong home in the Mississippi Delta, where, on the eve of my thirty-seventh birthday, I had recently finished the fifth of five novels in as many years. It really wasn't much of a move: Memphis has always been the capital of the Delta, even though it lies about a dozen miles north of the Tennessee line. In fact, there scarcely had been a season of my life that I hadn't visited there, aside, that is, from college and five years during the war. ("The War," in my part of the country, means the one you served in — in my case, World War II — or the Civil War, the former mostly while it was ongoing and the latter unremittingly down the years since it began in 1861.)

Mr Cerf's offer had its attractions. For one thing, I had been fascinated by the subject from the start, reading first-hand accounts of that cataclysmic struggle, along with the wayward adventures of Tom Swift and Tarzan, before I entered my teens. One memory I treasure, from about the age of ten, was a visit to an old soldiers' home at Jefferson Davis' post-war residence, Beauvoir, down on the Gulf coast, where I saw perhaps half a dozen Confederate survivors. Those septuagenarian graybeards scarcely could have been more than drummer boys when, and if, they passed through their baptism of fire at about the same age as the awed young fellow who stood before them. I remember clearly that they had a sort of cackling merriment which I never forgot, and often used, when writing about them afterwards. For example, I have heard that on another visitors' day, two ladies stopped in front of a veteran who was seated because he had undergone the amputation of one of his legs in the conflict. "Oh, you poor man," one of the ladies remarked with long-faced compassion, looking down at the protruding stump, "you've lost your leg." He too looked down, but with feigned surprise. "Damned if I haven't!" he exclaimed. . . . They were like that, and the world was poorer when the last of them died, over in

Texas, soon after I first sat down to write about them at Mr Cerf's suggestion.

The other attraction, along of course with the immediate need for making at least the semblance of a living, was that I considered those five novels a consolidated block, and I wanted a pause, a time for coasting, for summing up and looking forward to what substance and form the next group of novels was to take. So I rode up to New York, talked it over with Mr Cerf and my agent, and signed the contract for the "Short History." It was to run roughly twice my normal annual output. But to show you how little I knew about the writing of history — after all, the facts were there; all I'd have to do was look them up and put them down — I reckoned I could write about twice as much history a year as I'd been doing fiction. Fiction was hard work, as I knew only too well from having done it; whereas history, well, there's not much to that, I told myself. Then I came home to Memphis and set out.

I began with some remedial reading, working at the same time, as I have always done, on an outline. Like a dancer preparing to do a dance, I wanted a solid platform to perform on, one I wouldn't worry about collapsing in case I took a notion to try a somersault or a high kick. But alas, I found within no more than a week or two that it just plain wouldn't do. There was just so much *of* it, all of it near my heart, and I saw that I would never be satisfied with concocting a highpoint summary of a drama that filled so large a space in my background. Far from coasting, I'd be fretting and cursing my fate throughout the year the book would keep me away from the novels I intended to get back to. In fact, I now perceived that I'd do better not to undertake it.

Still, I stayed with the reading and the outlining, and presently it began to open out for me. There was no denying it. I was hooked, and had been ever since I encountered those old codgers down at Beauvoir, a generation back, and by the books I'd read, Federal and Confederate, over the years. Somewhat daunted, if not dismayed, I went ahead and fleshed out the sketch of what I now knew would fill three volumes and require some six or seven years to complete. I sent my plan up to Random House, explaining what I now had in mind. I don't know how many meetings were held or who said what, but after ten days or so a letter came back, more or less saying, "Fine; much better that way; go ahead." So I did; for twenty years.

Once more, though, I had made grievous underestimations both of time and space. When finished, my text would run more than seven times longer than the originally proposed book, and the six or seven years of my new plan expanded to three times that span. In part this was because I now discovered, despite all the reading and the study that had gone before, there was much about the war that I had never explored or even suspected. I found reports of marginal but critical campaigns and scholarly studies of them, together with fugitive biographies of the men who designed and fought them, that swelled my reading list and increased my understanding. The source materials grew in ratio to the drawn-out search for information.

Moreover, my work habits did not change to match this sudden shift of fields. As I had done with the preceding novels, wanting nothing mechanical between me and the paper I was writing on — not even a fountain pen, let alone a typewriter — I used a dip pen and an inkwell. This anachronistic practice made me take my time, which was why I adopted it in the first place. Thus, I would never *write* fast; my very method precluded that — five hundred words was a decent day and a thousand was phenomenal — with the result that I sometimes felt as if I was using a teacup to bail out the Mississippi, which flowed directly under my blufftop window all through the writing of the first book. After four years of bailing, that volume was published in 1958 — forty years ago.

One thing I knew from the start, even before I took that ringside seat overlooking the aortic Mississippi, though I did not get around to putting it into words until I was well past Appomattox: "Any understanding of this nation has to be based, and I mean really based, on an understanding of the Civil War. I believe that firmly. It defined us. The Revolution did what it did. Our involvement in European wars, beginning with the First World War, did what it did. But the Civil War defined us as what we are and it opened us to being what we became, good and bad things. And it is very necessary, if you're going to understand the American Character in the twentieth century, to learn about this enormous catastrophe in the nineteenth century. It was the crossroads of our being, and it was a hell of a crossroads." Knowing this, I knew too the grave responsibility — not to mention presumptuousness — of undertaking to describe and sometimes even sit in judgment on the events and men involved in this blood-drenched contention. That was part of my decision to go all out, spread-eagle; to do the job full-scale or not at all. I saw that, for me, it would well be worth everything I had to give it.

Here again there was still another attraction — in this case an aesthetic, even a literary, one. For present-day Americans, the Civil War is what the Trojan War was for the Greeks who came after it, and I think it can be written about any number of times by any number of writers, in part or as a whole, much as the Greek dramatists did in their turn, some 2500 years ago, when they dipped into the *Iliad*. As a novelist, once my thoughts were focused in that direction, I fairly jumped at the chance; not, as you might have expected, to turn out a historical novel, but to try my hand at full-blown hard-fact history, which seemed to me not to have to be all that different, except that the material would come from researched documents rather than from memory or imagination. An honest novelist is as true to his "facts," once he has established them in his mind and conscience, as an honest historian is to the facts he gathers from sources he considers sound. Both are after the truth underlying the facts, a truth that can only emerge when the breath of life is breathed into the subject under the writer's hand. John Keats said it best, about two hundred years ago: "A fact is not a truth until you love it."

Moreover, there is the truth that emerges when order is imposed on facts by a process known as plotting. In fiction this is invented; in history it is discovered. It is there; all you have to do is find it. Events set down in parallel chronological columns—as I did on outsized poster boards for Lincoln and Davis, the Eastern and Western and Transmississippi theaters, politics and diplomacy—take on a shape of their own in their interactions. This is what is called a plot, the force that makes a book move under its own power. Strangely enough, or perhaps not strangely at all, this never failed to occur. Events and characters intertwined; all I had to do was look and listen. God is the greatest dramatist, by far.

I soon found myself engaged in a mammoth exercise in the handling of multiple plot, combined with a start-to-finish attempt at large-scale precision. It was here that my apprenticeship as a novelist, together with my study of the masters of that art, served me best. Gibbon learned from Fielding, much as Thucydides had from Euripides, and that in part is why I credit Mark Twain and William Faulkner—along with Homer and Marcel Proust—among the writers to whom I was most indebted for their assistance in facing the problem, defined so eloquently by John Keegan, of combining "the authority of academic discipline" with "the aesthetic freedom of genuine literature." The notion that I was engaged in an effort to meet this challenge brought me what is surely among the greatest pleasures a writer can know: the pleasure, that is, of putting his head on the pillow at night with the happy anticipation of getting back to his desk and his work next morning.

Much else drew me, of course, and high among the things that did was the wonderment of being in the company of U. S. Grant and R. E. Lee, Tecumseh Sherman and Stonewall Jackson, Phil Sheridan and Jeb Stuart, George Thomas and Bedford Forrest, John Reynolds and Pat Cleburne, David Farragut and Raphael Semmes, along with many others, all the way up to Abraham Lincoln and Jefferson Davis. What novelist or playwright could muster such a cast of characters? Nor was it only the upright who livened the scene. Edwin Stanton, for instance—a scoundrel if ever there was one, though he was a highly effective Secretary of War—also contributed to the overall effect; I rejoiced whenever he happened along, much I suppose as Dickens did when Bill Sikes or Uriah Heep appeared. Brave men and cowards, heroes and villains, quiet men and blowhards, all played their roles, and for the most part played them well. I had photo portraits of them mounted on an outsized sheet of beaverboard tacked to the wall beside my desk, and thus from time to time, with a quarter-circle turn of my chair, could look them in the eye as they stood or sat before me, seemingly in hope of returning to life if only I could summon them up with a wave of my inkpen wand. I don't suppose I ever accomplished that Lazarus feat, but I did come to know them intimately, and I shared the sadness of their men when they fell, as so many of them did, in the fire and smoke of battle.

The era in which it was written also helped shape the composition of this narrative. The time and place a historian looks back from has a lot to do with the way he sees what he's looking back at. Certainly this applied in my case. That first year of the total twenty of writing, 1954, was momentous in a number of instances that influenced my view of the way things had been, some ninety-odd years before. The French pulled out of Dien Bien Phu, the Senate defanged McCarthy, and the Supreme Court handed down its *Brown* decision, all resonant of the subject under my hand and contributory to my understanding of the reactions of the people involved. Moreover, such resonances continued and multiplied, especially in the civil rights struggle and the war in Vietnam and the protest marches and demonstrations. On down the line, the reaction to the assassination of John Kennedy gave me at least a notion of the nation's grief and anger when Booth's derringer interrupted the laughter in Ford's Theater, less than a week after Appomattox.

In this connection, throughout that compositional span, conditions that were close to intolerable for others were sometimes downright beneficial to me in my work. For example, such bias as I might have been supposed to harbor (after all, my great-grandfather commanded the Noxubee Cavalry at Shiloh, where the only significant contribution he made to Sidney Johnston's comeback effort was getting the tail shot off his horse) was considerably reduced by what was going on around me in the Deep South, particularly on the part of George Wallace, Ross Barnett, and Orval Faubus, governors respectively of Alabama, Mississippi, and Arkansas. They served a corrective purpose and I said so at the time. At the end of my second volume I expressed my gratitude to them "for helping to lessen my sectional bias by reproducing in their actions . . . much that was least admirable in the position my forebears occupied when they stood up to Lincoln. I suppose, or at any rate fervently hope, it is true that history never repeats itself, but I know from watching these three gentlemen that it can be terrifying in its approximations." Publication of that second volume was November 18, 1963. Four days later, down in Dallas, Lee Harvey Oswald turned me into a reluctant prophet.

By then I was ten years into the project. Not yet aware that I was only at the midpoint of the time between conception and completion, I took a year off, half in Washington, on a Ford Foundation grant, the other half on the Alabama coast, intending to build a house on the white sand beach, until I gave up the notion — threats of hurricanes and the Klan were contributory factors — and returned to Memphis to undertake a last long march toward victory and defeat.

It was as if I'd never been away. The war was still raging: Banks and

Taylor were scrabbling up and down Red River, Grant and Lee were at each other's throats in the Wilderness, and Sherman and Joe Johnston were performing their North Georgia minuet. Now as before, I held to my conviction that the closer a writer comes to the truth — poet or playwright, novelist or historian — the better the work will be, provided he doesn't entertain the notion that facts alone can communicate the truth. This is no plea for irresponsible elaboration, let alone distortion: I have never known a modern historical instance where the truth was not superior to distortion, by any standard and in every way, and I kept this mind from the outset, quite apart from the praise or blame that came my way.

Two compliments I found welcome all the same. One was when a reader declared that he couldn't tell which side I favored in the conflict, and the other was when someone asked, in regard to some exchange or event in the text, "Did you make that up?" This last was perhaps the highest compliment of all, since in many instances the invention would have required downright genius, perhaps by the greatest dramatist Himself. I do hope, however, that I managed to measure up to, or anyhow approximate, the first of the two. Though I do confess in part to the charge, leveled by a fellow historian I respect, that my heart seemed to beat somewhat faster in the course of a Confederate victory. That might be, but I hasten to add that Americans in general tend to pull for the underdog in a fight.

On the other hand, I cannot agree with one overgenerous reviewer who remarked, after closing the final volume that he was "convinced that no one need undertake this particular enterprise again." The Civil War, that hellish crossroads, needs to be examined and re-examined for every passing generation, since it defined us as we were when it began and determined what we would be when it ended. Reinterpretations abound, and should abound; Vietnam, for example — the second war some Americans have lost — affords new angles for viewing the one that tore us apart and then reunited us, closer than ever, just over a century before.

So here you have the Fortieth Anniversary edition of my original *The Civil War: A Narrative,* now fully illustrated. In this introduction I have touched but little on the causes, events, and results of the war. You'll find them explored in considerable detail in the pages that lie ahead. Take your time. God knows I took mine.

Shelby Foote

April 1998

Shelby Foote

Presidents Abraham Lincoln and
Jefferson Davis, born a year
and about 100 miles apart, led
their opposing nations in a bitter
four-year-long struggle.

O N E

Secession: Davis and Lincoln

1861 ★ ★ ★ ★ ★ **I**t was a **Monday in Washington,** January 21; Jefferson Davis rose from his seat in the Senate. South Carolina had left the Union a month before, followed by Mississippi, Florida, and Alabama, which seceded at the rate of one a day during the second week of the new year. Georgia went out eight days later; Louisiana and Texas were poised to go; few doubted that they would, along with others. For more than a decade there had been intensive discussion as to the legality of secession, but now the argument was no longer academic. A convention had been called for the first week in February, at Montgomery, Alabama, for the purpose of forming a confederacy of the departed states, however many there should be in addition to the five already gone. As a protest against the election of Abraham Lincoln, who had received not a single southern electoral vote, secession was a fact — to be reinforced, if necessary, by the sword. The senator from Mississippi rose. It was high noon. The occasion was momentous and expected; the galleries were crowded, hoop-skirted ladies and men in broadcloth come to hear him say farewell. He was going home.

By now he was one of the acknowledged spokesmen of secession, though it had not always been so. By nature he was a moderate, with a deep devotion to the Union. He had been for compromise so long as he believed compromise was possible; he reserved secession as a last resort. Yet now they were at

★

that stage. In a paper which he had helped to draft and which he had signed and sent as advice to his state in early December, his position had been explicit. "The argument is exhausted," it declared. "All hope of relief in the Union . . . is extinguished." At last he was for disunion, with a southern confederacy to follow.

During the twelve days since the secession of Mississippi he had remained in Washington, sick in mind and body, waiting for the news to reach him officially. He hoped he might be arrested as a traitor, thereby gaining a chance to test the right of secession in the federal courts. Now the news had been given him officially the day before, a Sunday, and he stayed to say goodbye. He had never doubted the right of secession. What he doubted was its wisdom. Yet now it was no longer a question even of wisdom; it was a question of necessity — meaning Honor. On the day before Lincoln's election, Davis had struck an organ tone that brought a storm of ap-

He was dressed in neat black broadcloth, cuffless trouser-legs crumpling over his boots, the coat full-skirted with wide lapels, a satin waistcoat framing the stiff white bosom of his shirt, a black silk handkerchief wound stockwise twice around the upturned collar and knotted loosely at the throat.

plause in his home state. "I glory in Mississippi's star!" he cried. "But before I would see it dishonored I would tear it from its place, to be set on the perilous ridge of battle as a sign around which her bravest and best shall meet the harvest home of death."

Thus he had spoken in November, but now in January, rising to say farewell, his manner held more of sadness than defiance. For a long moment after he rose he struck the accustomed preliminary stance of the orators of his day: high-stomached, almost sway-backed, the knuckles of one hand braced against the desk top, the other hand raised behind him with the wrist at the small of his back. He was dressed in neat black broadcloth, cuffless trouser-legs crumpling over his boots, the coat full-skirted with wide lapels, a satin waistcoat

★

framing the stiff white bosom of his shirt, a black silk handkerchief wound stockwise twice around the upturned collar and knotted loosely at the throat. Close-shaven except for the tuft of beard at the jut of the chin, the face was built economically close to the skull, and more than anything it expressed an iron control by the brain within that skull. He had been sick for the past month and he looked it. He looked in fact like a man who had emerged from a long bout with a fever; which was what he was, except that the fever had been a generation back, when he was twenty-seven, and now he was fifty-two. Beneath the high square forehead, etched with the fine crisscross lines of pain and overwork, the eyes were deep-set, gray and stern, large and lustrous, though one was partly covered by a film, a result of the neuralgia which had racked him all those years. The nose was aquiline, finely shaped, the nostrils broad and delicately chiseled. The cheeks were deeply hollowed beneath the too-high cheekbones and above the wide, determined jaw. His voice was low, with the warmth of the Deep South in it.

"I rise, Mr President, for the purpose of announcing to the Senate that I have satisfactory evidence that the State of Mississippi, by a solemn ordinance of her people in convention assembled, has declared her separation from the United States. Under these circumstances, of course, my functions terminate here. It has seemed to me proper, however, that I should appear in the Senate to announce that fact to my associates, and I will say but very little more."

His voice faltered at the outset, but soon it gathered volume and rang clear — "like a silver trumpet," according to his wife, who sat in the gallery. "Unshed tears were in it," she added, "and a plea for peace permeated every tone." Davis continued:

"It is known to senators who have served with me here, that I have for many years advocated, as an essential attribute of State sovereignty, the right of a State to secede from the Union. . . . If I had thought that Mississippi was acting without sufficient provocation . . . I should still, under my theory of government, because of my allegiance to the State of which I am a citizen, have been bound by her action."

He foresaw the founding of a nation, inheritor of the traditions of the American Revolution. "We but tread in the paths of our fathers when we proclaim our independence and take the hazard . . . not in hostility to others, not to injure any section of the country, not even for our own pecuniary benefit, but from the high and solemn motive of defending and protecting the rights we inherited, and which it is our duty to transmit unshorn to our children." England had been a lion; the Union might turn out to be a bear; in which case, "we will invoke the God of our fathers, who delivered them from the power of the lion, to protect us from the ravages of the bear; and thus, putting our trust in God and in our own firm hearts and strong arms, we will vindicate the right as best we may."

★

Davis glanced around the chamber, then continued. "I see now around me some with whom I have served long. There have been points of collision; but whatever of offense there has been to me, I leave here. I carry with me no hostile remembrance. . . . I go hence unencumbered by the remembrance of any injury received, and having discharged the duty of making the only reparation in my power for any injury received." He then spoke the final sentence to which all the rest had served as prologue. "Mr President and Senators, having made the announcement which the occasion seemed to me to require, it remains only for me to bid you a final adieu."

★ ★ ★ **F**or a moment there was silence. Then came the ovation, the sustained thunder of applause, the flutter of handkerchiefs and hum of comment. Davis shrank from this, however, or at any rate ignored it. As he resumed his seat he lowered his head and covered his face with his hands. Some in the gallery claimed his shoulders shook; he was weeping, they said. It may have been so, though he was not given to public tears. If so, it could have been from more than present tension. His life was crowded with glory, as a soldier, as a suitor, as a statesman; yet the glory was more than balanced by personal sorrow as a man. He had known tears in his time.

He was born in Christian County, Kentucky, within a year and a hundred miles of the man whose election had brought on the present furor. Like that man, he was a log-cabin boy, the youngest of ten children whose grandfather had been born in Philadelphia in 1702, the son of an immigrant Welshman who signed his name with an X. This grandfather moved to Georgia, where he married a widow who bore him one son, Samuel. Samuel raised and led an irregular militia company in the Revolution. After the war he married and moved northwest to south-central Kentucky, where he put up his own log house, farmed six hundred acres of land by the hard agronomy of the time, and supplied himself with children, naming the sons out of the Bible — Joseph, Samuel, Benjamin, and Isaac — until the tenth child, born in early June of 1808, whom he named for the red-headed President then in office, and gave him the middle name Finis in the belief, or perhaps the hope, that he was the last; which he was.

By the time the baby Jefferson was weaned the family was on the move again, south one thousand miles to Bayou Teche, Louisiana, only to find the climate unhealthy and to move again, three hundred miles northeast to Wilkinson County, Mississippi Territory, southeast of Natchez and forty miles from the Mississippi River. Here the patriarch stopped, for he prospered; he did not move again, and here Jefferson spent his early childhood.

The crop now was cotton, and though Samuel Davis had slaves, he was his own overseer, working alongside them in the field. It was a farm, not a plantation; he was a farmer, not a planter. In a region where the leading men

★

were Episcopalians and Federalists, he was a Baptist and a Democrat. Now his older children were coming of age, and at their marriages he gave them what he could, one Negro slave, and that was all. The youngest, called Little Jeff, began his education when he was six. For the next fifteen years he attended one school after another, first a log schoolhouse within walking distance of home, then a Dominican institution in Kentucky, Saint Thomas Aquinas, where he was still called Little Jeff because he was the smallest pupil there. He asked to become a Roman Catholic but the priest told him to wait and learn, which he did, and either forgot or changed his mind. Then, his mother having grown lonesome for her last-born, he came home to the Mississippi schoolhouse where he had started.

*Confederate President Jefferson Davis
was born in this clapboard-sided log cabin
in Christian County, Kentucky, in 1808.*

★

He did not like it. One hot fall day he rebelled; he would not go. Very well, his father said, but he could not be idle, and sent him to the field with the work gang. Two days later Jeff was back at his desk. "The heat of the sun and the physical labor, in conjunction with the implied equality with the other cotton pickers, convinced me that school was the lesser evil." Thus he later explained his early decision to work with his head, not his hands. In continuation of this decision, just before his fourteenth birthday he left once more for Kentucky, entering Transylvania University, an excellent school, one of the few in the country to live up to a high-sounding name. Under competent professors he continued his studies in Latin and Greek and mathematics, including trigonometry, and explored the mysteries of sacred and profane history and natural philosophy — meaning chemistry and physics — with surveying and oratory thrown in for good measure. While he was there his father died and his oldest brother, Joseph, twenty-four years his senior, assumed the role of guardian.

"The heat of the sun and the physical labor, in conjunction with the implied equality with the other cotton pickers, convinced me that school was the lesser evil."

— Jefferson Davis

Not long before his death, the father had secured for his youngest son an appointment to West Point, signed by the Secretary of War, and thus for the first time the names were linked: Jefferson Davis, John C. Calhoun. Joseph Davis by now had become what his father had never been — a planter, with a planter's views, a planter's way of life. Jefferson inclined toward the University of Virginia, but Joseph persuaded him to give the Academy a try. It was in the tradition for the younger sons of prominent southern families to go there; if at the end of a year he found he did not like it he could transfer. So Davis attended West Point, and found he liked it.

Up to now he had shown no special inclination to study. Alert and affectionate, he was of a mischievous disposition, enjoyed a practical joke, and sought the admiration of his fellows rather more than the esteem of his professors. Now at the Academy he continued along this course, learning something of tavern life in the process. "O Benny Haven's, O!" he sang, linking arms and clinking tankards. He found he liked the military comradeship, the thought of unrequited death on lonely, far-off battlefields:

★

"To our comrades who have fallen, one cup before we go;

They poured their life-blood freely out pro bono publico.

No marble points the stranger to where they rest below;

They lie neglected — far away from Benny Haven's, O!"

Brought before a court martial for out-of-bounds drinking of "spirituous liquors," he made the defense of a strict constructionist: 1) visiting Benny Haven's was not *officially* prohibited in the regulations, and 2) malt liquors were not "spirituous" in the first place. The defense was successful; he was not dismissed, and he emerged from the scrape a stricter constructionist than ever. He also got to know his fellow cadets. Leonidas Polk was his roommate; Joseph E. Johnston was said to have been his opponent in a fist fight over a girl; along with others, he admired the open manliness of Albert Sidney Johnston, the high-born rectitude of Robert E. Lee.

Davis himself was admired, even liked. Witnesses spoke of his well-shaped head, his self-esteem, his determination and personal mastery. A "florid young fellow," he had "beautiful blue eyes, a graceful figure." In his studies he did less well, receiving his lowest marks in mathematics and deportment, his highest in rhetoric and moral philosophy, including constitutional law. But the highs could not pull up the lows. He stood well below the middle of his class, still a private at the close of his senior year, and graduated in 1828, twenty-third in a class of thirty-four.

★ ★ ★ As a second lieutenant, U.S. Army, he now began a seven-year adventure, serving in Wisconsin, Iowa, Illinois, Missouri, where he learned to fight Indians, build forts, scout, and lead a simple social existence. He had liked West Point; he found he liked this even better. Soon he proved himself a superior junior officer, quick-witted and resourceful — as when once with a few men he was chased by a band of Indians after scalps; both parties being in canoes, he improvised a sail and drew away. In a winter of deep snow he came down with pneumonia, and though he won that fight as well, his susceptibility to colds and neuralgia dated from then. He was promoted to first lieutenant within four years, and when Black Hawk was captured in 1832, Davis was appointed by his colonel, Zachary Taylor, to escort the prisoner to Jefferson Barracks.

Thus Colonel Taylor, called "Old Rough and Ready," showed his approval of Davis as a soldier. But as a son-in-law, it developed, he wanted no part of him. The lieutenant had met the colonel's daughter, sixteen-year-old Knox Taylor, brown-haired and blue-eyed like himself, though later the color of his own eyes would deepen to gray. Love came quickly, and his letters to her show a man unseen before or after. "By my dreams I have been lately almost crazed, for they were of you," he wrote to her, and also thus: "Kind, dear letter; I have kissed it often and often, and it has driven away mad notions from my brain." The girl accepted his suit, but the father did not; Taylor wanted no soldier son-in-law, apparently especially not this one. Therefore Davis, who had spent the past seven years as a man of action, proposed to challenge the colonel to a duel. Dissuaded from this, he remained a man of action still. He resigned his commission, went straight to Louisville, and married the girl. The wedding was held at the home of an aunt she was visiting. "After the service everybody cried but Davis," a witness remarked, adding that they "thought this most peculiar."

As it turned out, he was reserving his tears. The young couple did not wait to attempt a reconciliation with her father; perhaps they depended on time to accomplish this. Instead they took a steamboat south to Davis Bend, Mississippi, below Vicksburg, where Joseph Davis, the guardian elder brother, had prospered on a plantation called The Hurricane. He presented them with an adjoining 800-acre place and fourteen slaves on credit. Davis put in a cotton crop, but before the harvest time came round they were both down with fever. They were confined to separate rooms, each too sick to be told of the other's condition, though Davis managed to make it to the door of his bride's room in time to see her die. She had been a wife not quite three months, and as she died she sang snatches of "Fairy Bells," a favorite air; she had had it from her mother. Now those tears which he had not shed at the wedding came to scald his eyes. He was too sick to attend the funeral; the doctor believed he would not be long behind her.

The doctor was wrong, though Davis never lost the drawn, gaunt look of a fever convalescent. He returned to the plantation; then, finding it too crowded with recent memories, left for Cuba, thought to be a fine climate and landscape for restoring broken hearts. The sea bathing at least did his health much good, and he returned by way of New York and Washington, renewing acquaintances with old friends now on the rise and gaining some notion of how much he had missed on the frontier. Then he came home to Mississippi. He would be a planter and, at last, a student.

He found a ready tutor awaiting him. Joseph Davis had got a law degree in Kentucky, had set up practice in Natchez, and, prospering, had bought the land which in that section practically amounted to a patent of nobility. By now, in his middle fifties, he was the wealthiest planter in the state, the "leading philosopher" — whatever that meant — and the possessor of the finest library, which he gladly made available to his idolized younger brother. Davis soon had the Constitution by heart and went deeply into *Elliot's Debates,* theories of government as argued by the framers. He read John Locke and Adam Smith, *The Federalist* and the works of Thomas Jefferson. Shakespeare and Swift lent

Jefferson Davis often sought refuge at The Hurricane (left), the plantation of his guardian brother Joseph (above), some twenty-four years his senior. His own plantation, Brierfield, was not far away.

him what an orator might need of cadenced beauty and invective; Byron and Scott were there at hand, along with the best English magazines and the leading American newspapers. He read them all, and discussed them with his brother.

Also there was the plantation; Brierfield, he called it. Here too he worked and learned, making certain innovations in the labor system. The overseer was a Negro, James Pemberton. No slave was ever punished except after a formal trial by an all-Negro jury, Davis only reserving the right to temper the severity of the judgment. James was always James, never Jim; "It is disrespect to give a nickname," Davis said, and the overseer repaid him with frankness, loyalty, and efficiency. Once when something went amiss and the master asked him why, James replied: "I rather think, sir, through my neglect."

Davis gained all this from his decade of seclusion and study; but he gained something else as well. Up to now, his four years at West Point, brief and interrupted as they were, had been the longest period he had spent at any one place in his life. His school years had been various indeed, with instructors ranging from log-cabin teachers to Catholic priests and New England scholars. When a Virginian or a Carolinian spoke of his "country," he meant Virginia or Carolina. It was not so with Davis. Tennessee and Kentucky were as familiar to him as Mississippi; the whole South, as a region, formed his background; he was thirty before he knew a real home in any real sense of the word. Now at last he had this, too, though still with a feeling of being somewhat apart. Like his brother Joseph and his father before him, he was a Democrat, and while this was true of the majority of the people in his state, it was by no means true of the majority in his class, who were Federalists or Whigs.

Then history intervened for him and solved this problem too. Previously the cotton capitalists had thought their interests coincided with the interests of capitalists in general. Now anti-slavery and pro-tariff agitation was beginning to teach them otherwise. In 1844, the year when Davis emerged from seclusion, the upheaval was accomplished. Repudiating Jefferson and Jackson, the Democrats went over to the Whigs, who came to meet them, creating what Calhoun had been after from the start: a solid South. Davis caught the movement at its outset.

Before that, however, in the previous December, his brother produced one more item from the horn of plenty. He had a lawyer friend, W. B. Howell of Natchez, son of an eight-term governor of New Jersey. Howell had married a Kempe of Virginia and moved south to cotton country. Joseph Davis was an intimate of their house; their first son was named for him, and their seventeen-year-old daughter Varina called him Uncle Joe. Now he wrote to the girl's parents, inviting her to visit The Hurricane. She arrived by steamboat during the Christmas season, having just completed an education in the classics. She did not stay at The Hurricane; she stayed at his sister's plantation, fourteen miles away. Presently a horseman arrived with a message. He dismounted to give it to her, lingered briefly, then excused himself and rode off to a political meeting in Vicksburg. That night Varina wrote to her mother, giving her first impression of the horseman.

> *Today Uncle Joe sent, by his younger brother (did you know*
> *he had one?), an urgent invitation to me to go at once to The*
> *Hurricane. I do not know whether this Mr Jefferson Davis is*
> *young or old. He looks both at times; but I believe he is old, for*
> *from what I hear he is only two years younger than you are.*
> *He impresses me as a remarkable kind of man, but of uncertain*
> *temper, and has a way of taking for granted that everybody*
> *agrees with him when he expresses an opinion, which offends*
> *me; yet he is most agreeable and has a peculiarly sweet voice*
> *and a winning manner of asserting himself. The fact is, he is*
> *the kind of person I should expect to rescue one from a mad*
> *dog at any risk, but to insist upon a stoical indifference to the*
> *fright afterward. I do not think I shall ever like him as I do his*
> *brother Joe. Would you believe it, he is refined and cultivated,*
> *and yet he is a Democrat!*

This last was the principal difficulty between them. Varina was a Natchez girl, which meant not only that her background was Federalist, but also that she had led a life of gaiety quite unlike the daily round in the malarial bottoms of Davis Bend. The Christmas season was a merry one, however, and Joseph proved an excellent matchmaker, although a rather heavy-handed one. "By Jove, she is as beautiful as Venus!" he told his brother, adding: "As well as good looks, she has a mind that will fit her for any sphere that the man to whom she is married will feel proud to reach." Jefferson agreed, admiring the milk-pale skin, the raven hair, the generous mouth, the slender waist. "She is beautiful and she has a fine mind," he admitted, with some caution at the outset.

In the evenings there were readings from historians and orators, and the brothers marveled at the ease with which the girl pronounced and translated the Latin phrases and quotations that studded the texts. The conquest was nearly complete; there remained only the political difference. In the course of

Thirty-six-year-old Jefferson Davis married Varina Howell, just eighteen, in 1845. She proved a source of support throughout his tumultuous political career.

these discussions Varina wore a cameo brooch with a Whig device carved into the stone, a watchdog crouched by a strongbox. Then one day she appeared without it, and Davis knew he had won.

He left The Hurricane in late January, engaged. In February of the following year, 1845, they were married. Davis was thirty-six, Varina half that. They went to New Orleans on the wedding tour, enjoyed a fashionable Creole interlude, and returned after a few weeks to Brierfield.

★ ★ ★   **T**he house they moved into was a one-story frame twin-wing structure; Davis had planned and built it himself, with the help of James Pemberton. It had charm, but he and his young wife had little time to enjoy it. By then he had emerged from his shell in more ways than one. In 1843 he had run for the state legislature against Sergeant S. Prentiss, famous as an orator, a Whig in an overwhelmingly Whig district. Davis was defeated, though with credit and a growing reputation. The following year, taking time off from courtship, he stumped the state as an elector for James K. Polk. In the year of his marriage, Whigs and Democrats having coalesced, he was elected to Congress as representative-at-large. In Washington, his first act was to introduce a resolution that federal troops be withdrawn from federal forts, their posts to be taken by state recruits. It died in committee, and his congressional career was ended by the outbreak of the Mexican War.

Davis resigned his seat and came home to head a volunteer regiment, the Mississippi Rifles. Under the strict discipline of their West Point colonel, who saw to it that they were armed with a new model rifle, they were the crack outfit of Zachary Taylor's army, fighting bravely at Monterey and saving the day at Buena Vista, where Davis formed them in a V that broke the back of a Mexican cavalry charge and won the battle. He was wounded in the foot, came home on crutches, and at victory banquets in New Orleans and elsewhere heard himself proclaimed a military genius and the hero of the South. Hunched upon his crutches, he responded to such toasts with dignified modesty. Basically his outlook was unchanged. When Polk sent him a commission as a brigadier general of volunteers, Davis returned it promptly, remarking that the President had no authority to make such an appointment, that power inhering in the states alone. Perhaps all these honors were somewhat anticlimactic anyhow, coming as they did after the words General Taylor was supposed to have spoken to him at Buena Vista: "My daughter, sir, was a better judge of men than I was."

Honors fell thickly upon him now. Within sixty days the governor appointed him to the U.S. Senate. At a private banquet tendered before he left, he stood and heard the toasts go round: "Colonel Jeff Davis, the Game Cock of the South!" "Jeff Davis, the President of the Southern Confederacy!" Davis stood there, allowing no change of expression, no flush of emotion on his face. He took this stiffness, this coldness up to Washington and onto the floor of the Senate.

He would not unbend; he would engage in no log-rolling. In a cloakroom exchange, when he stated his case supporting a bill for removing obstructions from the river down near Vicksburg, another senator, who had his pet project too, interrupted to ask, "Will you vote for the Lake appropriations?" Davis responded: "Sir, I make no terms. I accept no compromises. If when I ask for an appropriation, the object shall be shown to be proper and the expenditure constitutional, I defy the gentleman, for his conscience' sake, to vote against it. If it shall appear to him otherwise, then I expect his opposition, and only ask that it shall be directly, fairly, and openly exerted. The case shall be presented on its single merit; on that I wish to stand or fall. I feel, sir, that I am incapable of sectional distinction upon such subjects. I abhor and reject all interested combinations." He would hammer thus at what he thought was wrong, and continue to hammer, icy cold and in measured terms, long after the opposition had been demolished, without considering the thoughts of the other man or the chance that he might be useful to him someday.

He was perhaps the best informed, probably the best educated, and certainly the most intellectual man in the Senate. Yet he too had to take his knocks. Supporting an army pay-increase bill, he remarked in passing that "a common blacksmith or tailor" could not be hired as a military engineer; whereupon Andrew Johnson of Tennessee — formerly a tailor — rose from his desk shouting that "an illegitimate, swaggering, bastard, scrub aristocracy" took much credit to itself, yet in fact had "neither talents nor information." Hot words in a Washington boarding house led to a fist fight between Davis and Henry S. Foote, his fellow senator from Mississippi. An Illinois congressman, W. H. Bissell, said in a speech that Davis's command had been a mile and a half from the blaze of battle at Buena Vista. Davis sent an immediate challenge, and Bissell, having the choice of weapons, named muskets loaded with ball and shot at fifteen paces, then went home, wrote his will, and said he would be ready in the morning. Friends intervening, Bissell explained that he had been referring to another quarter of the field and had not meant to question Davis's personal bravery anyhow; the duel was canceled. Davis made enemies in high places, as for example when he claimed that General Winfield Scott had overcharged $300 in mileage expenses. Scott later delivered himself of a judgment as to Davis: "He is not a cheap Judas. I do not think he would have sold the Saviour for thirty shillings. But for the successorship to Pontius Pilate he would have betrayed Christ and the Apostles and the whole Christian church." Sam Houston of Texas, speaking more briefly, declared that Davis was "ambitious as Lucifer and cold as a lizard."

Out of the rough-and-tumble of debate and acrimony, a more or less accepted part of political life at the time, Davis was winning a position as a leader in the Senate. Successor to Calhoun, he had become the spokesman for southern nationalism, which in those days meant not independence but domination from within the Union. This movement had been given impetus by the Mexican War. Up till then the future of the country pointed north and west, but now the needle trembled and suddenly swung south. The treaty signed at Guadalupe Hidalgo brought into the Union a new southwestern domain, seemingly ripe for slavery and the southern way of life: not only Texas down to the Rio Grande, the original strip of contention, but also the vast sun-cooked area that was to become Arizona, New Mexico, Nevada, Utah, part of Colorado, and California with its new-found gold. Here was room for expansion indeed, with more to follow; for the nationalists looked forward to taking what was left of Mexico, all of Central America south to Panama, and Yucatan and Cuba by annexation. Yet the North, so recently having learned the comfort of the saddle, had no intention of yielding the reins. The South would have to fight for this; and this the South was prepared to do, using States Rights for a spear and the Constitution for a shield. Jefferson Davis, who had formed his troops in a V at Buena Vista and continued the fight with a boot full of blood, took a position, now as then, at the apex of the wedge.

He lost the fight, and lost it quickly — betrayed, as he thought, from within his ranks. The North opposed this dream of southern expansion by opposing the extension of slavery, without which the new southwestern territory would be anything but southern. Attracted by the hope of so much gain, and goaded by the fear of such a loss, Davis and his cohorts adopted more drastic ac-

★

*Daniel Webster (left) of Massachusetts
joined fellow senator Henry Clay of Kentucky
in support of the Compromise of 1850.*

tions, including threats of secession. To give substance to this threat, he called the Nashville Convention of June 1850, and in conjunction with Albert Gallatin Brown of Mississippi, William Lowndes Yancey of Alabama, and Robert Barnwell Rhett of South Carolina, informed the North quite plainly that unless slavery was extended to the territories, the South would leave the Union. It was at this point that Davis was "betrayed," meaning that he discovered that he had outrun his constituents. Henry Clay proposed his Compromise, supported by Daniel Webster, and both houses of Congress gladly accepted it. California came in as a free state and the question of slavery was left to be settled by the various other territories at the time when they should apply for admission into the Union.

What was worse from Davis's point of view, the voters seemed to approve. All over the nation, even in Mississippi, there was rejoicing that disunion and war had been avoided. Davis could scarcely believe it; he must test it at the polls. So he resigned his seat in the Senate and went home to run for governor against Henry S. Foote, the senator with whom he had exchanged first tart remarks and finally blows. Now the issue was clearly drawn, for his opponent was a Unionist Whig of Natchez and had voted consistently against Davis, from the beginning down to the Compromise itself; the voters could make a clear-cut choice before all the world. This they did — repudiating Davis.

It was bad enough to be vanquished as the champion of secession, but to receive defeat at the hands of a man he detested as much as he detested Foote was gall and wormwood. At forty-three, in the hour of his glory and at the height of his prime, he was destroyed; or so he thought. At any rate he was through. He came home to Brierfield to plant cotton.

★ ★ ★ *T*hen history intervened again, as history always seemed to do for him. This time the muse took the form of Franklin Pierce, who in organizing a cabinet reached down from New Hampshire, all the way to Mississippi, and chose Jefferson Davis as his Secretary of War. They had been fellow officers in Mexico, friends in Congress, and shared a dislike of abolitionists. Whatever his reasons, Pierce chose well. Davis made perhaps the best War Secretary the country ever had, and though it included such capable men as William L. Marcy of New York and Caleb Cushing of Massachusetts, he dominated the cabinet in a time of strain and doubt.

Yet the man who returned to public life in 1853 was somewhat different from the man who had left it in 1851 at the behest of the voters. Rather chastened — though he kept his southern nationalism and clung to the spear of States Rights, the shield of the Constitution — he left the fire-eaters Yancey and Rhett behind him. He was no longer the impetuous champion of secession; he believed now that whatever was to be gained might best be accomplished within the Union. He strengthened the army, renovated the Military Academy, and came out strong for un-Jeffersonian internal improvements, including a Pacific Railway along a southern route through Memphis or Vicksburg, to be financed by a hundred-million-dollar federal appropriation. The Gadsden Purchase was a Davis project, ten million paid for a strip of Mexican soil necessary for the railroad right-of-way. Nor was his old imperialism dead. He still had designs on what was left of Mexico and on Central America, and he shocked the diplomats of Europe with a proclamation of his government's intention to annex Cuba. Above all, he was for the unlimited extension of slavery, with a revival of the slave trade if need be.

Returned to the Senate in 1857, he continued to work along these lines, once more a southern champion, not as a secessionist, but as a believer that the destiny of the nation pointed south. It was a stormy time, and much of the bitterness between the sections came to a head on the floor of the Senate, where northern invective and southern arrogance necessarily met. Here Texas senator Louis T. Wigfall, a duelist of note, would sneer at his northern colleagues as he told them, "The difficulty between you and us, gentlemen, is that you will not send the right sort of people here. Why will you not send either Christians or gentlemen?" Here, too, the anti-slavery Massachusetts senator Charles Sumner had his head broken by Congressman Preston Brooks of South Carolina, who, taking exception to remarks Sumner had made on the floor of the Senate regard-

★

ing a kinsman, caned him as he sat at his desk. Brooks explained that he attacked him sitting because, Sumner being the larger man, he would have had to shoot him if he had risen, and he did not want to kill him, only maim him. Sumner lay bleeding in the aisle among the gutta-percha fragments of the cane, and his enemies stood by and watched him bleed. Southern sympathizers sent Brooks walking sticks by the dozen, recommending their use on other abolitionists, and through the years of Sumner's convalescence Massachusetts let his desk stand empty as a reproach to southern hotheads, though these were in fact more likely to see the vacant seat as a warning to men like Sumner.

During this three-year furor, which led in the end to the disintegration of the Democratic Party and the resultant election of a Republican President, Davis remained as inflexible as ever. But his arguments now did not progress toward secession. They ended instead against a hard brick wall. He did not even claim to know the answers beyond debate. In 1860, speaking in Boston's Faneuil Hall while he and Mrs Davis were up there vacationing for his health — he was a chronic dyspeptic by now, racked by neuralgia through

SOUTHERN CHIVALRY — ARGUMENT versus CLUB'S.

Anti-slavery senator Charles Sumner of Massachusetts tries to ward off blows from South Carolina's Preston Brooks while southern sympathizers look on grinning.

★

sleepless nights and losing the sight of one eye — he stated his position as to slavery and southern nationalism, but announced that he remained opposed to secession; he still would not take the logical next step. He was much admired by the people of Massachusetts, many of whom despised the abolitionists as much as he did; but the people of Mississippi hardly knew what to make of him. "Davis is at sea," they said.

Then he looked back, and saw that instead of outrunning his constituents, this time he had let them outrun him. He hurried South, made his harvest-home-of-death speech on the eve of Lincoln's election, and returned to Washington, at last reconverted to secession. South Carolina left the Union, then Mississippi and the others, and opinion no longer mattered. As he said in his farewell, even if he had opposed his state's action, he still would have considered himself "bound."

Having spoken his adieu, he left the crowded chamber and, head lowered, went out into the street. That night Mrs Davis heard him pacing the floor. "May God have us in His holy keeping," she heard him say over and over as he paced, "and grant that before it is too late, peaceful councils may prevail."

★ ★ ★ *S*uch was Davis's way of saying farewell to his colleagues, speaking out of sadness and regret. It was not the way of others: Robert Toombs of Georgia, for example, whose state had seceded two days before Davis spoke. Two days later Toombs delivered his farewell. "The Union, sir, is dissolved," he told the Senate. A large, slack-mouthed man, he tossed his head in shaggy defiance as he spoke. "You see the glittering bayonet, and you hear the tramp of armed men from yon Capitol to the Rio Grande. It is a sight that gladdens the eye and cheers the hearts of other men ready to second them." In case there were those of the North who would maintain the Union by force: "Come and do it!" Toombs cried. "Georgia is on the war path! We are as ready to fight now as we ever shall be. Treason? Bah!" And with that he stalked out of the chamber, walked up to the Treasury, and demanded his salary due to date, plus mileage back to Georgia.

Thus Toombs. But Davis, having sent his wife home with their three children — Margaret aged six, Jeff three, and the year-old baby named for the guardian elder brother Joseph at Davis Bend — lingered in Washington another week, ill and confined to his bed for most of the time, still hoping he might be arrested as a traitor so as to test his claims in the federal courts, then took the train for Jackson, where Governor J. J. Pettus met him with a commission as major general of volunteers. It was the job Davis wanted. He believed there would be war, and he advised the governor to push the procurement of arms.

"The limit of our purchases should be our power to pay," he said. "We shall need all and many more than we can get."

★

"General," the governor protested, "you overrate the risk."

"I only wish I did," Davis said.

Awaiting the raising of his army, he went to Brierfield. In Alabama, now in early February, a convention was founding a Southern Confederacy, electing political leaders and formulating a new government. He was content, however, to leave such matters to those who were there. He considered his highest talents to be military and he had the position he wanted, commander of the Mississippi army, with advancement to come along with glory when the issue swung to war.

Then history beckoned again, assuming another of her guises. February 10; he and Mrs Davis were out in the garden, cutting a rose bush in the early blue spring weather, when a messenger approached with a telegram in his hand. Davis read it. In that moment of painful silence he seemed stricken; his face took on a look of calamity. Then he read the message to his wife. It was headed "Montgomery, Alabama," and dated the day before.

> *Sir:*
>
> *We are directed to inform you that you are this day unanimously elected President of the Provisional Government of the Confederate States of America, and to request you to come to Montgomery immediately. We send also a special messenger. Do not wait for him.*
>
> *R. Toombs,*
>
> *R. Barnwell Rhett . . .*

He spoke of it, Mrs Davis said, "as a man might speak of a sentence of death." Yet he wasted no time. He packed and left next day.

The train made many stops along the line and the people were out to meet him, in sunlight and by the glare of torches. They wanted a look at his face, the thin lips and determined jaw, the hollow cheeks with their jutting bones, the long skull behind the aquiline nose; "a wizard physiognomy," one called it. He brought forth cheers with confident words, but he had something else to say as well — something no one had told them before. He advised them to prepare for the long war that lay ahead. They did not believe him, apparently. Or if they did, they went on cheering anyhow.

He reached Montgomery Sunday night, February 17, and was driven from the station in a carriage, down the long torch-lit avenue to the old Exchange Hotel. The crowd followed through streets that had been decked as for a fair; they flowed until they were packed in a mass about the gallery of the hotel in time to see Davis dismount from the carriage and climb the steps; they cheered as he turned and looked at them. Then suddenly they fell silent. William Lowndes Yancey, short and rather seedy-looking alongside the erect and well-groomed Davis, had raised one hand. They cheered again when he brought it down, gesturing toward the tall man beside him, and said in a voice that rang above the expectant, torch-paled faces of the crowd: "The man and the hour have met."

* * * The day that Davis received the summons in the rose garden was Abraham Lincoln's last full day in Springfield, Illinois. He would be leaving tomorrow for Washington and his inauguration, the same day that Davis left for Montgomery and his. During the three months since the election, Springfield had changed from a sleepy, fairly typical western county seat and capital into a bustling, cadging hive of politicians, office seekers, reporters, committees representing "folks back home," and the plain downright curious with time on their hands, many of whom had come for no other reason than to breathe the same air with a man who had his name in all the papers. Some were lodged in railway cars on sidings; boarding houses were feeding double shifts.

All of these people wanted a look at Lincoln, and most of them wanted interviews, which they got. "I can't sleep nights," he was saying. His fingers throbbed from shaking hands and his face ached from smiling. He had leased the two-story family residence, sold the cow and the horse and buggy, and left the dog to be cared for by a neighbor; he and his wife and children were staying now at the Chenery House, where the President-elect himself had roped their trunks and addressed them to "A. Lincoln, The White House, Washington D.C." He was by nature a friendly man but his smile was becoming a grimace. "I am sick of office-holding already," he said on this final day in Illinois.

Change was predominant not only in Springfield; the Union appeared to be coming apart at the seams. Louisiana and Texas had brought the total of seceded states to seven. Banks and business firms were folding; the stock market declined and declined. James Buchanan, badly confused, was doing nothing in these last weeks of office. Having stated in his December message to Congress that while a state had no lawful right to secede, neither had the federal government any right to prevent it, privately he was saying that he was the last President of the United States.

North and South, Union men looked to Lincoln, whose election had been the signal for all this trouble. They wanted words of reassurance, words of threat, anything to slow the present trend, the drift toward chaos. Yet he said nothing. When a Missouri editor asked him for a statement, something he could print to make men listen, Lincoln wrote back: "I could say nothing which I have not already said, and which is in print and accessible to the public. . . . I am not at liberty to shift my ground; that is out of the question. If I thought a repetition would do any good I would make it. But my judgment is it would do positive harm. The secessionists, *per se* believing they had alarmed me, would clamor all the louder."

People hardly knew what to make of this tall, thin-chested, raw-boned man who spoke with the frontier in his voice, wore a stove-pipe hat as if to emphasize his six-foot four-inch height, and walked with a shambling western slouch, the big feet planted flat at every step, the big hands dangling from wrists that hung down out of the sleeves of his rusty tailcoat. Mr Lincoln, they called him, or Lincoln, never "Abe" as in the campaign literature. The seamed, leathery face was becoming familiar: the mole on the right cheek, the high narrow forehead with the unruly, coarse black shock of hair above it, barely grizzled: the pale gray eyes set deep in bruised sockets, the broad mouth somewhat quizzical with a protruding lower lip, the pointed chin behind its recent growth of scraggly beard, the wry neck — a clown face; a sad face, some observed on closer inspection, perhaps the saddest they had ever seen. It was hard to imagine a man like this in the White House, where Madison and Van Buren had kept court. He had more or less blundered into the Republican nomination, much as his Democratic opponents had blundered into defeat in the election which had followed. It had all come about as a result of linking accidents and crises, and the people, with their accustomed championing of the underdog, the dark horse, had enjoyed it at the time. Yet now that the nation was in truth a house divided, now that war loomed, they were not so sure. Down South, men were hearing speeches that fired their blood. Here it was not so; for there was only silence from Abraham Lincoln.

People hardly knew what to make of this tall, thin-chested, rawboned man who spoke with the frontier in his voice, wore a stove-pipe hat as if to emphasize his six-foot four-inch height, and walked with a shambling western slouch . . .

Congressman Horace Maynard, a Tennessee Unionist, believed he knew why. "I imagine that he keeps silence," Maynard said, "for the good and sufficient reason that he has nothing to say."

It was true that he had nothing to say at the time. He was waiting; he was drawing on one of his greatest virtues, patience. Though the Cotton South had gone out solid, the eight northernmost slave states remained loyal. Delaware and Maryland, Virginia and North Carolina, Kentucky and Tennessee, Missouri and Arkansas were banked between the hotheads, north and south, a double buffer, and though Lincoln had not received a single electoral vote from this whole area, he counted on the sound common sense of the people there. What was more — provided he did nothing to alienate the loyalty of the border states — he counted on Union sentiment in the departed states to bring them back into the family.

He had had much practice in just this kind of waiting. One of these days, while he was sitting in his office with a visitor, his son Willie came clattering in to demand a quarter. "I can't let you have a quarter," Lincoln said; "I can only spare five cents." He took five pennies from his pocket and stacked them on a corner of the desk. Willie had not asked for a nickel; he wanted a quarter. He sulked and went away, leaving the pennies on the desk. "He will be back after that in a few minutes," Lincoln told the visitor. "As soon as he finds I will give him no more, he will come and get it." They went on talking. Presently the boy returned, took the pennies from the desk, and quietly left. Patience had worked, where attempts at persuasion might have resulted in a flare-up. So with the departed states; self-interest and family ties might bring them back in time. Meanwhile Lincoln walked as softly as he could.

In this manner he had gotten through three of the four anxious months that lay between the election and inauguration, and on this final afternoon in Springfield he went down to his law office to pick up some books and papers and to say goodbye to his partner, William L. Herndon. Nine years his junior, Herndon was excitable, apt to fling off at a tangent, and Lincoln would calm him, saying, "Billy, you're too rampant." There had been times, too, when the older man had gone about collecting fees to pay the fine when his partner was about to be jailed for disorderly conduct on a spree. Now the two sat in the office, discussing business matters. Then came an awkward silence, which Lincoln broke by asking: "Billy, there's one thing I have for some time wanted you to tell me. . . . I want you to tell me how many times you have been drunk." Flustered, Herndon stammered, and Lincoln let it pass. This was the closest he ever came to delivering a temperance lecture.

They rose, walked downstairs, and paused on the boardwalk. Lincoln glanced up at the weathered law shingle: LINCOLN & HERNDON. "Let it hang there undisturbed," he said. "Give our clients to understand that the election of a President makes no change in the firm of Lincoln and Herndon. If I live I'm coming back some time, and then we'll go right on practicing law as if nothing ever happened." Again there was an awkward pause. Lincoln put his hand out. "Goodbye," he said, and went off down the street.

Herndon stood and watched him go, the tall, loose-jointed figure with the napless stove-pipe hat, the high-water pantaloons, the ill-fitting tailcoat bulging at the elbows from long wear. This junior partner was one of those who saw the sadness in Lincoln's face. "Melancholy dripped from him as he walked," he was to write. Herndon knew something else as well, something that had not been included in the campaign literature: "That man who thinks that Lincoln sat calmly down and gathered his robes about him, waiting for the people to call him, has a very erroneous knowledge of Lincoln. He was always calculating, and always planning ahead. His ambition was a little engine that knew no rest."

★ ★ ★ **T**hat day, as the sun went down and he returned to the Chenery House for his last sleep in Illinois, there were few who knew this side of him. There were gaps in the story that even Herndon could not fill, and other gaps that no one could fill, ever, though writers were to make him the subject of more biographies and memoirs, more brochures and poems than any other American. On the face of it the facts were simple enough, as he told a journalist who came seeking information about his boyhood years for a campaign biography: "Why, Scripps, it is a great piece of folly to attempt to make anything out of my early life. It can all be condensed into a single sentence, and that sentence you will find in Gray's *Elegy:* 'The short and simple annals of the poor.'"

He was born in the Kentucky wilderness of Daniel Boone, mid-February of 1809, in a one-room dirt-floor cabin put up that same winter by his father, Thomas Lincoln, a thick-chested man of average height, who passed on to Abraham only his coarse black hair and dark complexion. Originally from Virginia, Thomas was a wanderer like the Lincolns before him, who had come down out of New Jersey and Pennsylvania, and though in early manhood he could sign his name when necessary, later he either forgot or else he stopped taking the trouble; he made his X-mark like his wife, born Nancy Hanks.

In after years when Lincoln tried to trace his ancestry he could go no further back than his father's father, also named Abraham, who had been killed from ambush by an Indian. That was on his father's side. On his mother's he discovered only that she had been born out of wedlock to Lucy Hanks who later married a man named Sparrow. Nancy died of the milksick when Abraham was nine, and her body lay in another of those one-room cabins while her husband knocked together a coffin in the yard.

They were in Indiana by then, having come to the big woods after a

Thomas Lincoln had little appreciation for the humorous antics of his son Abraham, and their relationship was apparently a strained one.

previous move to Knob Creek, south of Louisville and beside the Cumberland Trail, along which pioneers with many children and few livestock marched north-westward. Thomas Lincoln joined them for the move across the Ohio, and when his wife died took another the following year: Sarah Bush Johnston, a widow with three children. She was called Sally Bush Lincoln now, tall and hard-working, a welcome addition to any frontier family, especially this one, which had been with-out a woman for almost a year. She brought to Abraham all the love and affection she had given her own. The boy returned it, and in later years, when his memory of Nancy Hanks Lincoln had paled, referred to the one who took her place as "my angel mother," saying: "All that I am I owe to my angel mother."

For one thing, she saw to it that the boy went to school. Previously he had not gone much deeper into learning than his ABC's, and only then at such times as his father felt he could spare him from his chores. Now at intervals he was able to fit in brief weeks of schooling, amounting in all to something un-der a year. They were "blab" schools, which meant that the pupils studied aloud at their desks and the master judged the extent of their concentration by the volume of their din. Between such periods of formal education he studied at home, ciphering on boards when he had no slate, and shaving them clean with a knife for an eraser. He developed a talent for mimicry, too, mounting a stump when out with a work gang and delivering mock orations and sermons. This earned him the laughter of the men, who would break off work to watch him, but his father disapproved of such interruptions and would speak to him sharply or cuff him off the stump.

He grew tall and angular, with long muscles, so that in his early teens he could grip an ax one-handed at the end of the helve and hold it out, untrembling. Neighbors testified to his skill with this implement, one saying: "He can sink an ax deeper into wood than any man I ever saw," and another: "If you heard him felling trees in a clearing, you would say there was three men at work by the way the trees fell." However, though he did his chores, including work his father hired him out to do, he developed no real liking for manual labor. He would rather be reading what few books he got his hands on: Parson Weems's *Life of Washington, Pilgrim's Progress, Æsop's Fables, Robinson Crusoe,* Grimshaw's *History of the United States,* and *The Kentucky Preceptor.* Sometimes he managed to combine the two, for in plowing he would stop at the end of a row, reading while he gave the horse a breather.

From a flatboat trip one thousand miles downriver to New Orleans, during which he learned to trim a deck and man a sweep, he returned in time for his twenty-first birthday and another family migration, from Indiana out to central Illinois, where he and a cousin hired out to split four thousand rails for their neighbors. Thus he came to manhood, a rail-splitter, wilderness-born and

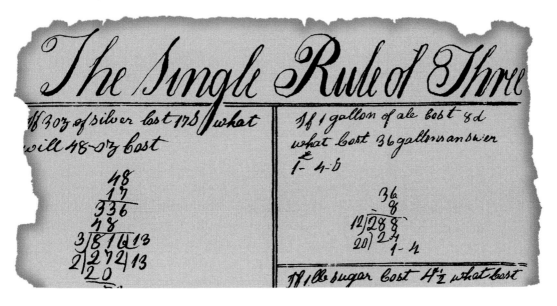

On this page from one of his early school workbooks, young Abraham worked out solutions to arithmetic problems.

frontier-raised. He was of the West, the new country out beyond the old, a product of a nation fulfilling a manifest destiny. It was in his walk, in his talk and in his character, indelibly. It would be with him wherever he went, along with the knowledge that he had survived in a region where "the Lord spared the fitten and the rest He seen fitten to let die."

He had never had much fondness for his father, and now that he was legally independent he struck out on his own. The family moved once more, deeper into Illinois, but Lincoln did not go with them. He took instead another flatboat trip down to New Orleans, and then came back to another kind of life. This was prairie country, with a rich soil and a future. Lincoln got a job clerking in a New Salem store at fifteen dollars a month plus a bed to sleep in. He defeated the leader of the regional toughs in a wrestling match, and when the leader's friends pitched in, Lincoln backed against a wall and dared them to come at him one by one; whereupon they acknowledged him as their new leader.

This last was rather in line with the life he had led before, but he found something new as well. He attended the New Salem Debating Society, and though at first the charter members snickered at his looks and awkwardness, presently they were admiring the logic and conciseness of his arguments. "All he lacked was culture," one of them said. Lincoln took such encouragement from his success that in the spring of 1832 he announced as a candidate for the state legislature.

The Black Hawk War interrupting his campaign, he enlisted and was elected captain by his fellow volunteers. Discipline was not strong among them; the new commander's first order to one of his men brought the reply, "You go to hell." They saw no action, and Lincoln afterwards joked about his military career, saying that all the blood he lost was to mosquitoes and all his charges were against wild-onion beds. When the company's thirty-day enlistment expired he reënlisted for another twenty days as a private, then came home and resumed his campaign for the legislature, two weeks remaining until election day. His first political speech was made at a country auction. Twenty-three years old, he stood on a box, wearing a frayed straw hat, a calico shirt, and pantaloons held up by a single-strap suspender. As he was about to speak, a fight broke out in the crowd. Lincoln stepped down, broke up the fight, then stepped back onto the box.

"Gentlemen and fellow citizens," he said, "I presume you all know who I am: I am humble Abraham Lincoln. I have been solicited by many friends to become a candidate for the legislature. My politics are short and sweet, like the old woman's dance. I am in favor of a national bank. I am in favor of the internal-improvements system and a high protective tariff. These are my sentiments and political principles. If elected, I shall be thankful; if not, it will be all the same."

Election day he ran eighth in a field of thirteen, but he received 277 of the 300 votes in the New Salem precinct.

★

★ ★ ★ *T*t was probably then that Lincoln determined to run for the same office next time around. Meanwhile there was a living to earn. He could always split rails and do odd jobs. These he did, and then went into partnership in a grocery store that failed, leaving him a debt beyond a thousand dollars; "the National Debt," he called it ruefully, and worked for years to pay it off. He became village postmaster, sometimes carrying letters in his hat, which became a habit. He studied surveying and worked a while at that. He also began the study of law, reading Blackstone and Chitty, and improved his education with borrowed books. His name was becoming more widely known; he was winning popularity by his great strength and his ability at telling funny stories, but mostly by his force of character. Then in the spring of 1834, when another legislature race came round, he conducted an all-out full-time campaign and was elected.

With borrowed money he bought his first tailor-made suit, paying sixty dollars for it, and left for the first of his four terms in the state law-making body, learning the rough-and-tumble give-and-take of western politics. Two years later he was licensed as an attorney, and soon afterwards moved to Springfield as a partner in a law firm. He said goodbye to the manual labor he had been so good at, yet had never really liked; from now on he would work with his head, as a leader of men. His ambition became what Herndon later called "a little engine."

Springfield was about to be declared the state capital, moved there from Vandalia largely through Lincoln's efforts in the legislature, and here he began to acquire that culture which the New Salem intellectuals had said was "all he lacked." The big, work-splayed hands were losing their horn-hard calluses. He settled down to the law, becoming in time an excellent trial lawyer and a capable stump debater at political rallies, even against such opponents as Stephen A. Douglas, the coming Little Giant. Socially, however, he was slow in getting started. About a month after his arrival he wrote in a letter: "I have been spoken to by but one woman since I've been here, and should not have been by her, if she could have avoided it." He was leery of the ladies, having once remarked, half-jokingly, "A woman is the only thing I am afraid of that I know will not hurt me." Nevertheless, by the time he was elected to his fourth term in the legislature, Lincoln was courting Mary Todd, a visitor from Lexington, Kentucky, and in early November of 1842 he married her.

It was an attraction of opposites, and as such it was stormy. At one point they broke off the engagement; she left Illinois and Lincoln had to go to Kentucky for a reconciliation before she would return to Springfield and marry him in her sister's parlor. If "culture" was what he was after, still, Lincoln again had moved in the proper direction. His wife, the great-granddaughter of a Revolutionary general, had attended a private academy in Lexington, where she

★

In 1842, at thirty-three, Lincoln married Kentucky belle Mary Todd, only twenty-four. The storminess of their courtship continued throughout their marriage.

learned to speak French, read music after a fashion, paint on china, and dance the sedate figures of the time. At twenty-four she was impulsive and vivacious, short and rather plump, looking especially so alongside her long lean husband, who was thirty-three. Lincoln seemed to take it calmly enough. Five days after the wedding he wrote to a lawyer friend: "Nothing new here, except my marrying, which to me is matter of profound wonder."

Their first child, Robert Todd, called Bob, was born the following year. Three others came in the course of the next decade, all sons: Edward and William and Thomas, called Eddy, Willie, Tad. Eddy died before he was five, and Tad had a cleft palate; he spoke with a lisp. The Lincolns lived a year in rented rooms, then moved into the $1500 white frame house which remained their home. They took their place in Springfield society, and Lincoln worked hard at law, riding the Eighth Judicial Circuit in all kinds of weather, a clean shirt and a change of underwear in his saddlebag, along with books and papers and a yellow flannel nightshirt. Fees averaged about five dollars a case, sometimes paid in groceries, which he was glad to get, since the cost of the house represented something beyond one year's total earnings.

Home life taught him patience, for his wife was high-strung as well as high-born. He called her Mother and met her fits of temper with forbear-

★

ance, which must have been the last thing she wanted at the time. When her temper got too hot he would walk off to his office and stay until it cooled. Accustomed to Negro house slaves in Kentucky, Mary Lincoln could not get along with Illinois hired girls, who were inclined to answer back. Lincoln did what he could here too, slipping the girls an extra weekly dollar for compensation. Once after a particularly bitter scene between mistress and maid, when Mrs Lincoln had left the room he patted the girl on the shoulder and gave her the same advice he had given himself: "Stay with her, Maria. Stay with her."

His law practice grew; he felt prepared to grow in other directions. Having completed his fourth term in the state legislature, he was ready to move on up the political ladder. He wrote to Whig associates in the district, "Now if you should hear anyone say that Lincoln don't want to go to Congress, I wish you as a personal friend of mine would tell him you have reason to believe he is mistaken. The truth is, I would like to go very much." In the backstage party scramble, however, he lost the nomination in 1842 and again in 1844. It was 1847 before he got to Congress. From a back row on the Whig side of the House he came to know the voices and faces of men he would know better, Ashmun of Massachusetts, Rhett of South Carolina, Smith of Indiana, Toombs and Stephens of Georgia, while a visit to the Senate would show him the elder statesmen Webster and Calhoun, along with newer men of note, such as Cameron of Pennsylvania and Davis of Mississippi.

The Mexican War had ended by then, and though Lincoln voted for whatever army supply bills came before the House, like most Whigs he attacked the motives behind the war, which now was being spoken of, by northern Whigs at least, as "infamous and wicked," an imperialist attempt to extend the slavery realm. This got him into trouble back home, where the Democratic papers began calling him a latter-day Benedict Arnold and the people read and noted all he did as a slur against the volunteers of his state. When Congress convened for his second session, Lincoln was the only Whig from Illinois. It was a hectic session anyhow, with tempers flaring over the question of slavery in the territories. He came home with no chance for reëlection, and did not try. He gave up politics, refusing even a spoils offer of the governorship of Oregon Territory, and returned to the practice of law, once more riding the circuit. Disheartened, he paused now to restore his soul through work and meditation.

★ ★ ★ *T*hough he did not believe at the outset that it would necessarily ever reach an end — indeed, he believed it would not; otherwise it could never have done for him what it did — this five-year "retreat," coming as it did between his fortieth and his forty-fifth years, 1849 to 1854, was his interlude of greatest growth. Like many, perhaps most, men of genius, Lincoln developed late.

It was a time for study, a time for self-improvement. He went back and drilled his way through the first six books of Euclid, as an exercise to discipline his mind. Not politics but the law was his main interest now. Riding the circuit he talked less and listened more. Together with a new understanding and a deeper reading of Shakespeare and the Bible, this brought him a profounder faith in people, including those who had rejected him and repudiated what he had to offer as a leader. Here, too, he was learning. This was the period in which he was reported to have said, "You can fool some of the people all the time, and all the people some of the time, but you can't fool all the people all the time."

Nonparticipation in public affairs did not mean a loss of interest in them. Lincoln read the papers more carefully now than he had ever done before, learning from them of the deaths of Calhoun, Clay, and Webster, whose passing marked the passing of an era. When the 1850 Compromise — as he and most men believed, including Clay who engineered it shortly before his death — settled the differences that had brought turmoil to the nation and fist fights to the floors of Congress while Lincoln himself was there, he breathed easier. But not for long. The conflict soon was heading up again. *Uncle Tom's Cabin* came from the presses in a stream; southern nationalists were announcing plans for the annexation of Cuba; the case of the slave Dred Scott, suing for his freedom, moved by legal osmosis through the courts; the Whigs seemed lost and the Democrats were splitting. Then Lincoln's old stump opponent, Stephen A. Douglas, who was four years younger than Lincoln but who had suffered no setback in political advancement, filling now his second term in the Senate, brought the crisis to a head.

Scarcely taller than Napoleon, but with all that monarch's driving ambition and belief in a private star, Douglas moved to repeal that part of the Missouri Compromise which served to restrict the extension of slavery. This came as a result of his championing a northern route for the proposed Pacific Railway. A southern route was also proposed and Douglas sought to effect a swap, reporting a bill for the organization of two new territories, Kansas and Nebraska, with the provision that the people there should determine for themselves as to the admission or exclusion of slavery, despite the fact that both areas lay well north of the 36°30' line drawn by the Compromise, which had guaranteed that the institution would be kept forever south of there. The Southerners were glad to abandon their New Mexico route for such a gain, provided the repeal was made not only implicit but explicit in the bill. Douglas was somewhat shocked (he brought a certain naivety to even his deepest plots) but soon agreed, and Secretary of War Jefferson Davis persuaded Franklin Pierce to make the bill an Administration issue. "Popular sovereignty," Douglas called it; "Squatter sovereignty," his opponents considered a better name. "It will raise a hell of a storm," Douglas predicted. It did indeed, though the Democrats managed to ram it through by late May of 1854, preparing the ground for Bleeding Kansas and the birth of the Republican Party that same year.

Another effect of the Kansas-Nebraska Bill was that it brought Lincoln out of retirement. It had raised even more of a storm than Douglas predicted, and not only in Congress. For when the senator came home to Illinois he saw through the train window his effigy being burned in courthouse squares, and when he came to explain his case before eight thousand people in Chicago, they jeered him off the rostrum. He left, shaking his fist in their faces, and set out to stump the state with a speech that confounded opposition orators and won back many of the voters. Then in early October he came to Springfield, packing the hall of the House of Representatives. After the speech — which had been as successful here as elsewhere in turning the jeers to cheers — the crowd filed out through the lobby and saw Abraham Lincoln standing on the staircase, announcing that he would reply to Douglas the following day and inviting the senator to be present, to answer if he cared.

Next day they were there, close-packed as yesterday; Douglas had a front-row seat. It was hot and Lincoln spoke in shirt sleeves, wearing no collar or tie. His voice was shrill as he began, though presently it settled to lower tones, interrupted from time to time by crackles and thunders of applause. Wet with sweat, his shirt clung to his shoulders and big arms. He had written his speech out beforehand, clarifying in his own mind his position as to slavery, which he saw as the nub of the issue — much to the discomfort of Douglas, who wanted to talk about "popular sovereignty," keeping the issue one of self-government, whereas Lincoln insisted on going beyond, making slavery the main question. Emerging from his long retirement, having restored his soul, he was asking himself and all men certain questions. And now the Lincoln music began to sound.

Stephen Douglas' support of "popular sovereignty" and the Kansas-Nebraska Bill helped bring Lincoln out of political retirement.

"The doctrine of self-government is right, absolutely and eternally right; but it has no just application, as here attempted. Or perhaps I should rather say that whether it has such just application depends upon whether a Negro is not or is a man. If he is not a man, why in that case he who is a man may, as a matter of self-government, do just as he pleases with him. But if the Negro is a man, is it not to that extent a total destruction of self-government to say that he too shall not govern himself? When the white man governs himself, that is self-government; but when he governs himself and also governs another man, that is more than self-government; that is despotism. If the Negro is a man, why then my ancient faith teaches me that 'all men are created equal,' and that there can be no moral right in connection with one man's making a slave of another."

He believed that it was a moral wrong; he had not come to believe that it was a legal wrong, though he believed that too would be clarified in time.

"Slavery is founded in the selfishness of man's nature, opposition to it in his love of justice. These principles are an eternal antagonism . . ."

— Abraham Lincoln

The words of his mouth came like meditations from his heart: "Slavery is founded in the selfishness of man's nature, opposition to it in his love of justice. These principles are an eternal antagonism, and when brought into collision so fiercely as slavery extension brings them, shocks and throes and convulsions must ceaselessly follow. Repeal the Missouri Compromise, repeal all compromises; repeal the Declaration of Independence, repeal all past history — you still cannot repeal human nature. It still will be the abundance of man's heart that slavery extension is wrong, and out of the abundance of his heart his mouth will continue to speak."

This, in part, was the speech that caused his name to be recognized throughout the Northwest, though personally he was still but little known outside his state. He repeated it twelve days later in Peoria, where shorthand reporters took it down for their papers, and continued to speak in central Illinois and in Chicago. Winning reëlection to the legislature, he presently had a chance at a seat in the U.S. Senate. His hopes were high and he resigned from the legislature to be eligible, but at the last minute he had to throw his votes to an anti-Nebraska Democrat to defeat the opposition.

Again he had failed, and again he regretted failing. Yet this time he

★

was not despondent. He kept working and waiting. His law practice boomed; he earned a five-thousand-dollar fee on a railroad case, and was retained to assist a high-powered group of big-city lawyers on a patents case in Cincinnati, but when they saw him come to town, wearing his usual rusty clothes and carrying a ball-handled blue cotton umbrella, they would scarcely speak to him. One of the attorneys, Edwin M. Stanton of Pittsburgh, was downright rude; "Where did that long-armed creature come from?" he asked within earshot. Lincoln went his way, taking no apparent umbrage.

Politically he was wary, too, writing to a friend: "Just now I fear to do anything, lest I do wrong." He had good cause for fear, and so had all men through this time of "shocks and throes and convulsions." Popular sovereignty was being tested in Kansas in a manner Douglas had not foreseen. Missouri border ruffians and hired abolitionist gunmen were cutting each other's throats for votes in the coming referendum; the Mormons were resisting federal authority in the West, and while a ruinous financial panic gripped the East, the Know-Nothing Party was sweeping New England with anti-foreigner, anti-Catholic appeals. The Whigs had foundered, the Democrats had split on all those rocks. Like many men just now, Lincoln hardly knew where he stood along party lines.

"I think I am a Whig," he wrote, "but others say there are no Whigs, and that I am an Abolitionist. . . . I am not a Know-Nothing. That is certain. How could I be? How can anyone who abhors the oppression of Negroes be in favor of degrading classes of white people? Our progress in degeneracy appears to me to be pretty rapid."

He was waiting and looking. And then he found the answer.

★ ★ ★ *T*t was 1856, a presidential election year. Out of the Nebraska crisis, two years before, the Republican Party had been born, a coalition of foundered Whigs and disaffected northern Democrats, largely abolitionist at the core. They made overtures to Lincoln but he dodged them at the time, not wanting a Radical tag attached to his name. Now, however, seeking to unify the anti-Nebraska elements in Illinois, he came to meet them. As a delegate to the state convention he caught fire and made what may have been the greatest speech of his career, though no one would ever really know, since the heat of his words seemed to burn them from men's memory, and in that conglomerate mass of gaping, howling old-line Whigs and bolted Democrats, Know-Nothings, Free Soilers and Abolitionists, even the shorthand reporters sat enthralled, forgetting to use their pencils. From now on he was a Republican; he would take his chances with the Radical tag.

At the national convention in Philadelphia he received 110 votes on the first ballot for the vice-presidential nomination, yielding them on the second to a New Jersey running mate for John C. Frémont of California. Lincoln had not favored Frémont, but he worked hard for him in the campaign that saw the election of the Democratic nominee James Buchanan, an elderly bachelor whose main advantage lay in the fact that he was the least controversial candidate, having been out of the country as Minister to England during the trying past three years. The Republicans were by no means dispirited at running second. They sniffed victory down the wind, in the race four years from now — provided only that the turmoil and sectional antagonism should continue, which seemed likely.

At this point the United States Supreme Court handed down a decision which appeared to cut the ground from under all their feet. The test case of the slave Dred Scott, suing for freedom on a plea that his master had taken him into a territory where slavery was forbidden by the Missouri Compromise, had at last reached the high court. In filing the majority opinion, Chief Justice Roger B. Taney dismissed Scott's lawyer's claim. A Negro, he said, was not a citizen of the United States, and therefore had no right to sue in a federal court. This was enough to enrage the Abolitionists, who secretly had sponsored the suit. But Taney went even further. The Missouri Compromise itself was void, he declared; Congress had no power over territories except to prepare for their admission to the Union; slaves being private property, Congress had no right to exclude them anywhere. According to this decision, "popular sovereignty" went into the discard, since obviously whatever powers Congress lacked would be lacked by any territorial legislature created by Congress.

The reaction was immediate and uproarious. Secession, formerly the threat of the South, now came as a cry from the North, particularly New England, where secessionist meetings were held in many towns. Douglas, on the other hand, digested the bitter dose as best he could, then announced that the decision was in fact a vindication of his repeal of the Compromise two years before, as well as a confirmation of the principles of popular sovereignty, since slavery, whether legal or not, could never thrive where the people did not welcome it. Lincoln did not mask his disappointment. He believed the decision was erroneous and harmful, but he respected the judgment of the Court and urged his followers to work toward the time when the five-four decision would be reversed. Meanwhile, during the off-year 1857, he prepared to run for the Senate against Douglas, whose third term would expire the following year.

Just then, unexpectedly, Douglas split with the Administration over the adoption of a constitution for Kansas. Threatened with expulsion from his party, he swung over to the Republicans on the issue, bringing many Democrats along with him. The Republicans were surprised and grateful, and it began to look as if Lincoln would be passed over again when nominating time came round. However, they were too accustomed to fighting the Little Giant to break off hostilities now. They nominated Lincoln at the state convention in mid-June. Lincoln was ready, and more than ready. He had not only prepared his acceptance, but

FRANK LESLIE'S ILLUSTRATED NEWSPAPER

Entered according to Act of Congress, in the year 1857, by FRANK LESLIE, in the Clerk's Office of the District Court for the Southern District of New York. (Copyrighted June 22, 1857.)

No. 82.—VOL. IV.]　　　NEW YORK, SATURDAY, JUNE 27, 1857.　　　[PRICE 6 CENTS.

TO TOURISTS AND TRAVELLERS.

We shall be happy to receive personal narratives, of land or sea, including adventures and incidents, from every person who pleases to correspond with our paper.

We take this opportunity of returning our thanks to our numerous artistic correspondents throughout the country, for the many sketches we are constantly receiving from them of the news of the day. We trust they will spare no pains to furnish us with drawings of events as they may occur. We would also remind them that it is necessary to send all sketches, if possible, by the earliest conveyance.

VISIT TO DRED SCOTT — HIS FAMILY — INCIDENTS OF HIS LIFE — DECISION OF THE SUPREME COURT.

WHILE standing in the Fair grounds at St. Louis, and engaged in conversation with a prominent citizen of that enterprising city, he suddenly asked us if we would not like to be introduced to Dred Scott. Upon expressing a desire to be thus honored, the gentleman called to an old negro who was standing near by, and our wish was gratified. Dred made a rude obeisance to our recognition, and seemed to enjoy the notice we expended upon him. We found him on examination to be a pure-blooded African, perhaps fifty years of age, with a shrewd, intelligent, good-natured face, of rather light frame, being not more than five feet six inches high. After some general remarks we expressed a wish to get his portrait (we had made

ELIZA AND LIZZIE, CHILDREN OF DRED SCOTT.

efforts before, through correspondents, and failed), and asked him if he would not go to Fitzgibbon's gallery and

have it taken. The gentleman present explained to Dred that it was proper he should have his likeness in the "great Illustrated paper of the country," overruled his many objections, which seemed to grow out of a superstitious feeling, and he promised to be at the gallery the next day. This appointment Dred did not keep. Determined not to be foiled, we sought an interview with Mr. Crane, Dred's lawyer, who promptly gave us a letter of introduction, explaining to Dred that it was to his advantage to have his picture taken to be engraved for our paper, and also directions where we could find his domicile. We found the place with difficulty, the streets in Dred's neighborhood being more clearly defined in the plan of the city than on the mother earth; we finally reached a wooden house, however, protected by a balcony that answered the description. Approaching the door, we saw a smart, tidy-looking negress, perhaps thirty years of age, who, with two female assistants, was busy ironing. To our question, "Is this where Dred Scott lives?" we received, rather hesitatingly, the answer, "Yes." Upon our asking if he was home, she said,

"What white man arter dad nigger for?—why don't white man 'tend to his own business, and let dat nigger 'lone? Some of dese days dey'll steal dat nigger—dat are a fact."

DRED SCOTT. PHOTOGRAPHED BY FITZGIBBON, OF ST. LOUIS.

HIS WIFE, HARRIET. PHOTOGRAPHED BY FITZGIBBON, OF ST. LOUIS.

Dred Scott and his family appeared on the front page of the June 27, 1857, issue of Frank Leslie's Illustrated Newspaper.

now for the first time he read a speech from manuscript, as if to emphasize his knowledge of the need for precision. It was at this point that Lincoln's political destiny and the destiny of the nation became one. The first paragraph once more summed up his thinking and struck the keynote for all that was to follow:

"If we could first know where we are, and whither we are tending, we could better judge what to do, and how to do it. We are now far into the fifth year since a policy was initiated with the avowed object and confident promise of putting an end to slavery agitation. Under the operation of that policy, that agitation has not only not ceased, but has constantly augmented. In my opinion it will not cease until a crisis shall have been reached and passed. 'A house divided against itself cannot stand.' I believe this government cannot endure permanently half slave and half free. I do not expect the Union to be dissolved — I do not expect the house to fall — but I do expect it will cease to be divided. It will become all one thing, or all the other. Either the opponents of slavery will arrest the further spread of it, and place it where the public mind shall be at rest in the belief that it is in the course of ultimate extinction, or its advocates will push it forward till it shall have become alike lawful in all the states, old as well as new, North as well as South."

"'A house divided against itself cannot stand.'
I believe this government cannot
endure permanently half slave and half free."

— Abraham Lincoln

Seizing upon this as proof of Lincoln's radicalism, and declaring that it proved him not only a proponent of sectional discord but also a reckless prophet of war, Douglas came home and launched an all-out campaign against the Republicans and the Democrats who had not walked out with him. He spoke in Chicago to a crowd that broke into frenzies of cheers, then set out to stump the state, traveling with a retinue of secretaries, stenographers, and influential admirers in a gaily bannered private car placed at his disposal by George B. McClellan, chief engineer of the Illinois Central, who also provided a flatcar mounting a brass cannon to boom the announcement that the Little Giant was coming down the line. Traveling unaccompanied on an ordinary ticket, Lincoln moved in his wake, sometimes on the same train, addressing the crowds attracted by the Douglas panoply. At last he made the arrangement formal, challenging his opponent to a series of debates. Douglas, with nothing to

★

gain, could not refuse. He agreed to meet Lincoln once in each of the seven congressional districts where they had not already spoken.

Thus the colorful Douglas-Lincoln debates got under way, the pudgy, well-tailored Douglas with his scowl, his luxurious mane of hair, gesturing aggressively as his voice wore to a froggy croak, and Lincoln in his clawhammer coat and straight-leg trousers, tall and earnest, with a shrill voice that reached the outer edges of the crowd, bending his knees while he led up to a point, then straightening them with a jerk, rising to his full height as he made it. Crowds turned out, ten to fifteen thousand strong, thronging the lonesome prairie towns. At Freeport, Lincoln threw Douglas upon the horns of a dilemma, asking: "Can the people of a United States Territory, in any lawful way . . . exclude slavery from its limits prior to the formation of a State Constitution?" If Douglas answered No he would offend the free-soil voters of Illinois. If he answered Yes he would make himself unacceptable to the South in the 1860 presidential campaign, toward which his ambition so clearly pointed. He made his choice; Yes, he said, defying both the Supreme Court and the South, and thereby cinched the present election and stored up trouble for the future.

★ ★ ★ *A*pproaching fifty, Lincoln again took defeat in his stride, turning once more to the practice of law to build up a flattened bank account. He was known throughout the nation now as a result of the cross-state debates. In his mail and in the newspapers there began to appear suggestions that he was presidential timber — to which he replied, sometimes forthrightly: "I must, in candor, say I do not think I am fit for the Presidency," sometimes less forthrightly: "I shall labor faithfully in the ranks, unless, as I think not probable, the judgment of the party shall assign me a different position." Through the long hot summer of 1859, past fifty now, he wrote letters and made speeches and did in general what he could to improve the party strategy, looking toward next year's elections.

Then in mid-October the telegraph clacked a message that drove all such thoughts from men's minds. John Brown, called Osawatomie Brown after a massacre staged in Kansas, had seized the federal arsenal at Harpers Ferry, Virginia, as the first step in leading a slave insurrection. His army counted eighteen men, including five Negroes; "One man and God can overturn the universe," he said. Captured by United States Marines under Colonel Robert E. Lee, U.S. Army, he was tried in a Virginia court and sentenced to be hanged in early December. He had the backing of several New England Abolitionists; they spent an anxious six weeks while the old fanatic kept their secret, close-mouthed behind his long gray beard. Seated on his coffin while he rode in a wagon to the gallows, he looked out at the hazy Blue Ridge Mountains. "This *is* a beautiful country," he said. "I never had the pleasure of really seeing it before." After the

John Brown's attempt to capture Harpers Ferry's U.S. arsenal (right below) ended when he was trapped in the firehouse behind the stone and wrought-iron fence (at left).

hanging the jailor unfolded a slip of paper Brown had left behind, a prophecy: "I John Brown am now quite certain that the crimes of this guilty land; will never be purged away; but with blood."

This too was added to the issues men were split on; John Brown's soul went marching, a symbol of good or evil, depending on the viewer. Douglas, back in Washington, was quick to claim that such incidents of lawlessness and bloodshed were outgrowths of the House Divided speech, and Lincoln's name was better known than ever. In late February, just past his fifty-first birthday, Lincoln traveled to New York for a speech at Cooper Union. The city audience thought him strange as he stood there, tall and awkward in a new broadcloth suit that hung

★

badly from having been folded in a satchel for the train ride. "Mr Cheerman," he began. Presently, however, the awkwardness was dropped, or else they forgot it. He spoke with calm authority, denying that the Republican Party was either sectional or radical, except as its opponents had made it so. Slavery was the issue, North and South, he said, probing once more for the heart of the matter.

"All they ask, we could readily grant, if we thought slavery right; all we ask, they could as readily grant, if they thought it wrong. Their thinking it right, and our thinking it wrong, is the precise fact upon which depends the whole controversy. Thinking it right, as they do, they are not to blame for desiring its full recognition as being right; but thinking it wrong, as we do, can we yield to them? Can we cast our votes with their view and against our own? In view of our moral, social, and political responsibilities can we do this?" He thought not. "If our sense of duty forbids this, then let us stand by our duty fearlessly and effectively. . . . Neither let us be slandered from our duty by false accusations against us, nor frightened from it by menaces of destruction to the government nor of dungeons to ourselves. Let us have faith that right makes might, and in that faith let us, to the end, dare to do our duty as we understand it."

That was the peroration, and the listeners surged from their seats to applaud him, waving handkerchiefs and hats as they came forward to wring his hand. Four New York newspapers printed the speech in full next morning, and Lincoln went on into New England, making a series of addresses there before returning to Springfield much enhanced. The time for presidential nominations was drawing close. When a friend asked if he would allow his name to be entered, Lincoln admitted: "The taste *is* in my mouth a little."

Chicago was the scene of the Republican national convention, the result of a political maneuver toward the close of the previous year by one of Lincoln's supporters, who, poker-faced, had suggested the western city as an ideal neutral site, since Illinois would have no candidate of her own. Now in mid-May, however, as the delegates converged upon the raw pine Wigwam put up to accommodate ten thousand in an atmosphere of victory foreseen, they found that Illinois had a candidate indeed, and something beyond the usual favorite son. Alongside such prominent men as William H. Seward of New York, Salmon P. Chase of Ohio, Edward Bates of Missouri, and Simon Cameron of Pennsylvania, Lincoln was comparatively unknown. Yet this had its advantages, since the shorter the public record a candidate presented, the smaller the target he would expose to the mud that was sure to be flung. Each of these men had disadvantages; Seward had spoken too often of the "irrepressible conflict," Chase had been too radical, Bates was tainted by Know-Nothingism, and Cameron was said to be a crook. Besides all this, Lincoln came from the critical Northwest, where the political scale was likely to be tipped.

His managers set up headquarters and got to work behind the

scenes, giving commitments, making deals. Then, on the eve of balloting, they received a wire from Springfield: "I authorize no bargains and will be bound by none." "Lincoln aint here and don't know what we have to meet," the managers said, and went on dickering right and left, promising cabinet posts and patronage, printing counterfeit admission tickets to pack the Wigwam nomination morning. The Seward yell was met by the Lincoln yawp. The New Yorker led on the first ballot. On the second there were readjustments as the others jockeyed for position; Lincoln was closing fast. On the third he swept in. The Wigwam vibrated with shouts and cheers, bells and whistles swelling the uproar while the news went out to the nation.

"Just think of such a sucker as me being President," Lincoln had said. Yet in Springfield when his friends came running, those who were not already with him in the newspaper office, they were somewhat taken aback at the new, calm, sure dignity which clothed him now like a garment.

★ ★ ★ *L*incoln himself did not campaign. No presidential candidate ever had, such action being considered incommensurate with the dignity of the office. Nor did two of his three opponents. But Douglas, the only one of the four who seemed to believe that the election might bring war, set forth to stump the country. All four were running on platforms that called for the preservation of the Union. The defeat of Lincoln depended solely on Douglas, however, since neither of the others could hope to carry the free states. Knowing this, Douglas worked with all his strength. Wherever he went he was met by Lincoln men, including Seward, Chase, and Bates. The Republican campaign for "Honest Abe, the Rail Splitter" was a colorful one, with pole raisings, barbecues, and torchlight parades. Douglas kept fighting. Then in August, when Lincoln supporters carried local elections in Maine and Vermont, and in October when Pennsylvania and Ohio followed suit, Douglas saw what was coming. He told his secretary, "Mr Lincoln is the next President. We must try to save the Union. I will go South."

He did go South in a final attempt to heal the three-way Democratic split, but there men would not listen either. On election day, November 6, though he ran closest to Lincoln in popular votes, he had the fewest electoral votes of all.

That night Lincoln sat in the Springfield telegraph office, watching the tabulations mount to a climax: Bell, 588,879; Breckinridge, 849,781; Douglas, 1,376,957; Lincoln, 1,866,452. The combined votes of his opponents outnumbered his own by almost a million; he would be a minority President, like the indecisive Buchanan now in office. He had carried none of the fifteen southern states, receiving not a single popular ballot in five of them, even from a crank, and no electoral votes at all. Yet he had carried all of the northern states except New Jersey, which he split with Douglas, so that the final elec-

*A white-suited Abraham Lincoln, at his
front door in Springfield, towers above the crowd
during a Republican rally in August of 1860.*

Illiterate herself, Sally Bush Lincoln insisted that Lincoln pursue his studies. She apparently foresaw her stepson's fate.

toral vote had a brighter aspect: Lincoln 180, Breckinridge 72, Bell 39, Douglas 12. Even if all the opposing popular votes had been concentrated on a single candidate, he would have received but eleven fewer electoral votes, which still would have left him more than he needed to win. Any way men figured it, North or South, barring assassination or an act of God, Abraham Lincoln would be President of the United States in March.

How many states would remain united was another question. South Carolina had warned that she would secede if Lincoln was elected. Now she did, and within three of the four months that lay between the election and the inauguration, six others followed her out. Lincoln in Springfield gave no assurance that he would seek a compromise or be willing to accept one. "Stand firm," he wrote privately to an Illinois senator. "The tug has to come, and better now than any time hereafter." "Hold firm, as with a chain of steel," he wrote to a friend in the House.

He had troubles enough, right there at home. "No bargains," he had wired his managers at the convention, but they had ignored him out of necessity. Now the claimants hedged him in, swarming into his home and office, plucking at his coat sleeve on the street.

The week before his departure for Washington he made a trip down

★

to Coles County to say goodbye to Sally Bush Lincoln, the stepmother who had done for him all she could. When his father had died there, nine years back, Lincoln had not attended the funeral; but he took time out for this. He kissed her and held her close, then came back to Springfield, closed his office the final day, said goodbye to his partner Herndon, and went to the Chenery House for his last sleep in Illinois.

★ ★ ★ *N*ext morning dawned cold and drizzly; 8 o'clock was leaving time. Lincoln and his party of fifteen, together with those who had come to say goodbye, assembled in the waiting room of the small brick depot. They felt unaccountably depressed; there was a gloom about the gathering, no laughter and few smiles as people came forward for handshakes and farewells. When the stub, funnel-stack locomotive blew the all-aboard they filed out of the station. The President-elect, and those who were going with him, boarded the single passenger car; those who were staying collected about the back platform, the rain making a steady murmur against the taut cotton or silk of their umbrellas. As he stood at the rail, chin down, Lincoln's look of sadness deepened. Tomorrow he would be fifty-two, one of the youngest men ever to fill the office he had won three months ago. Then he raised his head, and the people were hushed as he looked into their faces.

"My friends," he said quietly, above the murmur of the rain, "no one not in my situation can appreciate my feeling of sadness at this parting. To this place and the kindness of these people I owe everything. Here I have lived for a quarter of a century, and have passed from a young to an old man. Here my children have been born, and one is buried. I now leave, not knowing when, or whether ever, I may return, with a task before me greater than that which rested upon Washington. Without the assistance of that Divine Being who ever attended him, I cannot succeed. With that assistance I cannot fail. Trusting in Him who can go with me and remain with you and be everywhere for good, let us confidently hope that all will yet be well. To His care commending you, as I hope in your prayers you will commend me, I bid you an affectionate farewell."

The train pulled out and the people stood and watched it go, some with tears on their faces. Four years and two months later, still down in Coles County, Sally Bush Lincoln was to say: "I knowed when he went away he wasn't ever coming back alive."

★ ★ ★

★

Shelby Foote

*Fiery projectile trails light up the
night sky around Charleston as
Fort Sumter, shrouded in smoke,
duels with Confederate batteries
on shore on April 12, 1861.*

T W O

Sumter; Early Maneuvers

1861 ★ ★ ★ ★ ★ Throughout the twelve days of his roundabout trip to Washington, traversing five states along an itinerary that called for twenty speeches and an endless series of conferences with prominent men who boarded the train at every station, Lincoln's resolution to keep silent on the vital issues was made more difficult if not impossible. Determined to withhold his plans until the inauguration had given him the authority to act as well as declare, he attempted to say nothing even as he spoke. And in this he was surprisingly successful. He met the crowds with generalities and the dignitaries with jokes — to the confusion and outrage of both. He told the Ohio legislature, "There is nothing going wrong. It is a consoling circumstance that when we look out there is nothing that really hurts anybody. We entertain different views upon political questions, but nobody is suffering anything."

With seven states out of the Union, arsenals and mints seized along with vessels and forts, the Mississippi obstructed, the flag itself fired upon, this man could say there was nothing going wrong. His listeners shrugged and muttered at his ostrich policy. They had come prepared for cheers, and they did cheer him loudly each time he seemed ready to face the issue, as when he warned in New Jersey that if it became necessary "to put the foot down firmly" they must support him. Even so, his appearance was not reassuring to the Easterners. In New York he offended the sensibilities of many by wearing black kid gloves to the opera and letting his big hands dangle over the box rail. Taken in conjunction with the frontier accent and the shambling western gait, it made them wonder what manner of man they had entrusted with their destinies. Hostile papers called him "gorilla" and "baboon," and as caricature the words seemed unpleasantly fitting.

In Philadelphia, raising a flag at Independence Hall, he felt his breath quicken as he drew down on the halyard and saw the bright red and rippling blue of the bunting take the breeze. Turning to the crowd he touched a theme he would return to. "I have often inquired of myself what great principle or idea it was that kept this confederacy so long together. It was not the mere matter of the separation of the colonies from the mother land, but that something in the Declaration giving liberty, not alone to the people of this land, but hope to the world for all future time. It was that which gave promise that in due time the weights should be lifted from the shoulders of all men, and that all should have an equal chance." Men stood and listened with upturned faces, wanting fire for the tinder of their wrath, not ointment for their fears, and the music crept by them. It was not this they had come to hear.

So far Lincoln had seemed merely inadequate, inept, at worst a bumpkin; but now the trip was given a comic-opera finish, in which he was called to play the part not only of a fool but of a coward. Baltimore, the last scheduled stop before Washington, would mark his first entry into a slavery region as President-elect. The city had sent him no welcome message, as all the others had done, and apparently had made no official plans for receiving him or even observing his presence while he passed through. Unofficially, however, according to reports, there awaited him a reception quite different from any he had been given along the way. Bands of toughs, called Blood Tubs, roamed the streets, plotting his abduction or assassination. He would be stabbed or shot, or both; or he would be hustled aboard a boat and taken South, the ransom being southern independence. All this was no more than gossip until the night before the flag-raising ceremony in Philadelphia, when news came from reliable sources that much of it was fact. General Winfield Scott, head of the armed forces, wrote warnings; Senator Seward, slated for Secretary of State, sent his son with documentary evidence; and now came the railroad head with his detective, Allan Pinkerton, whose operatives had joined such Maryland bands, he said, and as members had taken deep and bloody oaths. Such threats and warnings had become familiar over the past three months, but hearing all this Lincoln was disturbed. The last thing he wanted just now was an "incident," least of all one with himself as a corpse to be squabbled over. His friends urged him to cancel the schedule and leave for Washington immediately. Lincoln refused, but agreed that if, after he had spoken at Philadelphia the next morning and at Harrisburg in the afternoon, no Baltimore delegation came to welcome him to that city, he would by-pass it or go through unobserved.

Next afternoon, when no such group had come to meet him, he returned to his hotel, put on an overcoat, stuffed a soft wool hat into his pocket, and went to the railroad station. There he boarded a special car, accompanied only by his friend Ward Hill Lamon, known to be a good man in a fight. As the train pulled out, all telegraph wires out of Harrisburg were cut. When the travelers reached Philadelphia about 10 o'clock that night, Pinkerton was waiting. He put them aboard the Baltimore train; they had berths reserved by a female operative for her "invalid brother" and his companion. At 3.30 in the morning the sleeping-car was drawn through the quiet Baltimore streets to Camden Station. While they waited, Lincoln heard a drunk bawling "Dixie" on the quay. Lamon, with his bulging eyes and sad frontier mustache, sat clutching four pistols and two large knives. At last the car was picked up by a train from the west, and Lincoln stepped onto the Washington platform at 6 o'clock in the morning. "You can't play that on me," a man said, coming forward. Lamon drew back his fist. "Don't strike him!" Lincoln cried, and caught his arm, recognizing Elihu Washburn, an Illinois congressman. They went to Willard's Hotel for breakfast.

Southern caricaturist Adalbert J. Volck lampooned Lincoln's alleged disguised passage through Baltimore.

Such was the manner in which the new leader entered his capital to take the oath of office. Though the friendly press was embarrassed to explain it, the hostile papers had a field day, using the basic facts of the incident as notes of a theme particularly suited for variations. The overcoat became "a long military cloak," draping the lanky form from heels to eyes, and the wool hat became a Scotch-plaid cap, a sort of tam-o'-shanter. Cartoonists drew "fugitive sketches" showing Lincoln with his hair on end, the elongated figure surrounded by squiggles to show how he quaked as he ran from the threats of the Blood Tubs. "Only an attack of ager," they had his friends explaining. Before long, the Scotch-plaid pattern was transferred from the cap to the cloak, which at last became a garment he had borrowed from his wife, whom he left at the mercy of imaginary assassins. In the North there was shame behind the laughter and the sighs. Elation was high in the South, where people found themselves confirmed in their decision to leave a

> *"They have gambled me all around, bought and sold me a hundred times. I cannot begin to fill all the pledges made in my name."*
>
> ⌐ Abraham Lincoln

Union which soon would have such a coward for its leader. Certainly no one could picture Jefferson Davis fleeing from threats to his safety, in a plaid disguise and surrounded by squiggles of fear.

Mrs Lincoln and the children arrived that afternoon, and the family moved into Parlor 6, Willard's finest, which between now and the inauguration became a Little White House. To Parlor 6 came the public figures, resembling their photographs except for a third-dimensional grossness of the flesh, and the office seekers, importunate or demanding, oily or brash, as they had come to Springfield. Here as there, Lincoln could say of the men who had engineered his nomination in Chicago, "They have gambled me all around, bought and sold me a hundred times. I cannot begin to fill all the pledges made in my name."

The card-writing stand in the lobby offered a line of cockades for buttonholes or hatbands, "suitable for all shades of political sentiment," while elsewhere in the rambling structure a Peace Convention was meeting behind closed doors, the delegates mostly old men who talked and fussed, advancing the views of their twenty-one states — six of them from the buffer region, but none from the Cotton South — until at last they gave up and dispersed, having come to nothing. Washington was a southern city, surrounded by slave states, and the military patrolled the streets, drilled and paraded and bivouacked in vacant lots, so that townspeople, waking to the crash of sunrise guns and blare of bugles, threw up their windows and leaned out in nightcaps, thinking the war had begun. Congress was into its closing days, and finally in early March adjourned, having left the incoming President no authority to assemble the militia or call for volunteers, no matter what emergency might arise.

Inauguration day broke fair, but soon a cold wind shook the early flowers and the sky was overcast. Then this too yielded to a change. The wind scoured the clouds away and dropped, so that by noon, when President Buchanan called for Lincoln at Willard's, the sky was clear and summer-blue. Along streets lined with soldiers, including riflemen posted at upper-story windows and cannoneers braced at attention beside their guns, the silver-haired sixty-nine-year-old bachelor and his high-shouldered successor rode in sunshine to the Capitol. From the unfinished dome, disfigured by scaffolds, a derrick ex-

★

tended a skeleton arm. A bronze Freedom lay on the grass, the huge figure of a woman holding a sword in one hand and a wreath in the other, awaiting the dome's completion when she would be hoisted to its summit. In the Senate chamber Buchanan and Lincoln watched the swearing-in of Vice President Hannibal Hamlin of Maine, so dark-skinned that campaign rumors had had him a mulatto; then proceeded to a temporary platform on the east portico, where they gazed out upon a crowd of ten thousand.

Lincoln wore new black clothes, a tall hat, and carried a gold-headed ebony cane. As he rose to deliver the inaugural address, Stephen Douglas leaned forward from among the dignitaries and took the hat, holding it while Lincoln adjusted his spectacles and read from a manuscript he took out of his pocket. A first draft had been written at Springfield; since then, by a process of collaboration, it had been strengthened in places and watered down in others.

In front of the unfinished Capitol, a crowd of thousands of people gathered to watch the inauguration of Abraham Lincoln as the sixteenth President of the United States on March 4, 1861.

★

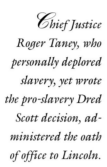

Chief Justice Roger Taney, who personally deplored slavery, yet wrote the pro-slavery Dred Scott decision, administered the oath of office to Lincoln.

Now, after months of silence and straddling many issues, he could speak, and his first words were spoken for southern ears.

"I have no purpose, directly or indirectly, to interfere with the institution of slavery in the states where it exists. I believe I have no lawful right to do so, and I have no inclination to do so." However, he denied that there could be any constitutional right to secession. "It is safe to assert that no government proper ever had a provision in its organic law for its own termination. . . . No state upon its own mere motion can lawfully get out of the Union." Then followed sterner words. "I shall take care, as the Constitution itself expressly enjoins upon me, that the laws of the Union be faithfully executed in all the states. Doing this I deem to be only a simple duty on my part; and I shall perform it, so far as practicable, unless my rightful masters, the American people, shall withhold the requisite means, or in some authoritative manner direct the contrary. . . . The power confided in me will be used to hold, occupy and possess the property and places belonging to the government, and to collect the duties and imposts."

Having clarified this, he returned to the question of secession, which he considered not only unlawful, but unwise. "Physically speaking, we cannot separate. . . . A husband and wife may be divorced, and go out of the presence and beyond the reach of each other; but the different parts of our country cannot do this. They cannot but remain face to face, and intercourse, either amicable or hostile, must continue between them." War, too, would be unwise. "Sup-

★

pose you go to war, you cannot fight always; and when, after much loss on both sides and no gain on either, you cease fighting, the identical old questions as to terms of intercourse are again upon you." The issue lay as in a balance, which they could tip if they chose. "In your hands, my dissatisfied fellow countrymen, and not in mine, is the momentous issue of civil war. The government will not assail you. You can have no conflict without being yourselves the aggressors. You have no oath registered in heaven to destroy the government, while I shall have the most solemn one to 'preserve, protect and defend' it."

He then read the final paragraph, written in collaboration with Seward. "I am loath to close. We are not enemies, but friends. We must not be enemies. Though passion may have strained, it must not break our bonds of affection. The mystic chords of memory, stretching from every battlefield and patriot grave to every living heart and hearthstone all over this broad land, will yet swell the chorus of the Union when again touched, as surely they will be, by the better angels of our nature."

Chief Justice Taney, tall and cave-chested, sepulchral in his flowing robes — "with the face of a galvanized corpse," one witness said — stepped forward and performed the function he had performed eight times already for eight other men. Extending the Bible with trembling hands, he administered the oath of office to Abraham Lincoln as sixteenth President of the United States, and minute guns began to thud their salutes throughout the city.

★ ★ ★ **R**eactions to this address followed in general the preconceptions of its hearers, who detected what they sought. Extremists at opposite ends found it diabolical or too mild, while the mass of people occupying the center on both sides saw in Lincoln's words a confirmation of all that they were willing to believe. He was conciliatory or cunning, depending on the angle he was seen from. Southerners, comparing it to the inaugural delivered by Jefferson Davis in Montgomery two weeks before, congratulated themselves on the results; for Davis had spoken with the calmness and noncontention of a man describing an established fact, seeking neither approval nor confirmation among his enemies.

Standing on the portico of the Alabama capitol, in the heart of the slave country, he did not mention slavery: an omission he had scarcely committed in fifteen years of public speaking. Nor did he waste breath on the possibility of reconciliation with the old government, remarking merely that in the event of any attempt at coercion "the suffering of millions will bear testimony to the folly

"The audience was large and brilliant," wrote Jefferson Davis of his inauguration, pictured here, in Montgomery, Alabama, February 18, 1861.

and wickedness" of those who tried it. He spoke, rather, of agriculture and the tariff, both in Jeffersonian terms, and closed with the calm confidence of his beginning: "It is joyous in the midst of perilous times to look around upon a people united in heart, where one purpose of high resolve animates and actuates the whole, where the sacrifices to be made are not weighed in the balance against honor and right and liberty and equality. Obstacles may retard, but they cannot long prevent the progress of a movement sanctified by its justice and sustained by a virtuous people. Reverently let us invoke the God of our fathers to guide

★

and protect us in our efforts to perpetuate the principles which by His blessing they were able to vindicate, establish, and transmit to their posterity. With the continuance of His favor, ever gratefully acknowledged, we may hopefully look forward to success, to peace, and to prosperity."

He had been chosen over such fire-eaters as Rhett and Yancey, Toombs and Howell Cobb, partly for reasons of compromise, but mainly on grounds that as a moderate he would be more attractive and less alarming to the people of the border states, still hanging back, conservative and easily shocked. Yet whatever their reasons for having chosen him, the people of the Deep South, watching him move among them, his lithe, rather boyish figure trim and erect in a suit of slate-gray homespun, believed they had chosen well. "Have you seen our President?" they asked, and the visitor heard pride in their tone. Charmed by the music of his oratory, the handsomeness of his clear-cut features, the dignity of his manner, they were thankful for the providence of history, which apparently gave every great movement the leader it deserved.

Such doubts as he had he kept to himself, or declared them only to his wife still back at Brierfield, writing to her two days after the inauguration: "The audience was large and brilliant. Upon my weary heart were showered smiles, plaudits, and flowers; but beyond them, I saw troubles and thorns innumerable.... We are without machinery, without means, and threatened by a powerful opposition; but I do not despond, and will not shrink from the task imposed upon me.... As soon as I can call an hour my own, I will look for a house and write you more fully."

Somehow he found both the time and the house, a plain two-story frame dwelling, and Mrs Davis and the children came to join him. "She is as witty as he is wise," one witness said. She was a great help at the levées and the less formal at-homes, having become in their senatorial years a more accomplished political manager than her husband, who had little time for anything but the exactions of his office. The croakers had already begun their chorus, though so far they were mostly limited to disappointed office seekers. Arriving, Mrs Davis had found him careworn, but when she expressed her concern, Davis told her plainly: "If we succeed we shall hear nothing of these malcontents. If we do not, then I shall be held accountable by friends as well as foes. I will do my best."

Rising early, he worked at home until breakfast, then went to his office, where he often stayed past midnight. He had need for all this labor, founding like Washington a new government, a new nation, except that whereas the earlier patriot had worked in a time of peace, with his war for independence safely won, Davis worked in a flurry against time, with possibly a harder war ahead. Like Washington, too, he lived without ostentation or pomp. His office was upstairs in the ugly red brick State House on a downtown corner, "The President" handwritten across a sheet of foolscap pasted to the door. He made himself accessible to all callers, and even at his busiest he was gracious, much as Jefferson had been.

Such aping of the earlier revolutionists was considered by the Confederates not as plagiarism, but simply as a claiming of what was their own, since most of those leaders had been southern in the first place, especially the ones who set the tone, including four of the first five, seven of the first ten, and nine of the first fifteen Presidents. In adopting a national standard, the present revolutionists' initial thought was to take the old flag with them, and the first name proposed for the new nation was The Southern United States of America. Except for certain elucidations, the lack of which had been at the root of the recent trouble, the Confederate Constitution was a replica of the one its framers had learned by heart and guarded as their most precious heritage. "We, the people of the United States," became "We, the people of the Confederate States, each state acting in its sovereign and independent character," and they assembled not "to form a more perfect Union," but "to form a permanent Federal government." There was no provision as to the right of secession. The lawmakers explained privately that there was no need for this, such a right being as implicit as the right to revolution, and to have included such a provision would have been to imply its necessity.

One important oversight was corrected, however. Where the founding fathers, living in a less pious age of reason, had omitted any reference to the Deity, the modern preamble invoked "the favor and guidance of Almighty God." Nor were more practical considerations neglected. The President and Vice President were elected to a six-year term, the former not eligible for reëlection. Congress was forbidden to pass a protective tariff or to appropriate money for internal improvements. Cabinet officers were to be given seats on the floor of Congress. Each law must deal with only one subject, announced in its title, and the President had the right to veto separate items in appropriation bills. Instead of requiring a three-fourths majority, amendments could be ratified by two-thirds of the states. While the newer document expressly prohibited any revival of the slave trade, those chattels referred to in the old one as "persons" now became outright "slaves," and in all territory acquired by the Confederacy, slavery was to be "recognized and protected" by both the federal and territorial governments.

Thus the paperwork foundation had been laid; the Confederacy was a going concern, one of the nations of earth. Whether it would remain so depended in a large part on the events of March and April, following the two inaugurals, particularly as these events affected the sympathies of the eight states in the two- to four-hundred-mile-deep neutral region which lay between the two countries. Davis knew this, of course, and knew as well that it would be the opposition's strategy to maneuver him into striking the first blow. This he was willing to do, provided the provocation to strike it was great enough to gain him the approval of the buffer states and the European powers. Actually, the odds

★

were with him, for the neutral states were slave states, bound to the South by ties of history and kinship, and it was to the interests of the nations of Europe to see a growing competitor split in two. Meanwhile what was needed was patience, which Davis knew was not his dominant virtue, and indeed was hardly a southern virtue at all. Therefore, though his people were united, as he said, by "one purpose of high resolve," he could also speak of his "weary heart" and "troubles and thorns innumerable."

Lincoln up in Washington had most of these troubles, including the problem of holding the border states, and a greater one as well. Having first made up his mind, he must then unite the North before he could move to divide and conquer the South. He had made up his mind; he had stated his position; "The Union is unbroken," he had said. Yet while Europe applauded the

---

*New Jersey was talking secession;
so was California, which along with Oregon
was considering the establishment of a new
Pacific nation; so, even, was New York City,
which beside being southern in sentiment would
have much to gain from independence.*

---

forthright manner in which the Confederacy had set itself in motion, Lincoln was confronted with division even among the states that had stayed loyal. New Jersey was talking secession; so was California, which along with Oregon was considering the establishment of a new Pacific nation; so, even, was New York City, which beside being southern in sentiment would have much to gain from independence. While moderates were advising sadly, "Let the erring sisters depart in peace," extremists were violently in favor of the split: "No union with slaveholders! Away with this foul thing! . . . The Union was not formed by force, nor can it be maintained by force."

On the other hand, whatever there was of native Union persuasion was sustained by economic considerations. Without the rod of a strong protective tariff, eastern manufacturers would lose their southern markets to the cheaper, largely superior products of England, and this was feared by the workers as well as the owners. The people of the Northwest remained staunchly pro-Union, faced as they were with loss of access to the lower Mississippi, that outlet to the Gulf which they had had for less than fifty years. Then too, following Lincoln's inaugural address, there was a growing belief that separation would solve no problems, but rather would add others of an international character, with the question of domination intensified. In early April the *New York Times* stated the proposition: "If the two sections can no longer live together, they can no longer live apart in quiet till it is determined which is master. No two civilizations ever did, or can, come into contact as the North and South threaten to do, without a trial of strength, in which the weaker goes to the wall. . . . We must remain master of the occasion and the dominant power on this continent." Reading this, there were men who faced responsibility; they believed they must accept it as members of a generation on trial. "A collision is inevitable," one said. "Why ought not we test our government instead of leaving it" — meaning the testing — "to our children?"

Walking the midnight corridors of the White House after the day-long din of office seekers and divided counsels, Lincoln knew that his first task was to unite all these discordant elements, and he knew, too, that the most effective way to do this was to await an act of aggression by the South, exerting in the interim just enough pressure to provoke such an action, without exerting

Robert Anderson, seated second from left, and eight other officers commanding Fort Sumter posed before the Confederate bombardment began.

★

enough to justify it. He had good cause to believe that he would not have long to wait. The longer the border states remained neutral, the less they were ashamed of their neutrality in the eyes of their sisters farther south; the Confederates were urged to force the issue. Roger Pryor, a smooth-shaven Virginian with long black hair that brushed his shoulders, a fire-eater irked that his state hung back, was speaking now from a Charleston balcony, advising the South Carolinians how to muster Virginia into their ranks "in less than an hour by Shrewsbury clock: Strike a blow!"

What Pryor had in mind was Fort Sumter, out in Charleston harbor, one of the four Federal forts still flying the Union flag in Confederate territory. Lincoln also had it in mind, along with the other three, all Florida forts: Pickens off Pensacola Bay, Taylor at Key West, and Jefferson in the Dry Tortugas. The crowd was delighted with Pryor's advice. So would Lincoln have been if he had heard him, for by now he saw Sumter as the answer to his need for uniting the North.

The garrison at Fort Sumter had originally occupied the more vulnerable Fort Moultrie on Sullivan's Island, but the night after Christmas, six days after South Carolina seceded, Major Robert Anderson removed his eighty-two men to the stronger fortress three miles out in the harbor. South Carolina protested to Washington, demanding as one nation to another that the troops return to Moultrie. Instead, Buchanan sent an unarmed merchant steamer, the *Star of the West,* with men and supplies to reinforce the fort; but when the Charleston gunners took her under fire, union jack and all, she turned back. That was that. Though they ringed the harbor with guns trained on Sumter and no longer allowed the garrison to buy food at local markets, the Carolinians fired no shot against the fort itself, nor did the Confederate authorities when they took over in March. Buchanan, with his after-me-the-deluge policy, left the situation for his successor to handle as he saw fit, including the question of whether to swallow the insult to the flag. On the day after his inauguration Lincoln received dispatches from Anderson announcing that he had not food enough to last six weeks, which meant that Lincoln had something less than that period of time in which to make up his mind whether to send supplies to the fort or let it go.

★ ★ ★ *D*uring this period, while Lincoln was making up his mind and seemed lost in indecision, there was played in Washington a drama of cross-purposes involving backstairs diplomacy and earnest misrepresentation. Secretary of State William H. Seward, leader of the Republican Party and a man of wide experience in public life, saw the new President as well-meaning but incompetent in such matters, a prairie lawyer fumbling toward disaster, and himself as the Administration's one hope to forestall civil war. He believed that if the pegs that held men's nerves screwed tight could somehow be loosened, or at any rate not screwed still tighter, the crisis would pass; the neutral states would remain loyal, and in time even the seceded states would return to the fold, penitent and convinced by consideration. He did not believe that Sumter should be reinforced or resupplied, since this would be exactly the sort of incident likely to increase the tension to the snapping point.

In this he was supported by most of his fellow cabinet members, for when Lincoln polled them on the issue — "Assuming it to be possible to now provision Fort Sumter, under all the circumstances is it wise to attempt it?" — they voted five-to-two to abandon the fort. The Army, too, had advised against any attempt at reinforcement, estimating that 20,000 troops would be required, a number far beyond its present means. Only the Navy seemed willing to undertake it. Lincoln himself, in spite of his inaugural statement that he would "hold, occupy and possess the property and places belonging to the government," seemed undecided or anyhow did not announce his decision. Seward believed he would come around in time, especially in the light of the odds among his counselors. Meanwhile he, Seward, would do what he could to spare the Southerners any additional provocation.

Three of them were in Washington now, sent there from Montgomery as commissioners to accomplish "the speedy adjustment of all questions growing out of separation, as the respective interests, geographical contiguity, and future welfare of the two nations may render necessary." They had much to offer and much to ask. The Confederate Congress having opened the navigation of the lower Mississippi to the northern states, they expected to secure in return the evacuation of Sumter and the Florida forts, along with much else. Lincoln, however, would not see them. To have done so would have been to give over the constitutional reasoning that what was taking place in Alabama was merely a "rebellion" by private persons, no more entitled to send representatives to the rightful government than any other band of outlaws. Being also an official person, Seward of course could not see them either, no matter how much good he thought would proceed from a face-to-face conciliatory talk. Yet he found a way at least to show them the extent to which he believed the government would go in proving it meant no harm in their direction.

On March 15, the day Lincoln polled his cabinet for its views on Sumter, U.S. Supreme Court Justice John A. Campbell of Alabama, who had not yet gone South, came into Seward's office to urge him to receive the Southerners. The Secretary regretfully declined, then added: "If Jefferson Davis had known the state of things here, he would not have sent those commissioners. The evacuation of Sumter is as much as the Administration can bear."

Justice Campbell was alert at once. Here was Seward, guaranteeing for the government, whose Secretary of State he was, the main concession the commissioners were seeking. To make this even more definite, Campbell re-

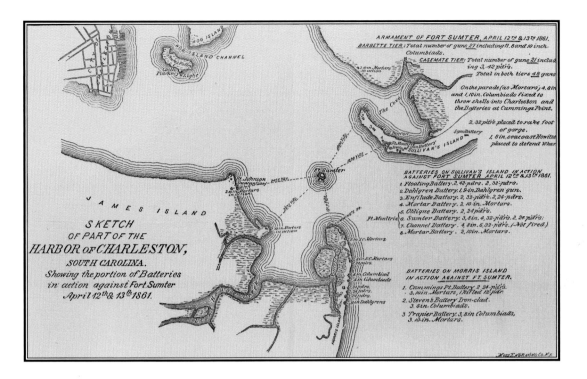

A map shows Sumter's strategic location in Charleston harbor, Confederate batteries, and the guns available to both sides.

marked that he would write to Davis at once. "And what shall I say to him on the subject of Fort Sumter?"

"You may say to him that before that letter reaches him — How far is it to Montgomery?"

"Three days."

"You may say to him that before that letter reaches him, the telegraph will have informed him that Sumter will have been evacuated."

Lincoln was still either making up his mind or reinforcing whatever decision he had already made. In this connection he sent three men down to Charleston to observe the situation and report on what they saw. The first two, both southern-born, were Illinois law associates. Both reported reconciliation impossible, and one — the faithful Lamon, who had come through Baltimore on the sleeping-car with Lincoln — went so far as to assure South Carolina's Governor Pickens that Sumter would be evacuated. The third, a high-ranking naval observer who secured an interview with Anderson at the fort, returned to declare that a relief expedition was feasible. Lincoln ordered him to assemble the necessary ships and to stand by for sailing orders; he would use him or not, depending on events. At the same time, in an interview with a member of the Virginia state convention — which had voted against leaving the Union, but remained in session, prepared to vote the other way if the Administration went against the grain of its sense of justice — Lincoln proposed a swap. If the convention would adjourn *sine die*, he would evacuate Sumter. "A state for a fort is no bad business," he said.

Nothing came of this, but at the end of March, when Lincoln again polled the cabinet on the question, the vote was three-to-three, one member being absent. Seward by now had begun to see that he might well have gone too far in his guarantees to the Confederate commissioners. When Justice Campbell returned on April 1 to ask why his promise of two weeks before had not been carried out, Seward replied with the straight-faced solemnity of a man delivering an April Fool pronouncement: "I am satisfied the government will not undertake to supply Fort Sumter without giving notice to Governor Pickens."

"What does this mean?" Campbell asked, taken aback. This was something quite different from the Secretary's former assurances. "Does the President design to supply Sumter?"

"No, I think not," Seward said. "It is a very irksome thing to him to surrender it. His ears are open to everyone, and they fill his head with schemes for its supply. I do not think he will adopt any of them. There is no design to reinforce it."

Campbell reported these developments to the Confederate commissioners, who saw them in a clearer light than Seward himself had done. Restating them in sterner terms, the following day they telegraphed their government in Montgomery: "The war wing presses on the President; he vibrates to that side. . . . Their form of notice to us may be that of a coward, who gives it when he strikes."

This, or something like this, was what followed; for though Lincoln himself had practiced no deception (at least not toward the Confederates) Seward's well-meant misrepresentations had led exactly to that effect. By now Lincoln was ready. On April 6 he signed an order dispatching the naval expedition to Fort Sumter. Yet Seward was still not quite through. The following day, when Justice Campbell asked him to confirm or deny rumors that such a fleet was about to sail, Seward replied by note: "Faith as to Sumter fully kept. Wait and see." Campbell thought that this applied to the original guarantee, whereas Seward only meant to repeat that there would be no action without warning; and this, too, was taken for deception on the part of the Federal government. For on the day after that, April 8, there appeared before Governor Pickens an envoy who read him the following message: "I am directed by the President of the

★

United States to notify you to expect an attempt will be made to supply Fort Sumter with provisions only, and that if such an attempt be not resisted, no effort to throw in men, arms, or ammunition will be made without further notice, or in case of an attack upon the fort."

Pickens could only forward the communication to the Confederate authorities at Montgomery. Lincoln had maneuvered them into the position of having either to back down on their threats or else to fire the first shot of the war. What was worse, in the eyes of the world, that first shot would be fired for the immediate purpose of keeping food from hungry men.

Davis assembled his cabinet and laid the message before them. Their reactions were varied. Robert Toombs, the fire-eater, was disturbed and said so: "The firing on that fort will inaugurate a civil war greater than any the world has yet seen, and I do not feel competent to advise you." He paced the room, head lowered, hands clasped beneath his coattails. "Mr President, at this time it is suicide, murder, and you will lose us every friend at the North. You will wantonly strike a hornets' nest which extends from mountains to ocean. Legions now quiet will swarm out and sting us to death. It is unnecessary. It puts us in the wrong. It is fatal."

Davis reasoned otherwise, and made his decision accordingly. It was not he who had forced the issue, but Lincoln, and this the world would see and know, along with the deception which had been practiced. Through his Secretary of War he sent the following message to General P. G. T. Beauregard, commanding the defenses at Charleston harbor:

> *If you have no doubt as to the authorized character*
> *of the agent who communicated to you the intention of*
> *the Washington government to supply Fort Sumter*
> *by force, you will at once demand its evacuation, and,*
> *if this is refused, proceed in such manner as you may*
> *determine to reduce it.*

Beauregard sent two men out to Sumter in a rowboat flying a flag of truce. They tendered Major Anderson a note demanding evacuation and stipulating the terms of surrender: "All proper facilities will be afforded for the removal of yourself and command, together with company arms and property, and all private property, to any post in the United States which you may select. The flag which you have upheld so long and with so much fortitude, under the most trying circumstances, may be saluted by you on taking it down."

★

Anderson received it sorrowfully. He was a Kentuckian married to a Georgian, and though he had been the military hero of the North since his exploit in the harbor the night after Christmas, he was torn between his love for the Union and his native state. If Kentucky seceded he would go to Europe, he said, desiring "to become a spectator of the contest, and not an actor." Approaching fifty-six, formerly Beauregard's artillery instructor at West Point, he had made the army his life; so that what he did he did from a sense of duty. The Confederates knew his thoughts, for they had intercepted his reply to Lincoln's dispatch informing him that Sumter would be relieved. "We shall strive to do our duty," he had written, "though I frankly say that my heart is not in the war, which I see is to be thus commenced." Therefore he read Beauregard's note sorrowfully, and sorrowfully replied that it was "a demand with which I regret that my sense of honor, and of my obligations to my government, prevent my compliance." Having written this, however, he remarked as he handed the note to the two aides, "Gentlemen, if you do not batter us to pieces, we shall be starved out in a few days."

Beauregard, hearing this last, telegraphed it immediately to Montgomery. Though he knew that it was only a question of time until the navy relief expedition would arrive to add the weight of its guns to those of the fort, and in spite of the danger that hot-headed South Carolina gunners might take matters in their own hands, Davis was glad to defer the opening shot. The Secretary of War wired back instructions for Beauregard to get Anderson to state a definite time for the surrender. Otherwise, he repeated, "reduce the fort."

It was now past midnight, the morning of April 12; there could be no delay, for advance units of the relief expedition had been sighted off the bar. This time four men went out in the white-flagged boat, empowered by Beauregard to make the decision without further conferences, according to Anderson's answer. He heard their demand and replied that he would evacuate the fort "by noon of the 15th instant" unless he received "controlling instructions from my government, or additional supplies." This last of course, with the relief fleet standing just outside the harbor—though Anderson did not know it had arrived—made the guarantee short-lived at best and therefore unacceptable to the aides, who announced that Beauregard would open fire "in one hour from this time." It was then 3.20 a.m. Anderson, about to test his former gunnery student in a manner neither had foreseen in the West Point classroom, shook the hands of the four men and told them in parting: "If we do not meet again in this world, I hope we may meet in the better one." Without returning to Beauregard's headquarters, they proceeded at once to Cummings Point and gave the order to fire.

One of the four was Roger Pryor, the Virginian who had spoken from a Charleston balcony just two days ago. "Strike a blow!" he had urged the Carolinians. Now when he was offered the honor of firing the first shot, he

*J*ust six days
after firing the first
shot on Fort Sumter,
Edmund Ruffin
sat in his Palmetto
Guard uniform for
this commemorative
photograph.

shook his head, his long hair swaying. "I could not fire the first gun of the war," he said, his voice as husky with emotion as Anderson's had been, back on the wharf at the fort. Another Virginian could and would—white-haired Edmund Ruffin, a farm-paper editor and old-line secessionist, sixty-seven years of age. At 4.30 he pulled a lanyard; the first shot of the war drew a red parabola against the sky and burst with a glare, outlining the dark pentagon of Fort Sumter.

Friday dawned crimson on the water as the siege got under way. Beauregard's forty-seven howitzers and mortars began a bombardment which the citizens of Charleston, together with people who had come from miles around by train and buggy, on horseback and afoot to see the show, watched from rooftops as from grandstand seats at a fireworks display, cheering as the gunnery grew less ragged and more accurate, until at last almost every shot was jarring the fort itself. Anderson had forty guns, but in the casemates which gave his cannoneers protection from the plunging shells of the encircling batteries he could man only flat-trajectory weapons firing nonexplosive shot. Beauregard's gunners got off more than 4000 rounds. As they struck the terreplein and rooted into the turf of the parade, their explosions shook the fort as if by earthquakes. Heated shot started fires, endangering the magazine. Presently the casemates were so filled with smoke that the cannoneers hugged the ground, breathing through wet handkerchiefs. Soon they were down to six guns. The issue was never in doubt; Anderson's was no more than a token re-

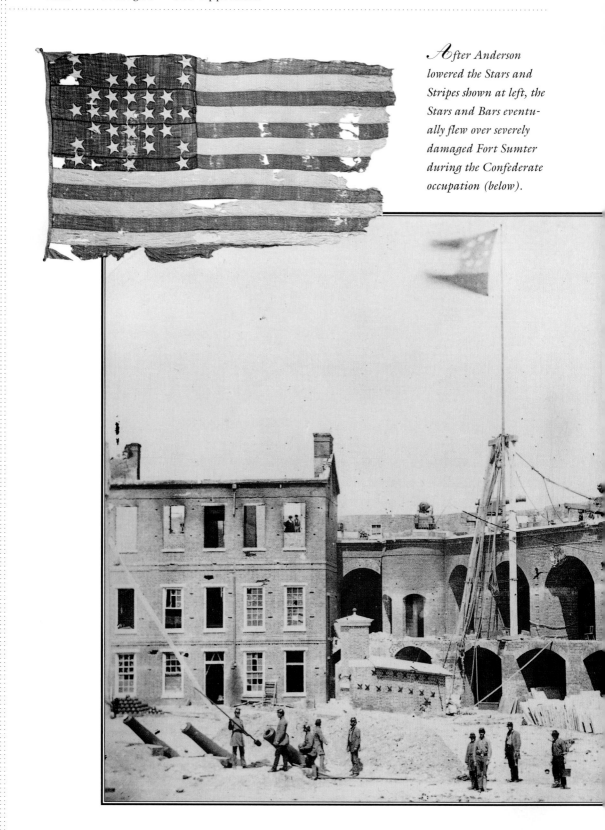

After Anderson lowered the Stars and Stripes shown at left, the Stars and Bars eventually flew over severely damaged Fort Sumter during the Confederate occupation (below).

sistance. Yet he continued firing, if for no other purpose than to prove that the defenders were still there. The flag was shot from its staff; a sergeant nailed it up again. Once, after a lull — which at first was thought to be preparatory to surrender — when the Union gunners resumed firing, the Confederates rose from behind their parapets and cheered them. Thus it continued, all through Friday and Friday night and into Saturday. The weary defenders were down to pork and water. Then at last, the conditions of honor satisfied, Anderson agreed to yield under the terms offered two days ago.

So far there had been no casualties on either side. The casualties came later, during the arrangement of the particulars of surrender and finally during the ceremony itself. The first was Roger Pryor, who apparently had recovered from his reluctance and was sent to the fort as one of Beauregard's emissaries. Sitting at a table in the unused hospital while the formal terms were being put to paper, he developed a thirst and poured himself a drink from a bottle which he found at his right hand. When he had tossed it off he read the label, and discovered that it was iodine of potassium. The Federal surgeon took him outside, very pale, his long hair hanging sideways, and laid him on the grass to apply the stomach pump that saved his life.

A second mishap, this time in the Unionist ranks and far more serious, occurred at 4 o'clock Sunday afternoon. While Anderson, in accordance with the capitulation terms, was firing a fifty-gun salute to his flag, an ember fell into some powder. One man was killed in the explosion and five were injured. Private Daniel Hough thus became the first fatality of the war, before a man had fallen in combat. The scorched and shot-torn flag was lowered and given to Anderson, who packed it among his effects — intending, he said, to have it wrapped about him as a winding sheet on his burying day — then marched his men, with flying colors and throbbing drums, to the wharf where they boarded a steamer from the relief expedition which had observed rather than shared their fight, but which at least could perform the service of taking them home once it was over.

As the weary artillerymen passed silently out of the harbor, Confederate soldiers lining the beaches removed their caps in salute. There was no cheering.

★

*L*incoln soon had cause to believe he had judged correctly. Sumter did indeed unite and electrify the North. That Sunday, when the news arrived by telegraph of the surrender in Charleston harbor, the White House was besieged by callers anxious to assure the President of their loyalty and support. Among them were senators and congressmen who pledged the resources of their states; their people, they said, would stand by the Union through fire and bloodshed. Among them was Stephen Douglas, who rose from his sickbed, the pallor of death already on his face, "to preserve the Union, maintain the government, and defend the capital." Thus he reported his pledge to the people afterwards, more than a million of whom had voted for him for President, never suspecting that he would be dead by early June. Now in mid-April Lincoln met him with outstretched hands and a smile.

Douglas was one among many throughout the nation. It was a time for oratory and easy promises. Businessmen formerly opposed to war as economically unsound now switched their line. They wanted it, now — as bloody as need be, so long as it was short and vigorous. In Pittsburgh, hangman's nooses dangled from lampposts inscribed "Death to Traitors!" Here as in other northern cities, secession sympathizers were bayed by angry crowds until they waved Union banners from their windows. Down in Knoxville, Tennessee, the loyal newspaper editor William G. Brownlow declared that he would "fight the Secession leaders till Hell froze over, and then fight them on the ice."

That same Sunday, in such a heady atmosphere of elation and indignation, Lincoln assembled his cabinet to frame a proclamation calling on the states for 75,000 militia to serve for ninety days against "combinations too powerful to be suppressed by the ordinary course of judicial proceedings." Technically it was not a declaration of war; only Congress could declare war, and Congress was not in session — a fact for which Lincoln was duly thankful, not wanting to be hampered. Though he called a special session for July 4, he expected to have the situation in hand by then. Meanwhile he proceeded unmolested, having determined in his own mind that extraordinary events called for extraordinary measures. The militia draft was issued the following day, April 15, to all the states and territories except the rebellious seven, apportioning the number of troops to be forwarded by each.

Here too, at first, the reply was thunderous. The northern states quickly oversubscribed their quotas; governor after northern governor wired forthright encouragement, asking only to be informed of the Administration's needs. Then Lincoln met a check. As he raised a pontifical hand, commanding "the persons composing the combinations aforesaid to disperse and retire peacefully to their respective abodes," he was given cause to think that he had perhaps outgeneraled himself. It soon became more or less obvious that, just as Davis had united the North by firing on Sumter, so had Lincoln united the South by issuing this demand for troops to be used against her kinsmen. This was true not only in the cotton states, where whatever remained of Union sentiment now vanished, but also in the states of the all-important buffer region, where Lincoln believed the victory balance hung. Telegram after telegram arrived from governors of the previously neutral states, each one bristling with moral indignation at the enormity of the proclamation, rather as if it had been in fact an invitation to fratricide or incest.

Governor Letcher of Virginia replied that since Lincoln had "chosen to inaugurate civil war," he would be sent no troops from Old Dominion. "The people of this Commonwealth are freemen, not slaves," Governor Rector answered for Arkansas, "and will defend to the last extremity their honor, lives, and property, against Northern mendacity and usurpation." Governor Ellis of North Carolina declared that his state would "be no party to this wicked violation of the laws of the country and this war upon the liberties of a free people." "Tennessee will furnish not a single man for the purpose of coercion," Governor Harris told Lincoln, "but fifty thousand if necessary for the defense of our rights and those of our Southern brothers."

In such hard words did these four governors reply to the call for troops. And their people backed them up. Virginia seceded within two days, followed by the other three, Arkansas and Tennessee and finally North Carolina. East of the Mississippi the area of the Confederacy was doubled, and her flag, which now could claim eleven stars, flew along a boundary that had leapfrogged northward two to four hundred miles, across soil that had been Union.

Four slave states still dangled in the balance, Delaware and Maryland, Kentucky and Missouri. The first two were cautious; Governor Burton of Delaware reported that his state had no militia and therefore could not comply with the call for troops, while Governor Hicks of Maryland replied that he would forward soldiers only for the defense of Washington. Lincoln was somewhat reassured by their cautiousness, which at least indicated that there would be no precipitate action on their part. He could take no such consolation from the other two wires he received. "I say, emphatically," Governor Magoffin responded, "Kentucky will furnish no troops for the wicked purpose of subduing her sister Southern states." Governor Jackson of Missouri sent the harshest reply of all: "Your requisition is illegal, unconstitutional, revolutionary, inhuman, diabolical, and cannot be complied with."

These were frets with which Lincoln would have to deal through the coming months, particularly the problem of holding onto his native state, Kentucky, with its critical location, its rivers and manpower, its horses and bluegrass cattle. "I think to lose Kentucky is nearly the same as to lose the whole game," he said. "Kentucky gone, we cannot hold Missouri, nor, as I think, Maryland. These all against us, and the job on our hands is too large for us. We would as well consent to separation at once, including the surrender of this capital."

Maryland compassed the District on three sides, while on the fourth, across the Potomac, lay hostile Virginia, whose troops were already on the march, their campfires gleaming on the southern bank. They had seized the arsenal at Harpers Ferry and the Norfolk navy yard, and now the Richmond *Examiner* proclaimed "one wild shout of fierce resolve to capture Washington City, at all and every human hazard. That filthy cage of unclean birds must and will be purified by fire." It seemed possible, even probable. Many of the army's best officers were resigning, going South along with hundreds of civil workers from the various departments.

The day of the proclamation passed, then another, and still another; not a volunteer arrived. The city was defenseless. On April 18, five hundred Pennsylvanians showed up, unarmed, untrained. They had met cold stares in Baltimore, but the troops who arrived next day, the 6th Massachusetts, met something worse. A crowd of southern sympathizers threw bricks and stones and fired into their ranks as they changed trains. They returned the fire, killing twelve citizens and wounding many more, then packed their four dead in ice for shipment north, and came on into Washington, bearing their seventeen wounded on stretchers. Three days later, when a Baltimore committee called on the President to protest the "pollution" of Maryland soil, Lincoln replied that he must have troops to defend the capital. "Our men are not moles, and cannot dig under the earth," he told them. "They are not birds, and cannot fly through the air. There is no way but to march across, and that they must do." So the Baltimore delegation went back and clipped the telegraph lines, tore up railroad tracks, and wrecked the bridges. Washington was cut off from the outside world.

It was now a deserted city, the public buildings barricaded with sandbags and barrels of flour, howitzers frowning from porticoes. The Willard's thousand guests had shrunk to fifty, its corridors as empty as the avenues outside. Many among the few who remained flaunted secession badges, preparing to welcome their southern friends. Virginia's Colonel T. J. Jackson had 8000 men at Harpers Ferry, while Beauregard, the conqueror of Sumter, was reported nearing Alexandria with 15,000 more. If they effected a junction, all Lincoln had to throw in their path was the handful from Pennsylvania and Massachusetts, five companies of the former, a regiment of the latter, quartered in the House of Representatives and the Senate Chamber.

They had arrived on Thursday and Friday. Saturday and Sunday passed, then Monday, and still there was no further sign of the 75,000 Lincoln had called for. "Why don't they come? Why don't they come?" he muttered, pacing his office, peering out through the window. Tuesday brought a little mail, the first in days, and also a few newspapers telling of northern enthusiasm and the dispatching of troops to Washington: Rhode Islanders and New York's 7th Regiment. Lincoln could scarcely credit these reports, and Wednesday when officers and men who had been wounded in the Baltimore fracas called at the White House he thanked them for their presence in the capital, then added: "I don't believe there is any North! The 7th Regiment is a myth; Rhode Island is not known in our geography any longer. You are the only northern realities!"

Then on Thursday, April 25, the piercing shriek of a locomotive broke the noonday stillness of the city. The 7th New York arrived, followed by 1200 Rhode Island militiamen and an equal number from Massachusetts, whose volunteer mechanics had repaired a crippled engine and relaid the torn-up Annapolis track. A route had been opened to the north.

By the end of the month, Washington had 10,000 troops for its defense, with more on the way. Lincoln could breathe easier. An iron hand was laid on Baltimore, securing Maryland to the Union. Major Robert Anderson,

Men of the 6th Massachusetts fire on a mob of rock-throwing secessionists during the Baltimore riot of April 19, 1861.

★

the returned hero of Sumter, was promoted to brigadier general and sent to assert the Federal claim to his native Kentucky. Major General John C. Frémont, the California Pathfinder and the Republican Party's first presidential candidate, was sent to perform a like function in Missouri. Before long, Lincoln could even assume the offensive.

Harpers Ferry was recaptured, Arlington Heights and Alexandria occupied. Confederate campfires no longer gleamed across the Potomac; the fires there now were Federal. Fortress Monroe, at the tip of the York-James peninsula, was reinforced, and an attack was launched against western Virginia, across the Ohio. Within another month, so quickly had despair been overcome and mobilization completed, there began to be heard in the North a cry that would grow familiar: "On to Richmond!"

★ ★ ★   **T**hat city was the southern capital now, moved there from Montgomery toward the end of May at the climax of the fervor following Sumter and the northern call for troops. Vice President Alexander H. Stephens voiced the defiance of the Confederacy, crying: "Lincoln may bring his 75,000 troops against us. We fight for our homes, our fathers and mothers, our wives, brothers, sisters, sons, and daughters!...We can call out a million of peoples if need be, and when they are cut down we can call another, and still another, until the last man of the South finds a bloody grave."

Davis, with a sidelong glance at Europe and what history might say, reinforced the defensive character of these words in a message to Congress, called into extra session on April 29. Though desirous of peace "at any sacrifice, save that of honor and independence," he said, the South would "meet" — not *wage* — the war now launched by Lincoln. "All we ask is to be let alone," he added. Spoken before the assembly, the words had a defiant ring like those of Stephens. Read off the printed page, however, they sounded somewhat plaintive.

When Congress voted to accept Virginia's invitation to transfer the national capital to Richmond, Davis at first opposed the move. In the event of all-out war, which he expected, the strategic risk would be less disconcerting in the Deep South area, where the revolution had had its birth, than on the frontier, near the jar of battle. Yet when he was overruled by the politicians, who were finding Montgomery uncomfortable and dull, he acceded gracefully, even cheerfully, and made the two-day train trip without ceremony or a special car. He took instead a seat in the rear coach of a regular train and remained unrecognized by his fellow passengers until he was called to their attention by cheers from station platforms along the way.

In Richmond the Virginians, offering something more of pomp, met him at the station with a carriage drawn by four white horses. When a tossed bouquet fell into the street during the ride to the hotel, the President ordered the vehicle stopped, dismounted to pick up the flowers, and handed them to a lady in the carriage before signaling the coachman to drive on. This was noted with approval by the Virginians, already won by the dignified simplicity of his manner, which was tested further at luncheon in the hotel dining room, when a group of ladies stood around the table and fanned him while he ate. Davis proved equal even to this, and afterwards at the Fair Grounds, having gotten through the ordeal of a handshaking ceremony more exhausting than the two-day train ride, he made a short informal speech in which he called his listeners "the last best hope of liberty." "The country relies upon you," he told them. "Upon you rest the hopes of our people; and I have only to say, my friends, that to the last breath of my life I am wholly your own."

Here as in Montgomery—also a city of seven hills; Our Rome, Virginians called their capital—the people congratulated themselves on having inherited such a President. At St Paul's, the first Sunday after secession, the words of the First Lesson had come with all the force of a prophecy: "I will remove far off from you the northern army, and will drive him into a land barren and desolate ... and his stink shall come up, and his ill savour." Now they seemed to have found the man to lead them through its accomplishment. Originally they had had doubts, wondering how a Westerner could head a people so conscious of having furnished the best leaders of the past, but now that they had seen him they were reassured. Daily he rode out to inspect the training camps, sometimes with his staff, more often with a single aide. "Mr Davis rode a beautiful gray horse," a witness wrote of one of these excursions. "His worst enemy will allow that he is a consummate rider, graceful and easy in the saddle."

He devoted most of his energy to organizing an army: work for which his years at West Point and in Mexico, as well as his experience as Pierce's capable Secretary of War, had prepared him well. War was an extension of state-craft, to be resorted to when diplomacy failed its purpose; but Davis took the aphorism one step further, believing that a nation's military policy should logically duplicate its political intentions. Lincoln had more or less maneuvered him into firing the first shot, and while Davis did not regret his action in the case of Sumter, he did not intend to give his opponent another chance to brand him an aggressor in the eyes of history and Europe. "All we ask is to be let alone," he had announced. Therefore, while Lincoln was gathering the resources and manpower of the North in response to the shout, "On to Richmond," Davis chose to meet the challenge by interposing troops where they blocked the more obvious paths of invasion.

Federal troops at right rush to support artillerists at Big Bethel. The gun was saved, although the clash became a Union rout.

All this time, men were being forwarded to Richmond by the states. By mid-July he had three small armies in the Virginia theater: Beauregard, with 23,000 northward beyond the important rail junction at Manassas, facing a Union army of 35,000; Joseph E. Johnston with 11,000 near the Potomac end of the Shenandoah Valley, facing the 14,000 who had retaken Harpers Ferry; and J. B. Magruder, with about 5000 down on the York-James peninsula, facing 15,000 at Fortress Monroe, which the North could reinforce by sea. Outnumbered at every point, with just under 40,000 opposing well over 60,000 troops, the Confederates yet held the interior lines and could thereby move reinforcements from army to army, across any arc of the circle, in much less time than the Federals beyond the long perimeter would require.

Already there had been clashes of arms. Down the Peninsula—at Big Bethel, northwest of Newport News—Major General Benjamin F. Butler attacked one of Magruder's outposts, seven Union regiments against 1400 Confederates. The attackers became confused, firing into one another's ranks until artillery drove them back. Casualties were 76 for the Federals, eight for the Confederates; which, the latter felt, came within a hair of proving their claim that one southern fighting man was worth ten Yankee hirelings. Yet there had been reverses, too. Johnston had abandoned Harpers Ferry in mid-June: a strategic withdrawal, he called it, under pressure from superior numbers. But when the Union commander, Major General Robert Patterson, a sixty-nine-year-old veteran of the War of 1812, crossed the river in early July there was a sharp clash at Falling Waters, casualties being about a dozen on each side, not including fifty Northerners taken prisoner. This too was felt to be a credit to southern arms, considering the odds, even though more of Virginia's "sacred soil" had been yielded to the invader. At the far-off western end of the state the advantage was clearly with the enemy, but this was blamed on bungling and mismanagement of brave troops. All in all, the Confederates were confident and saw far more reasons for pride than despair in the odds. The victories were glorious; the reverses were explicable. Besides, it was said in discussions on the home front, all this was mere jockeying for position, West Pointism, preliminaries leading up to the one big fight that would end the war and establish southern independence for all time.

The first Confederate council of war was held July 14 in the parlor of the Spotswood Hotel, where Davis had temporary quarters. Beauregard, as became the popular conqueror of Sumter, sent an aide down from Manassas to propose a plan of Napoleonic simplicity and brilliance. Reinforced by 20,000 men from Johnston, he would fall upon and shatter the Union army to his front; this accomplished, he would send the reinforcements, plus 10,000 of his own men, back to Johnston, who then could crush the smaller army facing him in the Valley and march through Maryland against Washington from the north, while Beauregard assailed it from the south; together they would dictate peace to Lincoln in the White House. This was opposed by Robert E. Lee, the President's military assistant since the consolidation into the national army of the Virginia forces he had commanded. The handsome Virginian, his dark mustache and hair touched with gray, opposed such an offensive, not only on the obvious grounds that Johnston, already facing long odds in the Valley, had in his whole army barely more than half the number of troops Beauregard was asking to have sent eastward, but also on grounds that the Federal army would retire within its Washington fortifications until it had built up strength enough to sally forth and turn the tables on the Confederates, using Beauregard's own plan against him and Johnston. Davis accepted Lee's judgment, finding that it coincided with his own, and sent the aide back to his chief with instructions to await the Federal advance.

It was not long in coming. On the 17th Beauregard telegraphed that his outposts were under attack; the northern army was on the march. Davis promptly wired Johnston, suggesting that he reinforce Beauregard at Manassas by giving Patterson the slip; which Johnston did, arriving by noon of the 20th with the leading elements of his army while the rest were still en route. The first big battle of the war was about to be fought.

★ ★ ★

Shelby Foote

*M*assive war rallies like this
one in New York took place in cities
and towns on both sides of the
Mason-Dixon line in the weeks after
the bombardment of Fort Sumter.

T H R E E

Statistics North and South

1861 ★ ★ ★ ★ ★ **C**hristmas Eve of the year before, **William Tecumseh Sherman,** super-intendent of the Louisiana State Military Academy, was having supper in his quarters with the school's professor of Latin and Greek, a Virginian named Boyd, when a servant entered with an Alexandria newspaper that told of the secession of South Carolina. Sherman was an Ohioan, a West Pointer and a former army officer, forty years old, red-bearded, tall and thin, with sunken temples and a fidgety manner. He had come South because he liked it, as well as for reasons of health, being twenty pounds underweight and possibly consumptive; the room had a smell of niter paper, which he burned for his asthma. Rapidly he read the story beneath the black headline announcing the dissolution of the Union, then tossed it into Boyd's lap and strode up and down the room while the professor read it. Finally he stopped pacing and stood in front of his friend's chair, shaking a bony finger in the Virginian's face as if he had the whole fire-eating South there in the room.

"You people of the South don't know what you are doing," he declared. "This country will be drenched in blood, and God only knows how it will end. It is all folly, madness, a crime against civilization! You people speak so lightly of war; you don't know what you're talking about. War is a terrible thing!" He resumed his pacing, still talking. "You mistake, too, the people of the

*"You people of the South don't know
what you are doing. This country
will be drenched in blood, and God only knows
how it will end. It is all folly, madness,
a crime against civilization! You people speak
so lightly of war; you don't know what
you're talking about. War is a terrible thing!"*

— William T. Sherman

North. They are a peaceable people but an earnest people, and they will fight, too. They are not going to let this country be destroyed without a mighty effort to save it. . . . Besides, where are your men and appliances of war to contend against them? The North can make a steam engine, locomotive or railway car; hardly a yard of cloth or a pair of shoes can you make. You are rushing into war with one of the most powerful, ingeniously mechanical and determined people on earth — right at your doors." Then he delivered a prophecy. "You are bound to fail. Only in your spirit and determination are you prepared for war. In all else you are totally unprepared, with a bad cause to start with. At first you will make headway, but as your limited resources begin to fail, shut out from the markets of Europe as you will be, your cause will begin to wane. If your people will but stop and think, they must see that in the end you will surely fail."

★

In February he resigned from the academy and came north, stopping off in Washington to see his brother John, a senator, who took him for a visit with the President. It was late March by then; Lincoln was at his busiest, harried by office seekers and conflicting counsels on Sumter. When the senator introduced his brother as a competent witness just arrived from the South, Lincoln said, "Ah. How are they getting along down there?"

"They think they are getting along swimmingly," Sherman told him. "They are preparing for war."

"Oh, well," Lincoln said, "I guess we'll manage to keep house."

Sherman left in disgust. In reply to his brother's plea that he stay and resume his military career, Sherman flung out against him and all politicians: "You have got things in a hell of a fix, and you may get them out as best you can!"

He went to St Louis and accepted a position as head of a streetcar company. However, when Sumter was fired on he returned to Washington, and after refusing a brigadier's commission — saying, to Lincoln's amazement, that he would rather work up to such rank — accepted command of one of the newly organized regiments of regulars. As he came down the White House steps he met a West Point friend and fellow Ohioan, Irvin McDowell, wearing stars on his shoulder straps.

"Hello, Sherman," McDowell said. "What did you ask for?"

"A colonelcy."

"What? You should have asked for a brigadier general's rank. You're just as fit for it as I am."

"I know it," Sherman snapped.

In his anguished tirade on Christmas Eve, comparing the resources of the two regions about to be at war, the waspish Ohio colonel had made a strong case, mostly within the bounds of truth. Yet he could have made a still stronger case, entirely within such bounds, by the use of statistics from the 1860 census. According to this, the southern population was nine million, the northern twenty million, and in the disparity of available manpower for the armies the odds were even longer, rising from better than two-to-one to almost four-to-one. White males between the ages of fifteen and forty numbered 1,140,000 in the South, compared to 4,070,000 in the North: a difference mainly due to the fact that more than three and one-half million out of the total southern population were Negroes. While these of course would contribute to the overall strength, by service as agricultural workers and diggers of intrenchments, their value was about offset by the fact that the North would be open to immigration — particularly from Germany and Ireland, both of which would furnish men in considerable numbers — as well as by the additional fact that the Negroes themselves would constitute a recruitable body for the invaders; 186,017, nearly all of them southern, were to enroll in the northern armies before the finish.

Sherman, however, had underrated the manufacturing capacity of the South. For the past decade the Tredegar Iron Works in Richmond had been building locomotives for domestic and foreign use, as well as projectiles and cannon for the U.S. Navy, and only the previous year a steam fire engine produced for the Russian government had been exhibited in the North before being shipped abroad. All the same, the colonel was mainly right. It was in just this field that the odds were longest. The North had 110,000 manufacturing establishments, the South 18,000 — 1,300,000 industrial workers, compared to 110,000 — Massachusetts alone producing over sixty percent more manufactured goods than the whole Confederacy, Pennsylvania nearly twice as much, and New York more than twice. Only in land area — and only then in a special sense — could the South, with its eleven states, out-statistic the twenty-two states of the North: 780,000 square miles as opposed to 670,000 in the area including Texas and the first tier of states west of the Mississippi. Yet this was a doubtful advantage at best, as might be seen by comparing the railway systems. The South had

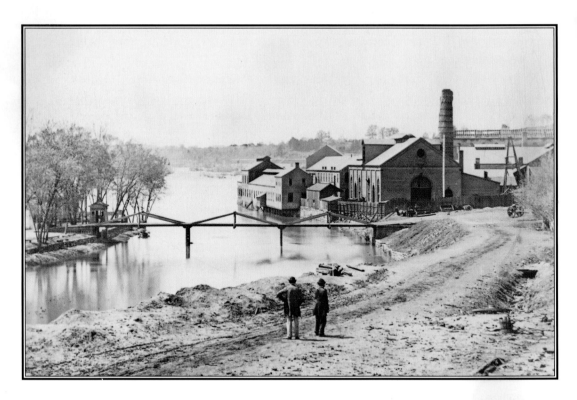

Richmond's Tredegar Iron Works was the more important of the Confederacy's two first-class foundries and machine shops.

★

9000 miles, the North 22,000, in both cases about a mile of track to every thousand persons. The North, with better than double the mileage in an area somewhat smaller, was obviously better able to move and feed her armies.

Statistically, therefore, Sherman had solid ground for his judgment, "You are bound to fail." Yet wars were seldom begun or even waged according to statistics. Nor were they always won on such a basis. The South had the proud example of the American Revolution, where the odds were even longer against those in rebellion. Now as then, she could reason, the nations of Europe, hungry for produce for their mills, would welcome the establishment of a new, tariff-free market for their goods, as well as the crippling of a growing competitor. And now among the nations offering aid there would be not only France, as in the earlier war for independence, but also the former adversary England, who was most powerful in just those directions where the Confederacy was statistically most weak.

What was more, aside from the likelihood of foreign intervention, there were other advantages not listed in those tables dribbling decimals down the pages. Principal among these, in the southern mind at any rate, was the worth of the individual soldier. The Southerner, being accustomed to command under the plantation system, as well as to the rigors of outdoor living and the use of horse and gun, would obviously make the superior trooper or infantryman or cannoneer. If the North took pride in her million-odd industrial workers, the South could not see it so; "pasty-faced mechanics," she called such, and accounted them a downright liability in any army, jumpy and apt to run from the first danger.

Such beliefs, though in fact they appeared to be borne out in the opening days of the conflict, were mostly prejudices and as such might be discounted by an opponent. There were other considerations, more likely to appeal to a professional soldier such as Sherman. Strategically, the South would fight a defensive war, and to her accordingly would proceed all the advantages of the defensive: advantages which had been increasing in ratio to the improvement of modern weapons, until now it was believed and taught that the attacking force on any given field should outnumber the defenders in a proportion of at least two-to-one; three-to-one, some authorities insisted, when the defenders had had time to prepare, which surely would be the case in the matter at hand. A study of the map would show additional difficulties for the North, particularly in the theater lying between the two capitals, where the rivers ran east and west across the line of march, presenting a series of obstacles to the invader. (In the West it would be otherwise; there the rivers ran north and south for the most part, broad highways for invasion; but few were looking westward in those days.) The northern objective, announced early in the war by the man who would be her leading general, was "unconditional surrender."

Against this stern demand, southern soldiers would fight in defense of their homes, with all the fervor and desperation accompanying such a position.

The contrast, of course, would be as true on the home front as in the armies, together with the additional knowledge on both sides that the North could stop fighting at any time, with no loss of independence or personal liberty: whereas the South would lose not only her national existence, but would have to submit, in the course of peace, to any terms the victor might exact under a government that would interpret, and even rewrite, the Constitution in whatever manner seemed most to its advantage. Under such conditions, given the American pride and the American love of liberty and self-government, it seemed certain that the South would fight with all her strength. Whether the North, driven by no such necessities, would exert herself to a similar extent in a war of conquest remained to be seen.

All this, or something like it, must have occurred to Sherman in the months after he left Louisiana for Washington, where he heard Lincoln say with a shrug, "Oh well, I guess we'll manage to keep house." So far had he revised his opinion since that Christmas Eve in his rooms with Professor Boyd, that before the new year was out he informed the Secretary of War that 200,000 troops would be required to put down the rebellion in the Mississippi Valley alone. And it must have gone to convince him even further of a lack of northern awareness and determination when, under suspicion of insanity, he was removed from command of troops for this remark.

★ ★ ★ On the eve of the great battle for which both North and South were now preparing, Lincoln declared in his July message to Congress: "So large an army as the government now has on foot was never before known, without a soldier in it but who has taken his place there of his own free choice. But more than this, there are many single regiments whose members, one and another, possess full practical knowledge of all the arts, sciences, professions, and whatever else, whether useful or elegant, is known to the world; and there is scarcely one from which there could not be selected a President, a Cabinet, a Congress, and perhaps a Court, abundantly competent to administer the government itself. Nor do I say this is not true also in the army of our late friends, now adversaries in this contest."

This estimate of the American volunteer, though pleasant to contemplate before the shock of battle, was discovered to be far beyond the mark, North and South, especially by drill instructors charged with teaching him the manual of arms and parade ground evolutions of the line — in the course of which it often appeared that, far from being the paragon Lincoln discerned, he did not know his left foot from his right, nor his backside from his front. He took cold easily, filling the nighttime barracks and tent camps with the racking uproar of his coughs. He was short-winded and queasy in the stomach, littering the roadsides in the course of conditioning marches, like so many corpses scattered along the way. What was worse, he showed a surprising bewilderment in learning to handle his rifle.

Yet these were but the shortcomings of recruits throughout the world and down the ages, back to the time of the crossbow and the spear. New problems were encountered, peculiar to the two opposing armies. The soldiers of a

The one characteristic they shared beyond all others was a lack of preparedness and an ignorance of what they had to face. Arming themselves with bowie knives and bullet-stopping Bibles, they somehow managed at the same time to believe that the war would be bloodless.

northern outfit, sleeping for the first time in the open, had their democratic sensibilities offended when their officers rolled themselves in their blankets a few paces apart from the line of enlisted men. On the other hand, accustomed as they were to instances of caste in civilian life, Southerners had no objections to such privileges of rank. The outrage was intensified, however, when a former social relationship was upset, so that an overseer or a storekeeper, say, was placed above a planter in the army hierarchy. "God damn you, I own niggers up the country!" might be the reply to a distasteful order, while officers were sometimes called to account because of the tone in which they gave commands to certain highborn privates.

Such problems were individual, and as such would be solved by time or cease to matter. Even at the outset it was clear to the discerning eye that the two armies were more alike than different. For all the talk of States Rights and the Union, men volunteered for much the same reasons on both sides: in search of glory or excitement, or from fear of being thought afraid, but mostly because it was the thing to do. The one characteristic they shared beyond all others was a lack of preparedness and an ignorance of what they had to face. Arming themselves with bowie knives and bullet-stopping Bibles, they somehow managed at the same time to believe that the war would be bloodless. Though it was in

★

Brothers (from left) Daniel, John, and Pleasant Chitwood, posed here with pistols and bowie knives, enlisted in a Georgia regiment at the beginning of the war.

Boston, it might have been in New Orleans or Atlanta that a mother said earnestly to the regimental commander as the volunteers entrained for the journey south: "We look to you, Colonel Gordon, to bring all of these young men back in safety to their homes."

All shared a belief that the war would be short, and some joined in haste, out of fear that it would be over before they got there. Uniforms were at first a matter of personal taste or the availability of materials, resulting in the following exchange:

"Who's that chap?"

"Guess he's the colonel."

"What sort of a way is that for a colonel to rig himself?"

"Morphodite rig, I guess."

"He aint no colonel; he's one of those new brigadier generals that aint got his uniform yet."

"Half general and half minister."

"Well, I said he was a morphodite."

They were not yet cynical; the soldiers of that war earned their cynicism. They were sentimental, and their favorite songs were sad ones that answered some deep-seated need: "The Dew is on the Blossom," "Lorena," "Aura Lea," "The Girl I Left Behind Me," and the tender "Home, Sweet Home." Yet they kept a biting sense of the ridiculous, which they directed against anything pompous. Northern troops, for example, could poke fun at their favorite battle hymn:

★

Mary had a little lamb,

Its fleece was white as snow,

Shouting the Battle-Cry of Freedom!

And everywhere that Mary went

The lamb was sure to go,

Shouting the Battle-Cry of Freedom!

Some of their other marching songs were briefer, more sardonic, pretending to a roughness which they had not yet acquired:

Saw my leg off,

Saw my leg off,

Saw my leg off

    SHORT!!!

Confederates hardly needed to parody their favorite, "Dixie." The verses were already rollicksome enough:

Old Missus marry Will de Weaver,

William was a gay deceiver —

Look away, look away, look away,

    Dixie land!

But when he put his arm around 'er

He smile as fierce as a forty pounder;

Look away, look away, look away,

    Dixie land!

Northern troops, however, had a stanza of their own for the southern tune:

I wish I was in Saint Law County,

Two years up and I had my bounty,

Away! Look away! Dixie land!

Southern soldiers objected to such onerous details as guard duty; they had joined the army to fight Yankees, not walk a post and miss their sleep. Similarly, Northerners were glad of a chance to move against the Rebels, yet on practice marches they claimed the right to break ranks for berry-picking along the roadside. At this time there was no agreement in either army as to what the war was about, though on both sides there was a general feeling that each was meeting some sort of challenge flung out by the other. They were rather in the position of two men who, having reached that stage of an argument where one has said to the other, "Step outside," find that the subject of dispute has faded into the background while they concern themselves with the actual fight at hand.

Perhaps the best definition of the conflict was given in conversation by a civilian, James M. Mason of Virginia: "I look upon it then, sir, as a war of sentiment and opinion by one form of society against another form of society." No soldier would have argued with this; but few would have found it satisfactory. They wanted something more immediate and less comprehensive. The formulation of some such definition and identification became the problem of opposing statesmen. Meanwhile, perhaps no soldier in either army gave a better answer — one more readily understandable to his fellow soldiers, at any rate — than a ragged Virginia private, pounced on by the Northerners in a retreat.

"What are you fighting for anyhow?" his captors asked, looking at him. They were genuinely puzzled, for he obviously owned no slaves and seemingly could have little interest in States Rights or even Independence.

"I'm fighting because you're down here," he said.

★ ★ ★   *C*hief among the statesmen seeking a more complex definition men could carry into battle were the two leaders, Davis in Richmond and Lincoln in Washington. At the outset it was the former who had the advantage in this respect, for in the southern mind the present contest was a Second American Revolution, fought for principles no less high, against a tyranny no less harsh. In the Confederate capital stood the white frame church where Patrick Henry had said, "Give me liberty or give me death," and eighty-five years later another Virginian, Colonel T. J. Jackson, commanding at Harpers Ferry, could voice the same thought no less nobly: "What is life without honor? Degradation is worse than death. We must think of the living and of those who are to come after us, and see that by God's blessing we transmit to them the freedom we have ourselves inherited."

The choice, then, lay between honor and degradation. There could be no middle ground. Southerners saw themselves as the guardians of the American tradition, which included the right to revolt, and therefore they launched a Conservative revolution. Davis in his inaugural had said, "Our present condition . . . illustrates the American idea that government rests upon the consent of

★

the governed. . . . The declared purpose of the compact of union from which we have withdrawn was 'to establish justice, insure domestic tranquillity, provide for the common defense, promote the general welfare, and secure the blessings of liberty to ourselves and posterity'; and when, in the judgment of the sovereign States now composing this Confederacy, it had been perverted from the purposes for which it was established, a peaceful appeal to the ballot box declared that, so far as they were concerned, the government created by that compact should cease to exist." For him, as for most Southerners, even those who deplored the war that was now upon them, there was no question of seeing the other side of the proposition. There was no other side. Mrs Davis had defined this outlook long ago: "If anyone disagrees with Mr Davis he resents it and ascribes the difference to the perversity of his opponent."

Afterwards in Richmond he repeated, "All we ask is to be let alone," a remark which the Virginia private was to translate into combat terms when he told his captors, "I'm fighting because you're down here." Davis knew as well as Lincoln that after the balance sheet was struck, after the advantages of the preponderance of manpower and matériel had been weighed against the advantages of the strategical defensive, what would decide the contest was the people's will to resist, on the home front as well as on the field of battle. Time after time he declared that the outcome could not be in doubt. Yet now, as he walked the capital streets, to and from the Spotswood and his office, or rode out to the training camps that ringed the seven-hilled city, though his step was lithe on the pavement and his figure erect in the saddle, he was showing the effects of months of strain.

Men looked at him and wondered. They had been of various minds about him all along, both North and South. Back at the outset, when he first was summoned to Montgomery, while the far-north Bangor *Democrat* was calling him "one of the very, very few gigantic minds which adorn the pages of history," old General Winfield Scott, commander-in-chief of all the Union armies, received the news of Davis' election with words of an entirely different nature. Perhaps recalling their squabble over a mileage report, Scott declared: "I am amazed that any man of judgment should hope for the success of any cause in which Jefferson Davis is a leader. There is contamination in his touch."

Lincoln, too, was careworn. A reporter who had known him during the prairie years, visiting the White House now, found "the same fund of humorous anecdote," but not "the old, free, lingering laugh." His face was seamed, eroded by responsibilities and disappointments, fast becoming the ambiguous tragedy mask of the Brady photographs. Loving the Union with what amounted in his own mind to a religious mysticism, he had overrated that feeling in the South; Sumter had cost him more than he had been prepared to pay for uniting the North. Through these months his main concern had been to avoid offending any faction — "My policy is to have no policy," he told his secretary — with the result that he offended all. Yet this was behind him now; Sumter at least had gained him that, and this perhaps was the greatest gain of all. He was free to evolve and follow a policy at last.

Unlike Davis, in doing this he not only did not find a course of action already laid out for him, with his only task being one of giving it the eloquence of words and the dignity of a firm example; he could not even follow a logical development of his own beliefs as he had announced them in the past, but must in fact reverse himself on certain tenets which he had expressed in words that returned to plague him now and in the years to come. At the time of the Mexican War he had spoken plainly for all to hear: "Any people anywhere being inclined and having the power have the right to rise up and shake off the existing government and form a new one that suits them better. This is a most valuable, a most sacred right — a right which we hope and believe is to liberate the world. Nor is this right confined to cases in which the whole people of an existing government may choose to exercise it. Any portion of such people that can may revolutionize and make their own so much of the territory as they inhabit."

He must raze before he could build, and this he was willing to do. Presently some among those who had criticized him for doing nothing began to wail that he did too much. And with good and relevant cause; for now that the issue was unalterably one of arms, Lincoln took unto himself powers far beyond any ever claimed by a Chief Executive. In late April, for security reasons, he authorized simultaneous raids on every telegraph office in the northern states, seizing the originals and copies of all telegrams sent or received during the past year. As a result of this and other measures, sometimes on no stronger evidence than the suspicions of an informer nursing a grudge, men were taken from their homes in the dead of night, thrown into dungeons, and held without explanation or communication with the outside world. Writs of habeas corpus were denied, including those issued by the Supreme Court of the United States. By the same authority, or in the absence of it, he took millions from the treasury and handed them to private individuals, instructing them to act as purchasing agents for procuring the implements of war at home and abroad. In early May, following the call for 75,000 militiamen, still without congressional sanction, he issued a proclamation increasing the regular army by more than 20,000, the navy by 18,000, and authorizing 42,034 three-year volunteers. On Independence Day, when Congress at last convened upon his call, he explained such extraordinary steps in his message to that body: "It became necessary for me to choose whether I should let the government fall into ruin, or whether . . . availing myself of the broader powers conferred by the Constitution in cases of insurrection, I would make an effort to save it."

Congress bowed its head and agreed. Though Americans grew pale in prison cells without knowing the charges under which they had been snatched from their homes or places of employment, there were guilty men among the innocent, and a dungeon was as good a place as any for a patriot to serve his country through a time of strain. Meanwhile the arsenals were being stocked and the ranks of the armed forces were being filled. By July 6, within three months of the first shot fired in anger, the Secretary of War could report that 64 volunteer regiments of 900 men each, together with 1200 regulars, were in readiness around Washington. These 60,000, composing not one-fourth of the men then under arms in the North, were prepared to march in all their might against the cockpit of the rebellion whenever the Commander in Chief saw fit to order the advance.

For Lincoln, as for "our late friends, now adversaries" to the south, this was a Second American Revolution; but by a different interpretation. The first had been fought to free the new world from the drag of Europe, and now on the verge of her greatest expansion the drag was being applied again, necessitating a second; the revolution, having been extended, must be secured once more by arms against those who would retard and roll it back. This was a war for democracy, for popular government, not only in a national but also in a universal sense.

"It became necessary for me to choose whether I should let the government fall into ruin, or whether . . . availing myself of the broader powers conferred by the Constitution in cases of insurrection, I would make an effort to save it."

— Abraham Lincoln

In that same Europe — though France had sold her revolutionary birthright, first for the starry glitter of one Napoleon, and again for the bourgeois security of a second — other nations were striving toward the freedom goal, and as they strove they looked across the water. Here the birthright had not been sold nor the experiment discontinued; here the struggle still went on, until now it faced the greatest test of all. Lincoln saw his country as the keeper of a trust.

On July 4 he said to Congress: "This is essentially a People's war. On the side of the Union it is a struggle for maintaining in the world that form and substance of government whose leading object is to elevate the condition of man, to lift artificial weights from all shoulders, to clear the paths of laudable pursuit for all, to afford all an unfettered start and a fair chance in the race of life. . . . Our popular government has often been called an experiment. Two points in it our people have already settled, the successful establishing and the successful administering of it. One still remains — its successful maintenance against a

★

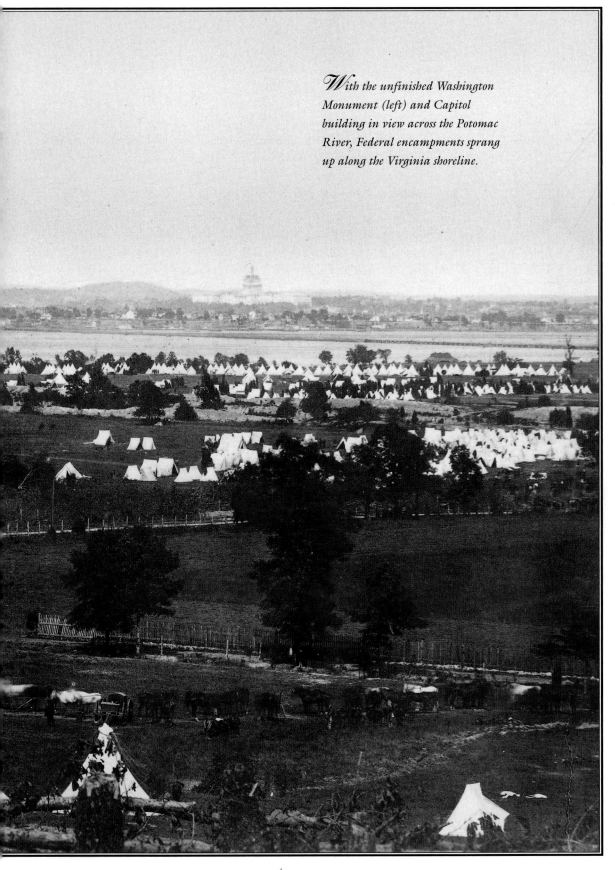

With the unfinished Washington Monument (left) and Capitol building in view across the Potomac River, Federal encampments sprang up along the Virginia shoreline.

formidable attempt to overthrow it. It is now for them to demonstrate to the world that those who can fairly carry an election can also suppress a rebellion, that ballots are the rightful and peaceful successors of bullets, and that when ballots have fairly and constitutionally decided, there can be no successful appeal except to ballots themselves at succeeding elections. Such will be a great lesson of peace, teaching men that what they cannot take by an election, neither can they take by war — teaching all the folly of being the beginners of a war."

In early May he had said to his young secretary, "For my part I consider the central idea pervading this struggle is the necessity that is upon us of proving that popular government is not an absurdity. We must settle this question now, whether in a free government the minority have the right to break up the government whenever they choose. If we fail it will go far to prove the incapacity of the people to govern themselves." Two months later, addressing Congress, he developed this theme, just as he was to continue to develop it through the coming months and years, walking the White House corridors at night, speaking from balconies and rear platforms to upturned faces, or looking out over new cemeteries created by this war: "The issue embraces more than the fate of these United States. It presents to the whole family of man the question whether . . . a government of the people, by the same people, can or cannot maintain its territorial integrity against its own domestic foes."

★ ★ ★ **T**hese days the military news was mostly good; Lincoln could take pride in the fact that so much had been done so quickly, the armies being strengthened and trained and permanent gains already being made. From northwest Virginia the news was not only good, it was spectacular. Here the contest was between Ohio and Virginia, and the advantage was all with the former. The Federal army had only to cross the Ohio and penetrate the settled river valleys, while the Confederates had to make long marches across the almost trackless Allegheny ridges: 8000 loyal troops against 4000 rebels in an area where the people wanted no part of secession. It was an ideal setting for the emergence of a national hero, and such a hero soon appeared.

At thirty-four, Major General George Brinton McClellan, commanding the Ohio volunteers, had earned both a military and a business reputation in the fifteen years since his graduation near the top of his Academy class, as a distinguished Mexican War soldier, official observer of the Crimean War, designer of the McClellan saddle, superintendent of the Illinois Central, and president of the Ohio & Mississippi Railroad. In late May, directing operations from Cincinnati, he sent troops to Grafton, east of Clarksburg on the B & O, who then marched southward thirty miles against Philippi, where they surprised the Confederates with a night attack, June 3; "the Philippi Races," it was called, for the rebels were demoralized and retreated through rain and darkness to the fastness of the mountains. Then McClellan came up.

"Soldiers!" he announced, in an address struck off on the portable printing press which was part of his camp equipment, "I have heard there was danger here. I have come to place myself at your head and share it with you. I fear now but one thing — that you will not find foemen worthy of your steel."

Seeking such foemen, he pressed the attack. When the southern commander, Brigadier General Robert S. Garnett, retreating up the Tygart Valley, divided his army to defend the passes at Rich Mountain and Laurel Hill, McClellan divided his army, too. Advancing one force to hold Garnett at the latter place, he swung widely to the right with the main body, marching by way of Buckhannon against the rebel detachment on Rich Mountain. Before that place he again divided his forces, sending Brigadier General William S. Rosecrans around by a little-used wagon trail to strike the enemy on the flank. "No prospect of a brilliant victory," he explained, "shall induce me to depart from my intention of gaining success by

Following the victory by Federal troops at Rich Mountain (below), Confederate General Robert Garnett was killed while retreating from an untenable position a few miles away.

maneuvering rather than by fighting. I will not throw these raw men of mine into the teeth of artillery and intrenchments if it is possible to avoid it."

Either way, it was brilliant. The flanking column made a rear attack and forced the surrender of the detachment, which in turn rendered Garnett's position on Laurel Hill untenable; he retreated northward and, having got the remnant of his army across Cheat River, was killed with the rear guard at Carrick's Ford, the first general officer to die in battle on either side. By mid-July the "brief but brilliant campaign," as McClellan called it in his report, was over. He telegraphed Washington: "Our success is complete, and secession is killed in this country." To his troops he issued an address beginning, "Soldiers of the Army of the West! I am more than satisfied with you." It was indeed brilliant, just as the youthful general said, and more; it was Napoleonic. The North had found an answer to the southern Beauregard.

★ ★ ★ *I*n Lincoln's mind, this western Virginia campaign also served to emphasize a lack of aggressiveness nearer Washington. Patterson had taken Harpers Ferry. Down on the James peninsula Ben Butler at least had shown fight; Big Bethel was better than nothing. But McDowell, with his army of 35,000 around Washington, had demonstrated no such spirit. In late June, responding to a request, he had submitted a plan to General Scott. While Patterson held Johnston fast in the Valley, McDowell proposed "to move against Manassas with a force of thirty thousand of all arms, organized into three columns, with a reserve of ten thousand." Though he warned that his new regiments were "exceedingly raw and the best of them, with few exceptions, not over steady in line," he added that he believed there was every chance of success "if they are well led."

Thus far, nothing had come of this; the old General-in-Chief did not believe in what he called "a little war by piecemeal." Lincoln, however — aware that the time of the three-month volunteers was about to expire before any more than a fraction of them had had a chance to fire a shot at anything in gray — saw in the plan exactly what he had been seeking. At a cabinet meeting, called soon afterwards, General Scott was overruled. McDowell was told to go forward as he proposed.

At first he intended to move on Monday, July 8, but problems of supply and organization delayed him until Tuesday, eight days later, when he issued his march order to the alerted regiments. "The troops will march to the front this afternoon," it began, and included warnings: "The three following things will not be pardonable in any commander: 1st. To come upon a battery or breastwork without a knowledge of its position. 2d. To be surprised. 3d. To fall back. Advance guards, with vedettes well in front and flankers and vigilance, will guard against the first and second."

*A*gainst his better judgment, a heavy,
white-haired Winfield Scott pens the order
for McDowell's march on Manassas.

So they set out, fifty regiments of infantry, ten batteries of field artillery, and one battalion of cavalry, shuffling the hot dust of the Virginia roads.
This marching column of approximately 1450 officers and 30,000 men, the
largest and finest army on the continent, was led by experienced soldiers and superbly equipped. All five of the division commanders and eight of the eleven
brigade commanders were regular army men, and over half of the 55 cannon
were rifled. Light marching order was prescribed and Fairfax Courthouse was
the immediate march objective, thirteen miles from Arlington, the point of departure. The start had been too late for the army to reach Fairfax that first day,
but orders were that it would be cleared by 8 a.m. Wednesday, Centreville being
the day's objective, another nine miles down the road and within striking distance of Manassas Junction, where the Confederates were massing.

Perhaps because the warning in the march order had made the leaders meticulous and over-ambush-conscious, and certainly because of the inexperience of the troops, no such schedule could be kept. Accordion-action in the

column caused the men to have to trot to keep up, equipment clanking, or stand in the stifling heat while the dust settled; they hooted and complained and fell out from time to time for berry-picking, just as they had done on practice marches. It was all the army could do to reach Fairfax Wednesday night, and at nightfall Thursday the column was just approaching Centreville, 22 miles from the starting point after two and one-half days on the road, stop and go but mostly stop. Then it was found that the men did not have in their haversacks the cooked rations McDowell's order had said "they must have." Friday was spent correcting this and other matters; Saturday was used up by reconnaissance, studying maps and locating approaches to and around the enemy assembled at Manassas. Beauregard thus had been presented with two days of grace, by which time McDowell heard a rumor that Johnston, out in the Valley, had given Patterson the slip and was at hand. He took the news with what calmness he had left, forwarded it to Washington, and set about completing his battle plan. Johnston or no Johnston, the attack was scheduled for first light, Sunday morning.

"You are green, it is true; but they are green also. You are all green alike."

— Abraham Lincoln

Lincoln in Washington and Davis in Richmond, one hundred miles apart, now were exposed for the first time to the ordeal of waiting for news of the outcome of a battle in progress between the two capitals. The northern President took it best. When McDowell had asked for a little more time for training, Lincoln told him, "You are green, it is true; but they are green also. You are all green alike." Now that the armies were arrayed and the guns were speaking, Lincoln kept this calmness. The Sunday morning news was reassuring; even old General Scott saw victory in the telegrams from Virginia. Lincoln attended church, came back for lunch and more exultant telegrams, and went for a carriage drive in the late afternoon, believing the battle won.

Davis, being more in the dark, experienced more alarm. Beauregard's wire on the 17th had told him, "The enemy has assailed my outposts in heavy force. I have fallen back on the line of Bull Run, and will make a stand at Mitchell's Ford." He spoke of retiring farther, possibly all the way to the Rappahannock, and closed with a plea for reinforcements for his 29 regiments and 29 guns, only nine of which were rifled. Davis sent what he could, including three regiments and a battery from Fredericksburg, and directed Johnston to move his army to Manassas "if practicable." Johnston's 18 regiments and 20 smooth-bore guns, even if they all arrived in time, would not bring Beauregard up to the reported strength of the Federals, for of the fifty regiments thus assembled to meet the fifty of the enemy, 1700 of the Valley soldiers — the equivalent of two regiments — were down with the measles. Presently, however, it seemed not to matter, or to be no more than a lost academic possibility. For that same Wednesday afternoon in Richmond another telegram arrived from Beauregard: "I believe this proposed movement of General Johnston is too late. Enemy will attack me in force tomorrow morning."

Thursday came and passed, and there was no attack. Then Friday came, and still the wire brought no word of battle. Davis kept busy, forwarding every corporal's guard he could lay hands on. At noon Saturday Johnston reached Manassas with the van of his army, the rest coming along behind as fast as the overworked railroad could transport them. Sunday came and Davis, a soldier himself, could wait no longer. He took a special northbound train.

In mid-afternoon, as it neared the Junction, there were so many signs of a defeat that the conductor would not permit the train to proceed, fearing it would be captured. But Davis was determined to go on. The engine was uncoupled and the President mounted the cab, riding toward the boom of guns and, now, the clatter of musketry. Beyond the Junction he secured a horse and continued north. Fugitives streamed around and past him, the wounded and the ones who had lost nerve. "Go back!" he told them. "Do your duty and you can save the day." Most of the powder-grimed men did not bother to answer the tall, clean civilian riding into the smoky uproar they had just come out of. Others shouted warnings of disaster. The battle had been lost, they cried; the army had been routed. Davis rode on toward the front.

★ ★ ★

*With a skirmish line in front,
Union troops move shoulder to
shoulder up Henry House Hill in
one of the last Federal attacks of the
Battle of First Manassas.*

F O U R

Manassas – Southern Triumph

1861 ★ ★ ★ ★ ★

*I*rvin McDowell had come a long way since he said to Sherman on the White House steps in April, "You should have asked for a brigadier general's rank. You're just as fit for it as I am." Now perhaps not even Sherman, still a colonel, commanding a brigade in his fellow Ohioan's army, would have replied as he did then. A West Pointer, in his early forties — he and Beauregard had been classmates — McDowell was six feet tall and heavy-set, with dark brown hair and a grizzled beard worn in the French style. He had attended military school in France and later spent a year's leave of absence there, so that, in addition to wearing a distinctive beard, he was one of the few regular army officers with a first-hand knowledge of the classical tactics texts, mostly French. His manner was modest and friendly in the main, but this was marred from time to time by a tendency to be impulsive and dogmatic in conversation, which offended many people. Some were appalled as well by his gargantuan appetite, one witness telling how he watched in dismay while McDowell, after a full meal, polished off a whole watermelon for dessert and pronounced it "monstrous fine!" He had a strong will along certain lines, as for instance in his belief that alcohol was an evil. Once when his horse fell on him and knocked him out, the surgeon who tried to administer some brandy found his teeth so firmly clamped that they could not be pried apart, and McDowell was proud that, even unconscious, he would not take liquor.

★

*Irvin McDowell (center, second step) and
staff pose at Robert E. Lee's Arlington, Virginia,
mansion before moving toward Manassas.*

Now, indeed, marching at the head of an army whose fitness for testing under fire he himself had doubted, he had need to clamp his teeth still tighter and call on all his self-control. Since setting out, prodded into motion by a civilian President who discounted the unpreparedness by remarking that the men of both armies were "green alike" — which did not at all take into account that one of them (McDowell's) would be required to execute a tactical march in the presence of the enemy — he had watched his fears come true. While congressmen and other members of Washington society, some of them accompanied by ladies with picnic hampers, harried the column with buggies and gigs, the troops went along with the lark, lending the march the holiday air of an outing. They not only broke ranks for berry-picking; they discarded their packs and "spare" equipment, including their cumbersome cartridge boxes, and ate up the rations intended to carry them through the fighting.

Re-issuing ammunition and food had cost him a day of valuable time, in addition to the one already lost in wretched marching, and now as he spent another day with his army brought up short at Centreville while he explored the roads and fords leading down to and across Bull Run, where the rebels were improving their position, the worst of his fears was rumored to be fact: Johnston had reached Manassas, leaving Patterson holding the bag out in the Valley. As he rose before daylight Sunday morning, having completed his reconnaissance, issued the orders for attack, and eaten his usual oversized supper the night before, it was no wonder he was experiencing the discomfort of an upset digestion. Even McDowell's iron stomach had gone back on him, cramping his midriff with twinges of pain and tightening the tension on his nerves.

Despite the twinges as he waited for the roar of guns to announce that the attack was rolling, there was confidence in his bearing. He felt that his tactical plan, based as it was on careful preparations, was a sound one. A study of the map had shown a battlefield resembling a spraddled X. Bull Run flowed from the northwest to the southeast to form one cross-member; Warrenton Turnpike ran arrow straight, southwest-northeast, to form the other. The stream was steep-banked, dominated by high ground and difficult to cross except at fords above and below a stone bridge spanning the run where the turnpike intersected it. McDowell had planned to attack on the left, that flank affording the best approach to Richmond; but when reconnaissance showed that the fords below the bridge were strongly held by rebel infantry and artillery, he looked to his right. Upstream, out the western arm of the X, he found what he was seeking. Cavalry patrols reported good crossings lightly held in that direction: one at Sudley Springs, all the way out the western arm, and another about halfway out. Both were suitable for wheeled vehicles, the troopers reported, which meant that the main effort, launched by way of these two crossings, could be supported by the superior Federal artillery. Now McDowell had his attack plan, and he committed it to paper.

Of his four divisions, each with about 8000 men, two would demonstrate against the run, while the other two executed a turning movement against the Confederate left flank. The First Division, under Brigadier General Daniel Tyler, would move "toward the stone bridge . . . to feint the main attack upon this point." The Fourth Division, under Colonel D. S. Miles, would be held in reserve near Centreville, at the tip of the eastern arm of the X, but one of its brigades would make a "false attack" on Blackburn's Ford, halfway down the eastern leg and midway between Centreville and Manassas. As the Second and Third Divisions, under Colonels David Hunter and S. P. Heintzelman, having made their turning movement and launched their attack, swept down the south bank of the stream, crumpling the Confederate line of battle, they would uncover the bridge and the fords, permitting the First and Fourth Divisions to cross the run and strengthen the main effort with fresh troops. This time there were no admonitions as to what would "not be pardonable"; the troops were to drive right through, with more of savagery than caution. Richmond lay beyond the roll of the southern horizon.

★

Sound as the plan was, it was also complicated, involving two feints by half the army and a flank attack by the other half, with the main effort to be made at right angles to the line of advance. McDowell knew that much depended on soldierly obedience to orders. Yet his commanders were regulars, and despite their clumsy performance on the long march, he felt that he could count on them for a short one. As a professional soldier he also knew that much would depend on luck, good and bad, but in this connection all he could do was hope for the former and guard against the latter. For one thing, to forestall delay he could order an early start, and this he did. The holding divisions were to leave their camps by 3 a.m. to open the demonstrations at Stone Bridge and Blackburn's Ford, while the turning column was to set out even earlier, at 2 o'clock, in order to clear Sudley Springs by 7 at the latest.

And so it was. The troops lurched into motion on schedule, some having had but very little sleep, others having had no sleep at all, and now again it was stop and go but mostly stop, just as on the other march, except that now there was the added confusion of darkness and bone-deep weariness as they stumbled over logs and roots and were stabbed at by branches in the woods, clanking as they ran to catch up or stood stock-still to breathe the thick dust of the "sacred soil." About 9.30 — two and one-half hours behind schedule — the head of the column reached Sudley Springs, where the men were halted to rest and drink. Away downstream, opposite the stone bridge and the ford, the guns of the other two divisions had been booming with false aggressiveness for more than three hours now.

★ ★ ★ **B**eauregard at Manassas, midway between the straddled feet of the X, had no intention of awaiting his classmate's pleasure. When Johnston had joined him Saturday with about half of his 9000 men, the rest being due to arrive in the night, the Creole general's spirits rose. Now that his army was about to be almost equal to the enemy's; he would attack. He made his dispositions accordingly, concentrating his regiments along the eastern leg of the X, from Stone Bridge down to Union Mills Ford, where the crossing would be made in force to envelop the Federal left and crush it while he marched on Centreville.

Thus Beauregard and McDowell, on opposite sides of Bull Run, had more or less identical plans, each intending to execute a turning movement by the right flank to strike his opponent's left. If both had moved according to plan, the two armies might have grappled and spun round and round, like a pair of dancers clutching each other and twirling to the accompaniment of cannon. However, this could only happen if both moved on schedule. And late as McDowell was, Beauregard was later.

In the first place there was trouble on the railroad from Manassas

*At Manassas, Union forces (blue)
advanced along and north of Warrenton
Turnpike while Confederate troops (red)
prepared to attack farther south along
Bull Run. Had both flanking moves gone
as planned, the armies would have fought
in a huge spiral.*

Gap, and though some of Johnston's men had been assigned a share in the for-ward movement, the remainder of them did not arrive that night. In the second place, the attack order was ambiguous and vague. There was to be an advance across the run, then an advance on Centreville, and though each section of the plan ended: "The order to advance will be given by the commander in chief," it was not clear to the brigade commanders just which advance was meant. They took it to mean the advance on the crossing, whereas Beauregard intended it to mean the second advance, after the crossing had been forced. Accordingly, early Sunday morning at Manassas, while Beauregard listened for the roar of guns, there was only silence from the right.

Then there arrived from Mitchell's Ford, two miles below Stone Bridge, a messenger who reported that the enemy had appeared in strength to the left front of that position; and as if to reinforce this information there came a sound of firing from the vicinity of the bridge. To guard against a crossing, Beauregard sent his reserve brigades, under Brigadier Generals Barnard Bee and T. J. Jackson, to strengthen the few troops he had stationed there, on the left flank of his army. All this time he listened for the boom of cannon to indicate that his attack was underway on the right. From that direction, all he heard was silence; but northward, from the direction of the bridge, the cannonade was swelling to a roar. At 8 o'clock Beauregard left his office at Manassas Junction to establish field headquarters on Lookout Hill, in the rear of Mitchell's Ford.

From there, of course, the roar of guns was louder, coming from both the left and right, Stone Bridge and Blackburn's Ford, but still there were no signs of an advance across the run. By 9 o'clock Beauregard had begun to suspect that the Federal main body was elsewhere, probably on one of his flanks, preparing to surprise him. Just then, as if in substantiation of his fears, a message arrived from a signal officer:

I see a body of troops crossing Bull Run about two miles above the Stone Bridge. The head of the column is in the woods on this side. The rear of the column is in the woods on the other side. About a half-mile of its length is visible in the open ground between. I can see both infantry and artillery.

Beauregard reacted fast. While a dust cloud floated up from that direc-tion to show the enemy in force, he sent couriers after Bee and Jackson, instruct-ing them to march above the bridge, and ordered Colonel Wade Hampton, just

Confederate Barnard Bee, wearing his national uniform here, rallied the collapsing southern left flank at First Bull Run but was mortally wounded in the battle.

arrived from Richmond with 600 South Carolinians, also to proceed to the exposed flank. When these commands joined the brigade of Colonel N. G. Evans, already posted near the bridge, he would have about 6500 men on the left: barely one-fourth of his army. Still, in spite of a rumor that the mystery column raising its ominous dust cloud might be Patterson, arrived from the Valley with 30,000 men, Beauregard was hoping that somehow the long overdue attack on the enemy left might have smashed through for a counterstroke. Then a message arrived from Brigadier General R. S. Ewell at Union Mills Ford. He had waited all this time for orders; now he was going forward without them. Beauregard despaired. This late, the attack could do no good; it would serve only to make those troops unavailable to help stem whatever success the enemy might achieve on the left. With his army so scattered, it hardly seemed possible to organize any sort of effective resistance. "My heart for a moment failed me," he said later.

Johnston was also there on Lookout Hill, the ranking Confederate, though so far he had left the dispositions in Beauregard's hands, being himself unfamiliar with the terrain. He watched with increasing concern as things went from bad to worse, the dust cloud spreading on the left while Beauregard did what he could to meet the challenge, recalling from across the run the brigades of Ewell, D. R. Jones, and James Longstreet. By 11 o'clock the fury beyond

Stone Bridge was approaching crescendo. The tearing clatter of musketry swelled the uproar of the guns, and powdersmoke boiled up dead-white out of the dust. Johnston, chafing under his self-imposed inaction, at last could bear it no longer. "The battle is there," he told Beauregard; "I am going!" And he went.

Beauregard was not far behind him. Remaining only long enough to order Brigadier General T. H. Holmes and Colonel Jubal Early to march their brigades to the left, he overtook Johnston soon after noon, the Virginian having paused to send a couple of unemployed batteries into action, and the two went on together, accompanied by their staffs. They rode past wounded and frightened men, dazed and blood-stained stragglers from the fight which they could hear but could not see until, climbing a wooded hill, they reached the crest at about 12.30, to find the battle raging below them, a panorama of jetting smoke and furious movement.

A few gray regiments were in action, their muskets flashing pink in the swirl of smoke. Others, shattered by the blue onslaught, were streaming for the rear. Across the line of their retreat a fresh Confederate brigade stood just behind the crest of a ridge adjoining the hill the generals watched from. Their ranks aligned steadily on both sides of a battery whose six guns were firing rapidly into the advancing mass of Federals, these troops had the determined, steadfast appearance of veterans. Otherwise the field had a look of impending disaster.

★ ★ ★ *M*cDowell at last had got his flanking divisions over the run at Sudley Springs, doubling the column to speed the crossing. It was smartly done, the blue ranks closely packed, water squelching in their shoes after their splash across the creek. But as they emerged from the woods about a mile south of the ford, Colonel Ambrose Burnside's Rhode Islanders heading the advance, they ran into fire from two Confederate regiments drawn up to meet them with two smooth-bore six-pounders barking aggressively on the flank. These were South Carolinians and Louisianians; their commander, Colonel Evans, charged with defending the stone bridge, had soon determined that the cannonade there was no more than a feint. Evans — called "Shanks" because of the thinness of his legs — was an old line soldier, resentful at having been stationed far to the left of where the main effort was intended. When he observed the dust cloud to the northwest, beyond the flank of the army, he saw his opportunity and acted on his own initiative. Leaving a handful to guard the bridge, he marched his thousand men upstream to block the path of 13,000 Federals.

The meeting engagement was sudden and furious, the gray troops having the advantage of firing the first volley. As they were beginning to come apart under pressure, they were joined by the Mississippians, Alabamians and Georgians in the brigade of General Bee, who like Evans had marched without

*T*homas J. Jackson, a thirty-three-year-old professor at Virginia Military Institute in this ambrotype, wore the blue frock coat at right at Manassas. Hailed for his tenacious stand on Henry House Hill, he was given the sobriquet "Stonewall."

orders toward the point of danger. All the cotton states were represented, presently reinforced by Hampton's Legion, which also came onto the field at a critical time. Then, as the tide turned again, the Federals exerting the pressure of their numbers, in war as in peace the fire-eaters looked to Virginia. On a ridge to their rear — as Johnston and Beauregard had observed, arriving at this moment — Jackson's Virginians were staunchly aligned on their guns.

"There is Jackson standing like a stone wall!" Bee shouted. "Let us determine to die here, and we will conquer."

Jackson too had arrived at a critical moment, but instead of rushing into the melee on the plain, he had formed his troops on the reverse slope of the ridge, protected from artillery and ready for whatever moved against them. When an officer came crying, "General! the day is going against us!" the stern-lipped Jackson calmly replied: "If you think so, sir, you had better not say anything about it." Another reported, "General, they are beating us back!" "Sir, we'll give them the bayonet," Jackson said.

Over the crest and down the hill, high on the western leg of the X, the battle raged around a small frame house where the eighty-year-old widow Judith Henry lay dying. When the Union troops came pounding south from Sudley Springs her invalid sons carried her on a mattress to the shelter of a ravine, but she begged so piteously to be allowed to die in her own bed that they brought her back, and there she had her wish. A shell killed her the instant they laid her down, and her body was riddled with bullets as the house began to flame.

In a dense blue mass, avenging the months of rebel boasting and insults to the flag, the Federal infantry roared to the attack. The advance had cleared the stone bridge now; Tyler's division poured across, adding its weight to the charge. Bee fell, shot as he rallied his men, who leaderless gave back before the cheering ranks of Federal attackers. On they came, their battle flags slanting forward in the sunlight, up the hill and over the crest, where Jackson's men stood sighting down their muskets. For a moment the blue soldiers were outlined black against the sky, and then it was as if the earth exploded in their faces. One volley struck them, then another, and the survivors stumbled back down the slope, where their officers were shouting for them to reform.

By now there were 18,000 Union troops on this quarter of the field. Supported by well-served rifled guns, the men who had been repulsed closed ranks and presently they charged again, up the slope and over the crest where the Virginians were waiting. But it was too late; the crisis had passed. Johnston and Beauregard had come down off the adjoining hill, Beauregard to ride along the battle line, replacing fallen commanders with members of his staff and making at intervals a speech in which, he said, he "sought to infuse into the hearts of my officers and men the confidence and determined spirit of resistance to this wicked invasion of the homes of a free people," while Johnston established a command post to the rear, at a road intersection where troops from the right and reinforcements from the Valley could be rushed to where the issue was in doubt. As fast as they came within reach he spurred them toward the fight on Henry Hill. There, while the battle raged on the forward slope — disintegrated by now into a strung-out, seemingly disconnected series of hand-to-hand skirmishes by knots of men clustered about their shot-ripped flags, each man fighting as if the outcome of the whole battle depended on himself alone — Beauregard used them to strengthen the line along the crest and to extend the left, where McDowell was attempting to envelop the Confederate defense.

The Union commander advanced two batteries of rifled guns, intending to support them with a regiment of New York Fire Zouaves. As these men in baggy trousers were forming off to the right, Colonel J. E. B. Stuart mistook them for an Alabama outfit, similarly clad, which he thought was fac-

She begged so piteously to be allowed to die in her own bed that they brought her back; and there she had her wish. A shell killed her the instant they laid her down. . . .

ing rear, about to retreat. "Don't run, boys; we're here!" he cried, riding toward them at the head of his cavalry regiment. By the time he saw his mistake, it was too late to turn back. So he charged, his troopers slashing at the white turbans of the men in blue and scarlet, who panicked and scattered in gaudy confusion, leaving the eleven guns unsupported, and a Virginia infantry regiment ran forward to deliver at seventy yards a volley that toppled every cannoneer. The guns were out of action.

Back on the crest, having watched all this, the Confederates were cheering. Jackson rode up and down his line. "Steady, men; all's well," he kept saying. Then, as the Federal infantry pushed forward again, he gave his troops instructions: "Hold your fire until they're on you. Then fire and give them the bayonet. And when you charge, yell like furies!"

By now Beauregard had what he had been building toward. Johnston had been feeding him men, including Brigadier General Kirby Smith's brigade from the Valley army, just off the cars from Manassas Gap, and Beauregard had built a solid line along both flanks of Jackson, extending the left westward until it not only met the threat from that direction, but overlapped the Federal right. The general was ready and so were his men, heartened by their recent success and

This sketch portrays the chaotic Federal flight from the Manassas battlefield that became known as the "Great Skedaddle."

the arrival of reinforcements. About 3.30, as if by signal, the gray line surged forward. "Yell like furies," Jackson had told his soldiers, and now they did. From flank to flank, for the first time in the war, the weird halloo of the rebel yell went up, as if twenty thousand foxhunters were closing on a quarry.

The Federals had watched the rebel line as it thickened and lengthened to their front and on their flank. Now the opposing forces were roughly equal. But the blue troops did not know this; they only knew that the enemy was receiving reinforcements, while they themselves got none. "Where are *our* reserves?" they asked in consternation after the scattering of the zouaves and the loss of their two most effective batteries near the center of the field. Wearied by thirteen hours of marching on dusty roads at night and fighting under a July sun, they began to reason that they had been too thoroughly mismanaged for mere incompetence to account for all the blunders. They were angry and dismayed, and from point to point along the front a strange cry broke out: "Betrayed! We are betrayed! Sold out!" When the long gray line sprang at them, bayonets snapping and glinting in the sunlight as the shrill, unearthly quaver of the rebel yell came surging down the slope, they faltered. Then they broke. They turned and fled past officers on horseback flailing the smoke with sabers while screaming for them to stand. They ran and they kept on running, many of them throwing down their rifles in order to travel lighter and run faster. "Betrayed! Sold out!" some shouted hoarsely as they fled, explaining — as all men apparently always must — the logic behind their fear.

★

Panic on the road between Bulls run Centerville

So far the retreat was mainly sullen, with more grim anger than panic in the ranks. It had not yet become a rout, though the Southerners were doing what they could to make it one. Kirby Smith had ridden down the line as his troops came off the cars to form for battle within the sound of guns and the sight of smoke boiling over the northward ridge. "This is the signal, men," he cried, the back of his hand to the bill of his cap; "the watchword is Sumter!" It didn't make much sense but it sounded fine, and the Valley soldiers cheered him riding past. He was wounded as soon as he reached the field; Colonel Arnold Elzey took command. Coming presently into sight of a mass of infantry drawn across the road ahead — whether Union or Confederate none could tell with the naked eye — Elzey halted the column. As he raised his binoculars a breeze stirred the drifting smoke; flags rippled stiffly from their staffs. "Stars and Stripes! Stars and Stripes! Give it to them, boys!" he yelled, and led his regiments forward at a run. Early's brigade had come up, too, their cheers swelling the din on the left as the whole gray line, curving away northeastward along the crest of Henry Hill, came whooping down upon the startled men in blue.

While his flanking column fell back over the run, McDowell did what he could to save the day. Two brigades, withdrawn from the fords below Stone Bridge, along with the one reserve brigade and some regiments just arrived from Alexandria, were combined to form a rally line near Centreville, in hopes that the retreaters from the crushed right flank would fall in here to challenge the Confederate counterattack. But it was no use. Anger was fast giving way to panic as the retreat gathered momentum. These men were bound for the Potomac, along a road that had been traveled prophetically that morning by a regiment of infantry and a battery of field artillery; their enlistments expiring today, they had declined any share in the battle, and deaf alike to pleas and jeers had returned to Washington for discharge. Panic was contagious. Troops from the proposed rally line fell in with the skulkers going past, and now the more or less sullen retreat became a rout, the column once more harried by the carriages and victorias of the junketing politicians who had driven out to see the Union reëstablished. Now, somehow, across the run and down the western leg of that spraddled X, in a roiling cauldron of dust and smoke with fitful, pinkish-yellow stabs of fire mixed in, the carefree lark had been transmuted into something out of a nightmare. "Turn back! Turn back! We are whipped!" the civilians heard the soldiers shout as they came surging up the pike. Darkness spread and the moon came out: a full moon like the one that had flooded the landscape two months ago, when the Grand Army crossed the Potomac to take potshots at an occasional scampering rebel.

Disorderly as the column was, it made good time. In that one night, returning north, McDowell's army covered more distance than it had managed to cover in three days of southward marching the week before.

★ ★ ★ **O**n the Confederate side there was disorganization, too. It was of a different kind, however, proceeding from the elation of victory rather than from the depression of defeat. The two were strangely alike. Belief that the battle was won produced very much the same effect, as far as concerted action went, as belief that the battle was lost. In either case it was over, and southern leaders could accomplish no more toward organizing pursuit along the turnpike than their northern counterparts could accomplish toward organizing a rally line across it. On the left, above Stone Bridge, the regiments were halted for realignment, all possibility of control being gone; while on the right, where the brigades had forced their way across the fords below the bridge, pursuit was abandoned and the men recalled to the south bank of the run to meet a false alarm of an attack at Union Mills. One brigadier, Longstreet — he had already crossed and recrossed the stream five times that day — was commanded to fall back just as he gave the order for his batteries to open fire on the retreating Federal column. Stuart's cavalry, swinging wide around Sudley Springs, should have been free to accomplish most; but the troopers soon were burdened with so many prisoners picked up along the way that they lost all mobility, and presently they dwindled to a squad. It was the same all along the line. Little could be done to gather the potential fruits of victory.

Even Jefferson Davis, braced for disaster as he rode from Manassas Junction through the backwash of the army, lost some measure of his self-control in the sudden release from anxiety when he emerged to find the Union soldiers fleeing from the charging men in gray. Meeting Colonel Elzey he conferred the first battlefield promotion of the war: "General Elzey, you are the Blücher of the day!" He joined the horseback chase toward Sudley Springs, and everywhere he encountered rejoicing and elation. In the gathering dusk, coming upon a body of men he thought were stragglers, he began a speech to rally them, only to learn that they were Jackson's Virginians, who had done so much to win the battle. Their commander was in a nearby dressing station, having a wounded finger bandaged. "Give me ten thousand men," he was saying, "and I would be in Washington tomorrow."

Davis rather thought so, too. He rode back to see Johnston and Beauregard at the latter's Manassas headquarters. The generals were as elated as their men; but when the President asked what forces were pushing the beaten enemy, they replied that the troops were confused and hungry and needed rest; pursuit had ended for the night. Davis was unwilling to reconcile himself to this, but presently a slow rain came on, turning the dust to mud all over eastern Virginia, and there was no longer even a question of the possibility of pursuit. Out on the field, along the turnpike and the run and in the angles of the X they formed, the drizzle soaked the dead and fell upon the wounded of both armies.

Among them was Major Roberdeau Wheat, commander of the Louisiana Tigers, who had opened the fight alongside Evans above Stone Bridge. He was a lawyer and had been a soldier of fortune, fighting with Carravajal in Mexico, Walker in Nicaragua, and Garibaldi in Sicily; but now a Union bullet had gone through both of his lungs and a surgeon told him he must die.

"I don't feel like dying yet," Wheat said.

The doctor insisted: "There is no instance on record of recovery from such a wound."

"Well, then," the lawyer-soldier replied, "I will put my case on record."

Next morning at breakfast Davis wrote out for Beauregard, subject to the approval of Congress, a promotion to full general. Then he returned to Richmond, where the bodies of General Bee and other leaders killed on yesterday's field were to lie in state, with honor guards and fitting obsequies. In spite of such causes for individual grief, the people in the capital were as elated as the soldiers around Manassas. Here as there, the feeling was that the Yankees had been shown for once and for all. The war was won. Independence was a fact beyond all doubt. Even the casualty lists, the source of their sorrow, reinforced their conviction of superiority to anything the North could bring against them.

The Confederates had lost almost two thousand, but the Union army had lost more than three thousand; 387 were dead in gray, 481 in blue. Only among the wounded were the Northerners outnumbered, 1582 to 1124, and this in itself was interpreted as a credit to the South; what, they asked, could be nobler than for a soldier to bleed for his country? However, they found the principal support for their opinion in the amount of captured equipment and the number of prisoners taken. Fifteen hundred Yankees had thrown down their arms and submitted to being marched away to prison, while in the Confederate ranks only eight were listed as missing, and no one believed that even these had surrendered. Equipment captured during the battle, or garnered from the field when the fighting was over, included 28 artillery pieces, 17 of them rifled, as well as 37 caissons, half a million rounds of small-arms ammunition, 500 muskets, and nine flags.

Later in the week, while southern outpost riders once more gazed across the Potomac at the spires of Washington, the wounded were brought to Richmond to be cared for — including Rob Wheat, who had put his case on record. The ladies turned out with an enthusiasm which sometimes tried the patience of the men. Asked if he wanted his face washed, one replied: "Well, ma'am, it's been washed twenty times already. But go ahead, if you want to." Prisoners came to Richmond, too, where a three-story tobacco warehouse had been hurriedly converted into a military prison. From the sidewalk, citizens tried to bribe the guards for a glimpse at a real live Yankee: especially New York Congressman Alfred Ely, who had strolled too near the scene of battle just as the lines gave way and was discovered trying to hide behind a tree. President Davis sent him two fine white wool blankets to keep him warm in the warehouse prison, and the people in general approved of such chivalry. They felt that they could afford to be magnanimous, now that the war was won.

★   ★   ★   *L*incoln, who had gone out for his Sunday drive believing the battle a Union victory, returned at sundown to find that the Secretary of State had come looking for him, white and shaky, and had left a message that McDowell had been whipped and was falling back. Hurrying to the War Department, he read a telegram confirming the bad news: "General McDowell's army in full retreat through Centreville. The day is lost. Save Washington and the remnants of this army." He returned to the White House and spent the night on a sofa in the cabinet room while bedraggled politicians, with the startled expressions of men emerging from nightmares, brought him eye-witness accounts of the disaster. Next morning, through windows lashed by rain, he watched his soldiers stagger up the streets, many of them so exhausted that they stumbled and slept in yards and on the steps of houses, oblivious to the pelting rain and the women who moved among them offering coffee.

General Scott and others with long faces soon arrived. "Sir, I am the greatest coward in America," Scott told one of them. "I deserve removal because I did not stand up, when my army was not in condition for fighting, and resist it to the last." Lincoln broke in: "Your conversation seems to imply that I forced you to fight this battle." The old general hesitated. He believed this was quite literally true, but he would not be rude. "I have never served a President who has been kinder to me than you have been," he said evasively, leaving Lincoln to draw from this what solace he could.

While Davis was soaring from anxiety to elation and Lincoln was moving in the opposite direction, downhill from elation to anxiety, others around the country and the world were reacting according to their natures. Horace Greeley, who had clamored for invasion, removed the banner "Forward to Richmond!" from the masthead of his New York *Tribune,* and after what he called "my seventh sleepless night — yours, too, doubtless" — wrote to Lincoln: "On every brow sits sullen, scorching, black despair. If it is best for the country and for mankind that we make peace with the rebels at once and on their own terms, do not shrink even from that." Tecumseh Sherman, reassembling his scattered brigade, wrote privately: "Nobody, no man, can save the country. Our men are not good soldiers. They brag, but don't perform, complain sadly if they don't get everything they want, and a march of a few miles uses them up. It will take a long time to overcome these things, and what is in store for us in the future I know not." One English journalist at least believed he could guess what was in store. "So short lived has been the American Union," the London *Times* observed, "that men who saw its rise may live to see its fall."

Allowing for journalistic license, "sullen, scorching, black despair" was scarcely an overstatement. All along the troubled line, from Missouri to the Atlantic, the gloom was lighted at only one point. In western Virginia, scene of the Philippi Races and the rout at Carrick's Ford, there was a commander with a Napoleonic flair who lifted men's hearts and brought cheers. Lincoln looked in that direction, the long sad face grown longer and sadder in the past few hours, and there he believed he found his man of destiny. On that same Monday, while fugitives from Sunday's battle still limped across Long Bridge and slept in the rain, he summoned him by telegraph:

General George B. McClellan

Beverly, Virginia:

Circumstances make your presence here necessary.

Charge Rosecrans or some other general with your

present department and come hither without delay.

★ ★ ★

★

Shelby Foote

*Routed Federals flee down the
face of Ball's Bluff and plunge
into the Potomac as Confederates
up the slope fire on them from
near point-blank range.*

Anderson, Frémont, McClellan

1861 ★ ★ ★ ★ ★ **L**incoln was already dealing with two men of destiny: Robert Anderson, the hero of Sumter, and John Charles Frémont, the California Pathfinder. They were to save Kentucky and Missouri for the Union, both having ties in the states to which they had been sent. Anderson was a Bluegrass native, and Frémont, though Georgia-born, had made important Missouri connections by eloping with the daughter of old Thomas Hart Benton, who lived long enough to be reconciled to the match.

In Kentucky the contest was political, swinging around the problem of the state's declared neutrality. Her sympathies were southern but her interests lay northward, beyond the Ohio, Lincoln having guaranteed the inviolability of her property in slaves. What was more, her desire for peace was reinforced by the knowledge that her "dark and bloody ground," as it was called, would be the scene of bitterest fighting if war came. Therefore, after the furor of Sumter and the departure into Confederate ranks of the eastern border states and Tennessee, the governor and both houses of the legislature announced that Kentucky would defend her borders, north and south, against invaders from either direction, and the people signified their approval in the special congressional election of late June, when nine out of the ten men sent to Washington were Unionists, and again in the August legislature races, which also were overwhelming Union victories.

Meanwhile Kentucky had become a recruiting ground for agents of

★

both armies. The state militia, under Simon Bolivar Buckner, a West Pointer and a wealthy Kentucky aristocrat, was the largest and probably the best-drilled body of nonregular troops in the country. Its 10,000 members were pro-Confederate, but this threat was countered by the Home Guard, swiftly organized under William Nelson, a six-foot five-inch, three-hundred-pound U.S. Navy lieutenant who distributed 10,000 "Lincoln rifles" among men of strong pro-Union beliefs. Whatever caution their political leaders might show, Kentuckians did not stand aside from individual bloodshed; 35,000 would fight for the South before the war was over, while more than twice that many would fight for the North, including 14,000 of her Negroes. Here the conflict was quite literally "a war of brothers." Senator John J. Crittenden typified the predicament of his state; he who had done so much for peace had two sons who became major generals in the opposing armies. Likewise Henry Clay, that other great compromiser, had three grandsons who fought to preserve the Union and four who enlisted on the other side. All over the state, instances such as these were reproduced and multiplied. Fathers and sons, brothers and cousins were split on issues that split the nation. Kentucky was in truth a house divided. The question was in which direction the house would fall.

After surrendering Sumter, Robert Anderson was sent west to keep his native Kentucky in the Union.

Commissioned a brigadier after the public acclaim that greeted him when he landed in New York from Fort Sumter, Anderson was sent west in late August. He had said that his heart was not in the struggle, that if Kentucky seceded he would go to Europe and wait the war out. But now that his native state expressed intentions of holding firm, he determined to take the field. Frail and aged beyond his fifty-six years, he was warned by his physicians that he might break under the stress of active duty: to which, according to a Washington newspaper interview, he replied that "the Union men of Kentucky were calling on him to lead them and that he must and would fall in a most glorious cause."

Out of respect for his state's declared neutrality, and despite his official designation as commander of the Military Department of Kentucky, he established headquarters in Cincinnati, just across the Ohio, and attempted to direct operations from there. He did little, for there was little he could do; which gave the impression that he was biding his time, waiting for the Bluegrass leaders to evolve their own decisions unmolested. Considering their touchy sensibilities — so violently in favor of peace that they were willing to fight for it — this was the best he could possibly have done. It was more, at any rate, than his opponent Leonidas Polk could do.

Polk was a West Pointer who had gone into the ministry and done well. Aged fifty-five at the outbreak of the war, he was Episcopal Bishop of Louisiana. Visiting Richmond in June he dropped by to see his Academy schoolmate Jefferson Davis, and when he emerged from the President's office he held, to his surprise, the commission of a Confederate major general and appointment to the command of troops in the Mississippi Valley. Northerners expressed horror at such sacrilege, but Southerners were delighted with this transfer from the Army of the Lord. Polk himself, considering his new duty temporary, did not resign his bishopric. He felt, he said, "like a man who has dropped his business when his house is on fire, to put it out; for as soon as the war is over I will return to my proper calling."

Just now, however, the bishop-general was alarmed at the development of events in Kentucky, which had gone from bad to worse from the Confederate point of view. Not only was the legislature pro-Unionist, but in mid-July, feeling that his position was somehow dishonorable or anyhow equivocal, Buckner resigned as head of the militia, which then disbanded, its guns and equipment passing into the hands of the Home Guard. At this rate Kentucky would soon be irretrievably gone. One of the first things Polk did when he arrived at his Memphis headquarters was to order a concentration of Confederate troops at Union City, in northwest Tennessee, prepared to cross the border and occupy Columbus, Kentucky — which Polk saw as the key to the upper Mississippi — whenever some Federal act of aggression made such a movement plausible.

Anderson, marking time in Cincinnati, would give him no such provocation, but Frémont, across the way, was more precipitate. On August 28 he instructed Brigadier General Ulysses S. Grant to take command of "a combined forward movement" and "to occupy Columbus, Ky. as soon as possible." That city's pro-southern citizens had already petitioned the Confederates to march to their defense, and now that he had an excuse Polk moved quickly. Not waiting to deal with an accomplished act of aggression, but hastening to forestall one, he ordered his troops to cross the border. They occupied Columbus on September 4, the day before the Federals were scheduled to arrive. Grant, thus checked, countered by crossing the border and occupying Paducah, strategically located at the junction of the Ohio and the Tennessee. Now both Confederate and Union soldiers, in rapid sequence, had violated Kentucky's declared neutrality.

The reaction, which was immediate, was directed mainly against the Southerners, since they had entered first and could make a less effective show of moral indignation. Anderson left Cincinnati at last, transferring his headquarters to Frankfort, where he appeared before the legislature on September 7 and was given an ovation. Four days later, though it sent no such angry communication to Grant or Frémont, this body issued a formal demand that the Confederacy withdraw its troops. When this injunction was not obeyed, it passed on the 18th an act creating a military force to expel them.

Neutrality was over. Politically, Kentucky had chosen the Union. She had a star in the Confederate flag and a secessionist legislature at Russellville, but these represented hardly anything more than the Kentuckians in the southern army. If she was to be reclaimed, if the northern boundary of the new nation was to reach the natural barrier of the Ohio, it would have to be accomplished by force of arms.

Much of the credit was due Anderson, who had waited. He had spoken of glory on setting out, but there had been little of that for him in his native Kentucky; he had said goodbye to glory in Charleston harbor. And now his physician's prediction came true. His health broke and he was given indefinite sick leave, Sherman replacing him in mid-October. Thus the Union's first man of destiny left the scene. Afterwards brevetted a major general and retired, he spent the war years in New York City, pointed out on the avenue as he took his daily constitutional, still the hero of Sumter, wearing a long military cloak across his shoulders to hide his stars. He read the war news in the papers and took a particular pride in the career of Sherman, who had served under him as a junior lieutenant in the peacetime army; "One of my boys," he called him.

★ ★ ★   *L*incoln's second man of destiny was quite different from the first, as indeed he had need to be. In Missouri the secession question had long since passed the political stage. Here there was bloodshed from the outset, and all through the last half of the opening year it was touch and go, a series of furious skirmishes, marches and countermarches by confused commanders, occupations, evacuations, and several full-scale battles. Jesse James studied tactics here, and Mark Twain skedaddled.

Whatever talents Frémont might show, and he was reputed to have many, the ability to wait and do nothing was not one of them. Heading westward on the day of McDowell's defeat on the plains of Manassas, he fell into Missouri's seething cauldron toward the end of July, when he established headquarters in St Louis. Apprised of the situation — disaffection throughout the state, bands of marauders roaming at will, Confederates massed along the southern border — he sent telegrams in all directions, from Washington D.C. out to California, calling for reinforcements. None were forthcoming, but apparently relieved just by the effort of having tried, Frémont settled down at once to making plans for the future.

Something of a mystic, he was a man of action, too, and within the widening circle of his glory he had a magnetism that drew men to him. With the help of such guides as Kit Carson he had explored and mapped the Rocky Mountain passes through which settlers came west. Under his leadership — the Pathfinder, they called him — they broke California loose from Mexico and joined her to the Union, rewarding Frémont by making him one of her first two senators, as well as one of her first millionaires, and subsequently the Republican Party's first presidential nominee. He was in France at the outbreak of war, but he came straight to Washington, where Lincoln made him a major general and sent him westward. His slender yet muscular body evidenced a youthfulness which the touches of gray in his hair and beard only served to emphasize by contrast, as if they represented not so much his forty-eight years, but rather the width of experience and adventure he had packed into them. His features were regular, his glance piercing. There was drama in his gestures, and his voice had overtones of music.

"I have given you carte blanche. You must use your own judgment, and do the best you can," Lincoln had told him, saying goodbye on the portico of the White House. And now in Missouri Frémont took him at his word.

While the news from Manassas dampened Unionist spirits, he continued to exorcise dismay with works and projects. After ordering intrenchments thrown around St Louis to secure it from attack, he occupied and fortified Cape Girardeau, above Cairo, as well as the railheads at Ironton and Rolla and the state capital at Jefferson City. Such actions were mainly defensive, but Frémont had offensive conceptions as well, and of these such occupations were a part. Poring over strategic maps in his headquarters, which he saw as the storm center of events, he looked beyond the present crisis and evolved a master plan for Federal efforts in the West. Whoever controlled the trunk controlled the tree; whoever held the Mississippi Valley, he discerned from his coign of vantage, "would hold the country by the heart." Missouri was only a starting point, elemental but essential to the plan, "of which the great object was the descent of the Mississippi River." With Memphis and Vicksburg lopped off, and finally New Orleans, the Confederacy would wither like a tree with a severed taproot.

★

Cairo was the key, and having secured it he went ahead. He began construction of 38 mortar boats and two gunboats to scour the rivers, and ordered Grant to seize Columbus, or, as it turned out — since Polk moved first, and thereby won the race and lost Kentucky — Paducah, which served as well. Whatever fit the plan got full attention; whatever did not fit got brushed aside. Some, in fact, found him too vague and exalted for their taste — Grant, for example, who recorded: "He sat in a room in full uniform with his maps before him. When you went in he would point out one line or another in a mysterious manner, never asking you to take a seat. You left without the least idea of what he meant or what he wanted you to do."

It was true that he was difficult to get at. To protect his privacy from obscure brigadiers like Grant while he worked eighteen hours a day in the three-story St Louis mansion which served as headquarters, he had a body-guard of 300 men, "the very best material Kentucky could afford; average height 5 feet 11½ inches, and measuring 40½ inches around the breast." Resplendent in feathers and loops of the gold braid known locally as "chicken guts," his personal staff included Hungarians and Italians with titles such as "adlatus to the chief" and names that were hardly pronounceable to a Missouri tongue; Emavic, Meizarras, Kalamaneuzze were three among many. The list ran long, causing one of his Confederate opponents to remark as he read it, "There's too much tail to that kite."

Whether he would soar or not, Frémont kept his gaze on far horizons. Down in the southwest corner of the state he had a compact, well-drilled army of 6000, including 1200 regulars and several batteries of artillery. Its commander, Brigadier General Nathaniel Lyon, had been active against rebellion from the start. Back in May, disguised in women's clothes, including a bonnet and veil to hide his red hair and whiskers, he had ridden in an open carriage to reconnoiter a secessionist camp. Afterwards he surrounded the place, forced its surrender under the muzzles of his guns, and marched the would-be Confederates off to prison, shooting down two dozen civilians when a crowd on the streets of St Louis attempted to interfere. By similar forthright action he had saved for the Union the arms in the Federal arsenal there. He was a hard-bitten, capable New Englander, forty-three years old, well acquainted with violence and well adapted for countering that particular brand of it being met with in Missouri. "I was born among the rocks," he once remarked.

So far, however, Lyon had no part in the plan Frémont was spending long hours evolving. In June he had led his troops southwest, intending to secure that section of the state and then move into Arkansas, with Little Rock as his goal. By early August he was beyond Springfield, near the border, but breakdowns along his line of supply had made his army ragged, ill-shod, low on ammunition, and disheartened. Frémont, intent on his master plan, could send no

★

Despite his feats as an explorer, flamboyant John C. Frémont proved an ineffective military commander and a political liability in Missouri.

reinforcements. What was worse, the Confederates encamped to Lyon's front around Cowskin Prairie were growing stronger every day. He estimated their strength at 20,000; it was "impractical to advance." On August 4 he reported: "I am under the painful necessity of retreating, and can at most only hope to make my retreat good. I am in too great haste to explain more fully." On the 6th he fell back to a position around Springfield, and the Confederates came on after him, pausing a few miles south before making the final pounce.

They were not as formidable as Lyon thought, and for several reasons. Though they numbered about 12,000 — twice the size of the Union force — for the most part they were miserably equipped and poorly organized, under commanders who were divided in their counsels and ambitions. The majority were Missouri militia led by Sterling Price, a fifty-two-year-old Virginia-born ex-governor who thought so little of West Pointers that he inserted a notice in the

★

papers, indignantly quashing a rumor that he had received a formal military education. His men had neither uniforms nor tents; many had no arms at all, while others had only shotguns or 1812-style flintlocks, and as substitutes for artillery projectiles they had laid in a stock of smooth stones, rusty chains, and iron rods to be shot from their eight antiquated cannon. The remainder, under Ben McCulloch of Tennessee, forty years old and a former Texas Ranger, were somewhat better equipped, being regular Confederate troops.

Price was a major general, McCulloch a brigadier, both veterans of the Mexican War; but the latter, who held his commission directly from Richmond, did not feel that the former should outrank him, and refused to combine the two forces unless the Missourian would yield command. Price, called Old Pap by his men — they asserted that their general had "won more battles in Mexico than McCulloch ever witnessed" — was so anxious to fall upon

He disposed his army for one of those complicated envelopments so popular in the early days of the war, when the generals and the soldiers they commanded were least capable of executing them.

Lyon that he agreed to the stipulation. As soon as Lyon began his retreat, McCulloch led the combined forces after him. They went into camp along Wilson's Creek, ten miles short of Springfield, where the Federals had halted. McCulloch drew up plans for attack. The movement began on August 9, but was called off because of threatening rain; the troops returned to camp and settled down to sleep, not bothering to put out pickets. At dawn the storm of Lyon's attack exploded in their rear.

The red-haired Federal was also a veteran of Mexico, where he had won promotion for valor, capturing three guns at Cerro Gordo. In the spirit of those days, instead of waiting to receive attack or risking being struck while in motion, he had decided to deliver a blow that would permit him to retreat unmolested. The fact that he was outnumbered two to one — three to one, as he thought — did not discourage this, but rather — in Lyon's eyes, at any rate — demanded it. He felt that his army would do a better job of delivering an attack than of standing to receive one. With his men somewhat heartened by a day's rest and the arrival of shoes from the railhead at Rolla, he distributed the shoes on the afternoon of the 9th and set out south for Springfield. Soon after midnight, the Confederates having averted a meeting engagement by turning back in the face of lowering weather, he had his troops within striking distance of the rebel camp on Wilson's Creek.

He had not minded the rain, and he counted the darkness a positive advantage. Under its cover he disposed his army for one of those complicated envelopments so popular in the early days of the war, when the generals and the soldiers they commanded were least capable of executing them. One column, under Colonel Franz Sigel — two regiments of infantry, two troops of cavalry, and a six-gun battery of artillery — was sent on a wide swing to hit the enemy rear, while Lyon struck in front with the main body, southward down the western bank where most of the rebels lay snug in their blankets. He detached one regiment of regulars — First Infantry, U.S. Army: about as regular as troops could be — sending them beyond the creek to handle whatever Confederates might have pitched their camps on that side.

Sigel set out; Lyon waited in the darkness. Nothing stirred in the rebel camp. As dawn paled the rising ground beyond the creek, the limbs of trees coming black against the sky, there was a sudden spatter of musketry — the skirmishers had opened fire — then the roar and flash of guns like summer lightning on the far horizon: Sigel had come up from the south and was in action, on time and in place. Lyon ordered the main body forward, east and west of the creek, closing the upper jaw of his tactical vise.

Everything was moiling confusion in the camps along the creek-bed, guns booming north and south as men came out of their blankets in various stages of undress, tousle-haired, half asleep, and badly frightened. Under the stress of that first panic many fled. Some returned, rather shamefaced. Others ran, and kept on running, right out of the war. Yet those who stood were hard-core men from Arkansas and Louisiana, Texas and Missouri, wanting only to be told what to do. McCulloch and his aides soon established a line of resistance, and these men fell in eagerly. Price had yielded the command, but he was there, too, his white hair streaming in the wind as he rode up and down the line of his rallied Missourians, shouting encouragement. Under such leadership, the Southerners assembled in time to meet the attack from both directions. The battle that followed set the pattern for all such encounters in the West.

Few of the romantic preconceptions as to brilliant maneuver and individual gallantry were realized. Fighting at close quarters because of the short-range Confederate flintlocks and muzzle-loading fowling pieces, a regiment would walk up to the firing line, deliver a volley, then reload and deliver another, continuing this until it dissolved and was replaced by another regiment, which repeated the process, melting away in the heat of that furnace and being in turn replaced. No fighting anywhere ever required greater courage, yet individual gallantry seemed strangely out of place. A plume in a man's hat, for example, accomplished nothing except to make him a more conspicuous target. Nor did the rebel yell ring out on the banks of Wilson's Creek. There was little cheering on either side; for a cheer seemed as oddly out of place as a plume. The men went about their deadly business of firing and reloading and melting away in a grim silence broken only by the rattling crash of musketry and the deeper roar of guns, with the screams of the injured sometimes piercing the din. Far from resembling panoplied war, it was more like reciprocal murder.

In such a battle the weight of numbers told. Sigel's surprise attack from the south became a rout almost as soon as he encountered resistance. His men broke, stampeded, and did not stop till they got back to Springfield, having abandoned their colors and all but one of their guns. To the north, Lyon's men were wavering, too. East of the creek the regulars, lacking reinforcements, were blasted off the field. The main body, west of the creek, stood manfully to their work for a while; but presently, the Confederates clustering thicker and thicker to their front, new regiments arriving after their success in dealing with other

*Mortally wounded, Union General
Nathaniel Lyon topples from his horse at
Wilson's Creek, Missouri, in August 1861.*

columns of attack, the Federals began to look back over their shoulders, apprehensive. Lyon rode among them, calling for them to stand firm in the face of gathering resistance. As he sought thus to rally them, a bullet creased his scalp. A second struck his thigh, a third his ankle. His horse was shot and fell dead under him. Stunned, Lyon limped slowly toward the rear, shaking his head. "I fear the day is lost," he said. Presently, though, recovering from the shock and depression, he secured another mount and rode again into the fight, at a place where the troops were about to give way. Swinging his hat he called for them to follow him, and when they rallied he led them forward. Near the point of deepest penetration, a bullet struck his heart and he went down. His men fled, shaken by the loss of their red-bearded leader.

It was Manassas all over again. Once the Federal troops gave way, they did not stand upon the order of their going, but retreated pell-mell to Springfield and then to Rolla, leaving their fallen comrades on the field: Kansas, Missouri, and Iowa farmboys, lying dead in their new shoes, and the brave Lyon, whose body McCulloch forwarded through the lines under a flag of truce, only to recapture it when the Unionists fell back from Springfield, abandoning it in its coffin in the courthouse.

The fighting had been bloody; "the severest battle since Waterloo," one participant called it. Within four hours each side had suffered about 1200 casualties. In one-third the time, and with less than one-third the number of troops involved, more than half as many men had fallen along Wilson's Creek as had fallen along Bull Run. Yet here too, as after that battle three weeks before, on the banks of that other rural stream 800 miles away, one side was about as disorganized by victory as the other was by defeat. Though there was broad open daylight for pursuit, the Confederates could not be put into column to press the retreating Federals. All the same, the battle was taken as further proof, if such was needed, of the obvious superiority of the southern fighting man, and in Missouri as in Virginia there was the feeling that, now that the Yankees had been shown what they were up against, there was no real need for giving chase.

In Richmond, President Davis announced the victory in much the same tone of quiet exultation he had used for the announcement in July. Then, out of respect for Missouri's "neutrality," he ordered McCulloch to return to Arkansas with his Confederate troops, awaiting an invitation from the secessionist legislature soon to assemble in Neosho, Lyon having scattered them from Jefferson City in July. Price and his native militiamen followed slowly as the Federals fell back. The battle was therefore inconclusive in results, since Lyon had been retreating anyhow.

One thing it did, at any rate. It removed Frémont's transfixed gaze from far horizons. The lopping descent of the Mississippi could never be accomplished without Missouri under control. Galvanized by reports of the battle, which indicated that he was in danger of losing his starting-point, he reacted first according to pattern, wiring the Secretary of War for reinforcements: "Let the governor of Ohio be ordered forthwith to send me what disposable force he has; also governors of Illinois, Indiana, and Wisconsin. Order the utmost promptitude." This done — though nothing came of it — he sent five regiments to strengthen the defeated men at Rolla, and declared martial law in St Louis. Other rebel columns were reported to be advancing, however, and all over the northern portion of the state, guerillas were coming out of hiding, emboldened by Confederate successes.

As the month wore on, Frémont realized that something had to be done to stem the tide. The week before the battle, Congress had passed a confiscation act prescribing certain penalties against persons in rebellion. Now Frémont issued a proclamation of his own, with real teeth in it, written in one night and printed for distribution the following morning. Drawing a line from Fort Leavenworth to Cape Girardeau, he directed that any unauthorized person found under arms north of this line would be tried by court martial, the sentence being death before a firing squad. In addition he announced as confiscated the property, real and personal, of all Missourians who should be "proved to have taken an active part with their enemies in the field." Nor was that all. "And their slaves, if any they have," he added, "are hereby declared freemen."

Emancipation: feared or hoped for, the word had been spoken at last. The reaction came from several directions: first from down in the southeast corner of the state, where the Missouri brigadier, M. Jeff Thompson, issued a proclamation of his own. "For every member of the Missouri State Guard, or soldier of our allies the Confederate States, who shall be put to death in pursuance of said order of General Frémont," he avowed, "I will *Hang, Draw* and *Quarter* a minion of said Abraham Lincoln . . . so help me God!" Throughout the North, on the other hand, antislavery radicals were delighted. They had wanted a proclamation such as Frémont's all along, and now they had a champion who said plainly, "War consists not only in battles, but in well-considered movements which bring the same results." In Kentucky the reaction was otherwise. A Unionist volunteer company threw down its arms on receiving the news, and the legislature balked on the verge of landing the state officially in the Federal camp. Lincoln thus was caught between two fires, having to offend either the abolitionist wing of his own party, which clamored for emancipation, or the loyal men of the border states, who had been promised nonintervention on the slavery question. Three of the latter wired from Louisville: "There is not a day to be lost in disavowing emancipation, or Kentucky is gone over the mill dam."

Lincoln was circumspect, threading his way. He wrote to Frémont "in a spirit of caution, and not of censure," explaining the predicament and requesting that the Pathfinder modify the edict so as to conform to the recent act of Congress. As for the use of firing squads, he reminded the general that the Confederates would retaliate "man for man, indefinitely," and directed that no shootings were to take place without presidential approval. Frémont waited six days, then replied that he would not "change or shade it. It was worth a victory in the field," he earnestly maintained. As Commander in Chief, Lincoln could *order* it modified; otherwise, the proclamation stood.

This letter was entrusted to no ordinary courier, but was taken to Washington by Jessie Benton Frémont, an illustrious father's ambitious daughter, who had been at her husband's elbow all the while. She arrived after two days and nights on the cars, and, despite the late hour at which she checked into Willard's, sent a note to the White House, asking when she might deliver the message. A card was brought: "Now, at once. A. Lincoln." She had not had time to rest or change her clothes, but she went immediately. The President was waiting. "Well?" he said.

She found his manner "hard," she later declared, and when she handed him the letter he smiled "with an expression not agreeable." When she attempted to reinforce her husband's defense of the proclamation, enlarging upon his explanation that the war must be won by more than the force of arms and that Europe would cheer a blow struck at slavery, Lincoln interrupted her lecture by remarking, "You are quite a female politician." At this she lost her temper and reminded Lincoln that the Pathfinder was beyond the ordinary run of soldiers. If the President wanted to "try titles," he would find Frémont a worthy adversary. "He is a man and I am his wife!" she added hotly. Lincoln had not doubted that Frémont was a man, or that Jessie was his wife; but having stirred up this hornets' nest, he mustered what tact he could to try to calm her. It was not enough. She "left in anger," he said afterwards, "flaunting her hand-kerchief before my face."

Returning westward she traveled in the wake of a letter addressed to her husband in St Louis. Signed "Your Obt Servt A Lincoln," it began: "Yours of the 8th, in answer to mine of the 2d instant, is just received," and remarked that while the President "perceived in general no objection" to the proclamation, he could not allow an Act of Congress to be overridden; therefore he would assume responsibility for revoking so much of Frémont's edict as failed to conform to that Act. "Your answer . . . expresses the preference on your part that I should make an open order for the modification, which I very cheerfully do." Thus he drew the teeth of the proclamation for the sake of the border Unionists, while for the sake of the abolitionists he explained that this was done, not because of its policy — to which he "perceived in general no objection" — but simply because it was unlawful, interfering as it did with the prerogative of Congress, where the most vociferous of the abolitionists sat.

Such wary action pacified the conservatives, but the antislavery radicals were by no means satisfied. In this first open break within his party Lincoln was assailed on the floor of the Senate, in the press, and from the pulpit. Protests were especially loud among the German emigrants in Missouri — "the St Louis Dutch," their enemies called them — whose devotion to the general was redoubled. Jessie Frémont's threat that her husband might set up for himself and try titles with the President began to seem quite possible.

Meanwhile, alarming reports of a different kind were arriving from the West, where $12,000,000 had gone down the drain for steamboats, fortifications, uniforms, food, and ice for sherry cobblers. Graft and extravagances were charged against the men surrounding Frémont — "a gang of California robbers and scoundrels," the head of a congressional investigating committee called them, adding that while the general refused to confer with men of honor and wisdom, these boodlers "rule, control and direct everything." Lincoln wrote to Major General David Hunter, who had commanded the flanking column at Manassas, saying of Frémont: "He needs to have by his side a man of large experience. Will you not, for me, take that place? Your rank is one grade too high to be ordered to it, but will you not serve the country and oblige me by taking it voluntarily?" Hunter knew well enough what was meant. He also knew an opportunity when he saw one; and he set out at once for St Louis.

There was a need for military wisdom and alertness, for bushwhackers were plundering the state while Price moved northward with his 15,000 militia, their shortage of arms somewhat repaired by 3000 Union rifles picked up after the fight at Wilson's Creek. At Lexington they besieged Mulligan's Irish Guard, 2800 men intrenched on the campus of the Masonic College. Price was low on percussion caps, but when a supply arrived in mid-September he attacked, keeping his casualties down by advancing his men behind water-soaked bales of hemp which they jimmied along as a sort of sliding breastwork. The Irish surrendered, and Price, with 3000 more rifles and a single-handed victory to his credit, issued a call for his fellow Missourians to flock to his standard: "Do I hear your shouts? Is that your war-cry which echoes through the land? Are you coming? Fifty thousand men! Missouri shall move to victory with the tread of a giant. Come on, my brave boys, 50,000 heroic, gallant, unconquerable, Southern men! We await your coming."

Once more Frémont was galvanized. "I am taking the field myself," he telegraphed Washington. "Please notify the President immediately." He assembled five divisions, 38,000 men, and set out after Price. He had not lost sight of his goal, however. "My plan is New Orleans straight," he wrote his wife, October 7 from Tipton, adding: "I think it can be done gloriously."

It might be done gloriously, but not by Frémont; Lincoln had marked him for destruction. Having found that the Pathfinder would not hesitate to embarrass him politically, the President sent observers to investigate his competence in other matters. In addition to the rumors of graft, the Adjutant General and the Secretary of War had both reported the general unfit for his post: an opinion shared by Brigadier General Samuel Curtis in St Louis, who wrote that Frémont lacked "the intelligence, the experience, and the sagacity necessary to his command." Such reports, in themselves, justified removal; but Jessie Frémont's threat, reinforced by warnings from observers — "[Frémont] does not intend to yield his command at your bidding," one flatly declared — made the problem of procedure a difficult one, and Lincoln continued to exercise caution. On October 28 he sent General Curtis two orders for delivery: one relieving Frémont, the other appointing Hunter in his place. Curtis was told to deliver them only on condition that Frémont had not won a battle or was not about to fight one; Lincoln would not risk the clamor that would follow the dismissal of a general on the eve of an engagement or the morrow of a victory.

"Fifty thousand men! Missouri shall move to victory with the tread of a giant. Come on, my brave boys, 50,000 heroic, gallant, unconquerable, Southern men!"

— Sterling Price

News of the order had leaked to the press, however, and Frémont, in camp southwest of Springfield, surrounded by his bodyguard and army, was forewarned. Disguised as a farmer with information about the rebels, a captain detailed by Curtis to deliver Lincoln's order got past Frémont's pickets at 5 a.m., November 1. At headquarters he was told that he could not see the general in person but that his information would be passed on. The captain declined, saying he would wait. He waited hours on end, and then at last was ushered into the presence. Removing the order from the lining of his coat, he handed it to the general. Frémont read it, then frowned. "Sir," he said, trembling with anger, "how did you get admission into my lines?"

There was one chance. A victory would abrogate the order and vindicate his generalship. He placed the disguised captain in arrest to prevent the spread of news of his relief, stirred up the camp, and prepared to fall upon the enemy to his front. But there was no enemy to his front. Undetected, Price had fallen back beyond his reach, recruits and all, and the captain-messenger, having overheard the password, had escaped. Next morning, rounding out one hundred days of glory, Frémont issued a farewell address, beginning: "Soldiers! I

★

regret to leave you," and requesting loyalty to his successor. Then he set out for St Louis to join his wife, who remarked when she received the news of his downfall: "Oh, if my husband had only been more positive! But he never did assert himself enough. That was his greatest fault."

———————⟡———————

★ ★ ★ ***W**hile these two men of destiny rose and fell,* a third was rising fast, and he kept rising. On the day Frémont received his dismissal, McClellan was appointed to head all the armies of the nation, superseding his old chieftain Winfield Scott. Much had been done in the three months since his arrival, five days after the Bull Run disaster. The army of 50,000 which he then found waiting for him — "a mere collection of regiments cowering on the banks of the Potomac," he called it — had grown to 168,000 well-trained, spirited men, superbly equipped and worshipful of the commander who had accomplished their transformation.

Out in western Virginia when he received the telegram ordering him to "come hither without delay," he rode sixty miles on horseback to the nearest

Officers and men of the Army of the Potomac celebrate McClellan's rise to general-in-chief with fireworks and a serenade at his Washington home in November 1861.

railway station and caught the train for the capital. Given command of the Washington army on the day after his arrival, he found the city "almost in condition to have been taken by a dash of a regiment of cavalry," and himself looked up to from all sides as the deliverer. "I find myself in a new and strange position here," he wrote his wife that evening; "President, cabinet, Gen. Scott, and all deferring to me. By some strange operation of magic I seem to have become the power of the land." With a strong belief in his ability to set things straight, he had gone to work at once. "I see already the main causes of our recent failure," he declared; "I am sure that I can remedy these, and am confident that I can lead these armies of men to victory."

Employing two regiments of regulars as military police — hard-faced men who had stood fast, taking up position after rear-guard position during the Bull Run retreat — he cleared the bars and hotel lobbies of stragglers and shirkers, requiring officers and men alike to show passes authorizing their absence from their outfits. The crests of the hills ringing the city were fortified, the slopes whitened overnight by tent camps that sprang up as the three-year volunteers arrived in answer to Lincoln's call for 400,000 on the morrow of Manassas. Soon the men within the encampments far outnumbered the population of the city they encircled. The clatter of musketry came from the firing ranges, a ragged uproar punctuated by the cries of sergeants on the drill fields: "Your *left!* Your *left!* Now you've *got* it; damn you, *hold* it! *Left!*" Thus McClellan set about restoring order, securing the defenses of the capital as a prelude to the offensive, which he intended to launch as soon as possible. "I shall carry this thing *en grand*," he wrote, "and crush the rebels in one campaign."

Rigid discipline was the order of the day, and the commander himself was on hand to see it inforced. Something new had come into the war; Little Mac, the soldiers called this man who had transformed them from a whipped mob into a hot-blooded army that seemed never to have known the taste of defeat. He brought out the best in them and restored their pride, and they hurrahed whenever he appeared on horseback, which he frequently did, accompanied by his staff, a glittering cavalcade that included two genuine princes of the blood: the Comte de Paris, pretender to the throne of France, and the Duc de Chartres, known respectively to their fellow officers as Captain Parry and Captain Chatters. There was also an American prince among them, John Jacob Astor, who lived in a style that outshone the Europeans, served by his own valet, steward, chef, and female companions whom he took driving four-in-hand, at once the glory and the despair of Washington society.

Yet even in such company as this, of foreign and domestic royalty, McClellan was dominant. The fame that had preceded him was enhanced by his arrival, and unlike Frémont, whose brilliant first impression soon wore thin, McClellan improved with acquaintance. He did not *seem* young; he *was* young, with all the vigor and clear-eyed forcefulness that went with being thirty-four. His eyes were blue, unclouded by suspicion, his glance direct. He wore his dark auburn hair parted far on the left and brushed straight across, adding a certain boyish charm to his air of forthright manliness. Clean-shaven save for a faint goatee and a heavy, rather straggly mustache which hid his mouth except when he threw back his head to laugh, he had strong, regular features that gave cartoonists little to catch hold of. He was of average height, five feet nine and one-half inches, yet was so robust and stockily built — his chest massive, his well-shaped head set firmly on a muscular neck; "a neck such as not one man in ten thousand possesses," an admirer wrote — that he seemed short. The Young Napoleon, journalists had begun to call him, and photographers posed him standing with folded arms, frowning into the lens as if he were dictating terms for the camera's surrender.

Galloping twelve hours a day or poring over paperwork by lamplight, he had in fact the Napoleonic touch. Men looking at him somehow saw themselves as they would have liked to be, and he could therefore draw on their best efforts. He could be firm or he could temper justice. When two regiments mutinied, declaring that their time was up and they were leaving, McClellan handled each in a different way. The ringleaders of one were sent to the Dry

Charismatic George McClellan, a brilliant military organizer, administrator, and trainer of men, was hailed as the "Young Napoleon."

Tortugas to serve out their enlistments at hard labor. In the other case he merely took away the regimental colors and kept them in the hall of his headquarters until the mutineers should earn by good behavior the right to have them back, which they presently did. Both regiments soon cheered him to the echo whenever he came riding through their camps.

Within ten days of his arrival he could write, "I have restored order completely." Training now entered a new phase, with emphasis on the development of unit pride, as the men learned to polish equipment to new degrees of brightness and step to parade-ground music. Reviews were staged, the massed columns swinging past reviewing stands, eyes-right, guidons snapping, where the generals and distinguished civilians stood and ladies in hoop skirts watched from under parasols. Then, for climax, McClellan himself rode down the line, his charger Dan Webster setting a pace that made the staff string out behind, the rather desperate faces of the junior officers at the rear affording much amusement to the men in ranks. Yet even they, who had sat up half the night, scrubbing and polishing cloth and leather, could see the purpose behind the panoply and the results that purpose yielded. The young general had an eye for everything. A dingy cartridge box or a special gleam on a pair of shoes could bring a sudden frown or a smile of pride, and the men were disconsolate or happy, depending on which expression flickered across the youthful face. They cheered him riding past, and when he acknowledged the cheers with his jaunty salute, they cheered again. Even the salute was something special. He "gave his cap a little twirl," one witness wrote, "which with his bow and smile seemed to carry a little of personal good fellowship even to the humblest private soldier. If the cheer was repeated he would turn in the saddle and repeat the salute." It was reciprocal. Between them they felt that they were forging the finest army the world had ever seen.

There was a Virginian here in Washington against whom he must also fight his way: Lieutenant General Winfield Scott, second only to the Father of his Country on the list of the nation's military heroes . . .

Yet all was not as confident in McClellan's mind as the soldiers judged from his manner on parade. In the small hours of the night, alone in his quarters, musing upon the example of McDowell, whose army had been wrecked on the very plains where the Confederates were still massing under the same victorious commanders, he took counsel of his fears. Soon after his arrival, in the flush of early confidence, he had written: "I flatter myself that Beauregard has gained his last victory." Now he wrote, "I have scarcely slept one moment for the last three nights, knowing well that the enemy intend some movement and fully recognizing our own weakness. If Beauregard does not attack tonight I shall look upon it as a dispensation of Providence. He ought to do it." The dispensation was granted, but that did not keep McClellan from complaining: "I am here in a terrible place. The enemy have from three to four times my force."

Such figures were not guesswork. They came from his chief of intelligence, Allan Pinkerton, the railroad detective who had herded Lincoln through Baltimore on the eve of inauguration, and they were detailed and explicit, based on reports from agents planted behind the rebel lines. Earlier in August, Pinkerton had shown his chief that the forces around Manassas amounted to beyond 100,000 men. This estimate grew steadily as the agents grew more industrious,

★

until by early October, as the days drew in and shadows lengthened, McClellan was reporting: "The enemy have a force on the Potomac not less than 150,000 strong, well drilled and equipped, ably commanded, and strongly intrenched."

What was worse — or was at least more irritating — it seemed to him that he not only had to contend with the threat of overwhelming numbers across the river, but there was a Virginian here in Washington against whom he must also fight his way: Lieutenant General Winfield Scott, second only to the Father of his Country on the list of the nation's military heroes and the first person Mc-Clellan had called on to pay his respects when he arrived. Scott had been a great man in his day, six feet four and a quarter inches tall, resplendent in epaulets of solid gold and wearing an aura of victory through two wars. Yet now, as he said himself, "broken down by many particular hurts, besides the general infirmities of age," he could no longer mount a horse and had to be assisted out of his chair before he could rise. When he would indicate troop positions on a wall map, an aide stood by to wield the pointer. "I have become an incumbrance to the Army as well as to myself," he confessed, with pain to his enormous pride.

McClellan's original feelings of veneration and pity ("It made me feel a little strangely when I went into the President's last evening with the old general leaning on me; I could see that many marked the contrast") had turned to resentment and exasperation as Scott continued to get in the way of his plans. Regular army officers commanding companies and battalions of regulars should not be transferred to lead brigades and divisions of volunteers; a hard core of trained regulars, officered by regulars, was needed. Divisions should not even be created; the brigade had been the largest unit in the army he took to Mexico, where he had accomplished maneuvers that now were described in the history books and tactics manuals. Ensconced between McClellan and Lincoln, and between McClellan and the War Department, Scott advanced these views and delayed the reorganization. Worst of all, the old general put little stock in the Pinkerton reports. Regardless of what was set down in black and white, he would not believe the Union army was outnumbered. When McClellan reported his fears for the safety of the capital, Scott protested: "Relying upon our numbers, our forts, and the Potomac River, I am confident in the opposite direction."

"He understands nothing, appreciates nothing," McClellan declared on August 8, and on the 9th: "Gen. Scott is the great obstacle. He will not comprehend the danger. I have to fight my way against him." Five days later he was saying outright, "Gen. Scott is the most dangerous antagonist I have." Plainly, the old general had to go. As McClellan had already told his wife, "The people call upon me to save the country. I must save it, and I cannot respect anything that is in the way." It was not his doing, he wrote. "I was called to it; my previous life seems to have been unwittingly directed to this great end."

With military acumen, he attacked where his adversary was weakest:

in his pride. Snubbing him in public and differing with him abruptly in private councils, he goaded him into such trembling fury that the old man requested to be placed on the retired list as soon as possible, "to seek the palliatives of physical pain and exertion." Lincoln felt he could not spare him yet, however, and asked him to stay on, which Scott reluctantly agreed to do. McClellan kept at him, and at last in early October at a War Department meeting Scott turned heavily in his chair, addressing McClellan who lounged in the doorway: "You were called here by my advice. The times require vigilance and activity. I am not active and never shall be again. When I proposed that you should come here to aid, not supersede me, you had my friendship and confidence. You still have my confidence."

A week before, there had been an incident which seemed to support the old man's opinion that the force across the river might not be as powerful as McClellan claimed. About halfway between Washington and Fairfax Courthouse, less than ten miles from the former, was Munson's Hill, the nearest enemy outpost, from which Confederate pickets could look out and see the unfinished dome of the Capitol itself. On the last day of August, on his own responsibility — partly because the rebels had been taking potshots, but mostly because he could no longer abide the impudence of their dominating an area where his men were learning to drill — a New Jersey colonel pushed his regiment forward against the height. This took courage, for the graybacks had a gun up there, black against the skyline. After a few shots and the fall of a few New Jersey boys, though the cannon itself was providentially silent, the colonel fell back, with at least the satisfaction of having protested. A month later, September 28, Johnston apparently having decided that the outpost could be captured or destroyed by a more determined push, the Federals woke to find the hill unoccupied. They went up somewhat cautiously, for the gun was still in position and it seemed unlikely that the rebels would abandon ordnance. Then the revelation came. The cannon was not iron but wood, a peeled log painted black, a Quaker gun.

There was general indignation as the newspapers spread word of how McClellan had been tricked, held at bay by the frown of a wooden cannon. Sightseers, riding out to Munson's Hill to be amused and to exercise their wit, could not see what was clear to army Intelligence: that if Johnston hadn't wanted them to think he was equipped with wooden guns he would never have left one in position when he drew back. With the swift, uncluttered logic of civilians, all they could see was the painted log itself, complete with a pair of rickety wagon wheels, and the fact that the Confederates had fallen back unpushed. Mutterings began to be heard against the Young Napoleon, especially among senators and businessmen, who wanted a short quick fight no matter how bloody. The daily bulletin, "All quiet along the Potomac," which had given the war its first indigenous popular song and which had been so reassuring through the weeks of unease that followed defeat, was greeted now with derision.

★

Then suddenly, as if to reinforce the army's caution, that quiet was shattered by proof that the rebels on the southern bank had something more than wooden ordnance.

★ ★ ★ *I*n late October, when the leaves were turning and a brisk promise of winter came down the wind, McClellan received word that Johnston was preparing to evacuate Leesburg, up the Potomac about two-thirds of the way to Harpers Ferry. This time he acted. If Old Joe was ready to fall back, Little Mac at least would give him a nudge to hasten his going.

First, though, he must determine if Johnston was really ready to leave. One division was sent up the Virginia shore to investigate, and another, training in Maryland opposite where the Confederates were reported to be sending their baggage to the rear, was told that it might have a share in the reconnaissance. The Union general across the river halted at Dranesville, ten miles short of Leesburg, content to do his observing from there. The commander on the Maryland side, however — Brigadier General Charles P. Stone, who read his instructions as permission to push things — believed that the best way to discover the enemy's strength was to provoke him into showing it. Accordingly, a couple of regiments were put across the Potomac at Edwards Ferry, while others were sent on a night march to complete the envelopment by crossing at Harrison's Island, three miles upstream.

Here the operation was necessarily slow, being made in three small boats with a combined capacity of 25 men. By dawn, one regiment was on the island, looking out across the other half of the river at the wooded Virginia bank. It reared up tall there, over a hundred feet, steep and mean-looking; Ball's Bluff, it was called, and from beyond its rim they heard a nervous popping of musketry, each shot as flat and distinct as a handclap, only more so. They were Massachusetts boys, and they looked at one another, wondering. No one had told them on the drill field or in bivouac that the war might be like this. They continued the crossing, still in groups of 25, herded by their officers, and took a meandering cow path up the bluff toward the hollow-sounding spatter of rifle fire.

At the top, in explanation of the firing — it had a sharper sound up here, less mysterious but considerably more deadly, with the occasional twang of a ricochet mixed in — they found another Massachusetts outfit drawn up in a glade, returning shots that were coming at them from beyond the brush and timber at the far end of the clearing. These men had crossed the river during the night; their colonel, a Boston lawyer, had taken a patrol almost to Leesburg without uncovering the rebel camp; but presently, coming under fire from scouts or pickets, he had drawn back to the glade above the bluff and assembled his troops to meet the threat that seemed to be building up beyond the brush.

★

Charles P. Stone, commander of the U.S. forces at Ball's Bluff, became the scapegoat for the Federal debacle there.

He and his men were glad to see their sister Bay State regiment arrive as reinforcements from the island, and he sent word to General Stone of what had happened. In reply the general instructed him to hold what he had: Colonel Edward D. Baker was crossing with his Pennsylvania regiment, and would take command when he arrived.

Baker was someone special, not only a colonel but a full-fledged senator, a one-time Illinois lawyer and an intimate friend of Abraham Lincoln, whose second son had been named for him. Veteran of the Mexican War and the California gold rush, in 1860 he had moved to Oregon at the invitation of the people, who promptly elected him to the U.S. Senate. There he became the

Administration's chief far-western spokesman, riding in the presidential carriage on inauguration day and introducing Lincoln for the inaugural address. He welcomed the nation's angry reaction to Sumter; "I want sudden, bold, forward, determined war," he told the Senate, and personally raised a Philadelphia regiment. He did not resign his Senate seat, however, and would not accept a major general's commission from his friend the Commander in Chief, since by law this would have required his resignation from Congress. From time to time he would return from the field, appearing in full uniform on the floor of the Senate, where he would unbuckle his sword, lay it across his desktop, and launch an oratorical attack upon those of his fellow lawmakers who appeared to favor any compromise with secession. At fifty he was clean-shaven and handsome, with a high forehead and a fondness for declaiming poetry. "Press where ye see my white plume shine amidst the ranks of war," he quoted as he took the field.

Now on this October 21, coming up the bluff with his Pennsylvanians, he was happy to be where bullets were flying. "I congratulate you, sir, on the prospect of a battle," he told the Massachusetts colonel, shaking hands as he assumed command. In point of fact, it was more than a prospect; he had a battle on his hands already, as he soon found out.

He had managed to get two guns across the river, and now he put them into action, shelling the brush from which the rebel sniping was getting more vicious all the time. Then he went back to the lip of the bluff and, peering down, saw a New York outfit known as the Tammany Regiment toiling up the cow path. This would make a total of four Union regiments on the field. Baker felt confident and expansive. Spotting the colonel at the head of the climbing column, he waved gaily and greeted him with a quotation from "The Lady of the Lake":

> *"One blast upon your bugle horn*
>
> *Is worth a thousand men."*

Reaching the top of the bluff, the New York colonel — a West Pointer and the only professional soldier on a field in charge of lawyers and politicians — was amazed to find Baker so confident and buoyant over a situation in which, to the military eye at any rate, the danger in front was exceeded only by the confusion in the rear. The Confederates, holding high ground beyond the brush and timber where their snipers were picking off men in the glade almost at will, obviously were building up to launching an attack; whereas the Federals, backed up to the rim of a steep drop with an unfordable river one hundred feet below, were doing little more than dodging bullets and listening to their senator-colonel sing out quotations from Walter Scott.

★

About this time, one of the two guns recoiled sharply and toppled backward off the bluff; the other was already silent, its cannoneers dropped or driven away by snipers. It seemed to the New Yorker that events were moving swiftly toward disaster. Suddenly Baker seemed to realize it, too. He hurried along the wavering line, calling for his soldiers to stand fast. Perhaps he had some counter-movement in mind. If so, no one ever learned it. For just then, by way of climax, he who had called for sudden, bold, forward, determined war received it in the form of a bullet through the brain, which left him not even time for a dying quotation.

The Confederates out in the brush were Mississippians and Virginians, three regiments of the former and one of the latter, brigaded under Shanks Evans, who had marched above the stone bridge at Bull Run to meet McDowell's flank attack head-on. Evans was not here today, but his men had absorbed what he had taught them. Maneuvering on familiar ground, they had allowed the Yankees to penetrate almost to their Leesburg camp, then had taken them under fire and followed them back to the bluff. There, while the Federals drew into a compact mass in the ten-acre glade above the river, with reinforcements coming up to render the mass even more compact and the target plumper, the Southerners kept up a galling fire, some of them even climbing trees to do so. All this while, two of the four regiments returning from a march to meet the empty threat downriver, their battle line was forming in the timber. There was no hurry. By now they saw clearly that the Yanks were too rattled to organize a charge, and they were enjoying their advantage thoroughly; particularly the Mississippians, who were reminded of turkey-shoots down home. It was late afternoon before the gray line was ready. Then their officers led them forward, and the rebel yell quavered above the crash of snapping brush and trampled saplings.

What followed was pandemonium. Colonel Baker had just fallen, and the troops drawn up to meet the onslaught were demoralized when a group of soldiers carried the colonel's body to the rear. They thought it was the beginning of a retreat. As it turned out, they were right. Remembering the limited capacity of the boats, each man wanted to be in the first wave heading for the Maryland shore and no man wanted to be among the last, with all those screeching fiends in gray concentrating their fire on him. "A kind of shiver ran through the huddled mass upon the brow of the cliff," a Confederate later wrote. Then, as he watched, "it gave way; rushed a few steps; then, in one wild, panic-stricken herd, rolled, leaped, tumbled over the precipice." The descent was steep, with jagged rocks, but they would not wait to take the roundabout cow path. They leaped and kept on leaping, some still clutching their muskets, and tumbled onto the heads and bayonets of the men below, with resultant screams of pain and terror. Presently, the witness added, "the side of the bluff was worn smooth by the number sliding down."

★

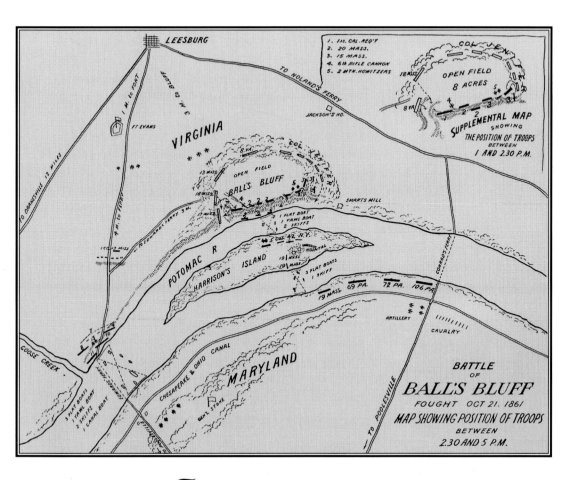

This period map shows the upper Potomac around Ball's Bluff, where Union and Confederate forces clashed in October 1861.

Some Confederates hesitated in pursuit, horrified at the results of the panic they had just been doing their utmost to create. They shook this off, however, and running to the rim of the bluff they fired into the huddled, leaping rout of blue-clad men as fast as they could manipulate ramrods and triggers. On the narrow bank and in the water — lashed by bullets until the surface boiled "as white as in a great hail storm," one declared — the scene was worse than the one back on the summit. The wounded had been coming down all day, to be ferried across for medical care and safety. Just as two such boatloads were leaving, their comrades came hurtling down the bluff. Making straight for the loaded boats, they filled them till they swamped and went all the way under, and those of the wounded too badly hurt to swim were swept away and drowned. A flatboat Colonel Baker had horsed out of a nearby canal, using it to get his guns across, was scrambled into until it was almost awash. The fugitives set out in this, but presently, live men ducking and dodging and shot men falling heavily on the gunwales, it capsized and thirty or forty were drowned. One skiff remained, a sheet-metal lifeboat, which soon was so riddled by bullets that it sank, and that left none.

It was dusk by now, the pearly gunsmoke turning blue, the pink stabs of muzzle-flashes deepening to scarlet as they stitched the lip of the bluff overhead. Marooned, many of the fugitives surrendered. A few removed their clothes and swam to safety across the bullet-lashed Potomac. Still others discovered a neck-deep ford leading over to Harrison's Island and got away in the darkness.

Confederate casualties were negligible, but Union losses approached 1000 — over 200 shot and more than 700 captured. Prominent men were among them, including a grandson of Paul Revere, a son of Oliver Wendell Holmes, and

---

As he stepped out into the street he stumbled, groping blindly, and almost fell. Orderlies and newspapermen jumped to help him, but he recovered his balance and went on alone, leaving them the memory of a weeping President.

---

a nephew of James Russell Lowell. Most prominent of all, however, was the senator from Oregon, Edward D. Baker, called Ned by his friend the President. Back in Washington, Lincoln was at army headquarters while the telegraph clicked off news of the disaster. When the death of Ned Baker came over the wire, Lincoln sat for five minutes, stunned, then made his way unaccompanied through the anteroom, breast heaving, tears streaming down his cheeks. As he stepped out into the street he stumbled, groping blindly, and almost fell. Orderlies and newspapermen jumped to help him, but he recovered his balance and went on alone, leaving them the memory of a weeping President.

Thus Lincoln received the news, with sorrow and tears. Baker's fellow congressmen received it otherwise. Their breasts heaved, too, but with quite different emotions. Men who had squirmed with impatience at the army's overcautiousness in coming to grips with the rebels now raged against a rashness which had snuffed out one of the Senate's brightest stars. Someone had blundered and blundered badly, and they were out to fix the blame, determined to revenge their martyred colleague. And their rage brought out of this clash on

Senator Benjamin Wade chaired the Joint Committee on the Conduct of the War, formed to investigate the Federal defeat at Ball's Bluff.

the bluff above the Potomac a new influence, a new force to shape the character of the conflict: the Joint Committee on the Conduct of the War. Senator Ben Wade of Ohio was its chairman, an all-out abolitionist with keen little jet-black eyes and bulldog flews, the upper lip overhanging the lower one at the corners of his mouth, a figure to frighten the disloyal or the inefficient or the merely unlucky. Congress was voting a million dollars a day for war expenses, and now they were out to get their money's worth, in the form of at least a share in its prosecution. "We must stir ourselves," Wade said, "on account of the expense."

Star-Chamber-like, the committee's meeting room was in the Capitol basement, and here the military were summoned to answer accusations without being faced by their accusers or even being allowed to learn their names. General Stone was the first. It was Stone who had ordered Baker across the river; whatever had happened there was clearly his fault. He was suspect anyhow. Back in September he had issued general orders admonishing his men "not to incite and encourage insubordination among the colored servants in the neighborhood of the camps." That in itself was enough for Wade; but further investigation turned up all sorts of things. There had been strange bonfires, mysterious messengers passing between the lines, and much else. Before long it became clear to the committee that Stone had sent those men across the river to get them butchered, probably after prearrangement with the enemy. He was called up, confronted with the evidence, such as it was — but not with the ones who gave it — and when he protested that he was the man who had guarded the capital through the dark week following Sumter ("I could have surrendered Washington," he reminded them) they were unimpressed. He was relieved of his command, placed in a cell at Fort Lafayette in New York harbor, and kept there under lock and key, an example to all who dared the wrath of the joint committee.

All this took time, a matter of months. The man they were really after was McClellan, who had Democratic leanings — it was true he had voted only once, but that once had been for Douglas — in addition to being a "soft war" man, with a concern for rebel property rights, including slaves. Beyond McClellan was Lincoln, who had some of the same attributes, and if they were not precisely after Lincoln's scalp — he had too many votes behind him for that — they intended at least to put some iron in his backbone. Stone was merely an opportunity that popped up, a chance to install the machine and test it, too, even as it was being installed. The trial run had worked out fine, with Stone lodged in a prison cell beyond the help of Lincoln or McClellan. Now they would pass on to bigger things. Ben Wade and his colleagues were out to make this fight a war to the knife, and Stone was their warning to anyone who might think otherwise.

McClellan was aware of this, of course, and was on guard. "I have a set of men to deal with unscrupulous and false," he told his wife. "If possible they will throw whatever blame there is on my shoulders, and I do not intend to be sacrificed by such people." It made him wary, coupled as it was with a belief that he was outnumbered by the enemy to his front. Ball's Bluff had reinforced that belief, and he felt a deep-down sadness.

"There is many a good fellow that wears the shoulder-straps going under the sod before this thing is over," he told Lincoln soon after they received word of Baker's death. Then he added, by way of consolation: "There is no loss too great to be repaired. If I should get knocked on the head, Mr President, you will put another man into my shoes."

"I want you to take care of yourself," Lincoln said.

Presently there was more cause than ever for him to want Little Mac to take care of himself. Within eleven days of the Ball's Bluff fiasco, General Scott having at last broken completely under the pointed snubs and contradictions, McClellan was given command of all the Union armies. The old Virginian's renewed application for retirement was accepted November 1. "Wherever I may spend my little remainder of life," he wrote, "my frequent and latest prayer will be, 'God save the Union.'" The same day, McClellan was appointed to fill his place, in addition to remaining in command of the Washington army.

Lincoln was worried that the young general might feel overburdened by the increased responsibility. So that evening — while out in Missouri the captain disguised as a farmer was being held incommunicado, having delivered the order relieving Frémont — Lincoln went to McClellan's headquarters to see how he was bearing up.

He found him in high spirits, glad to be out from under the dead weight of General Scott. Lincoln was pleased to find him so, but he wondered whether McClellan was fully aware of how much he was undertaking. After expressing his pleasure that the change had been made, the President added: "I should be perfectly satisfied if I thought this vast increase of responsibility would not embarrass you."

"It is a great relief, sir!" McClellan answered. "I feel as if several tons were taken from my shoulders today. I am now in contact with you and the Secretary. I am not embarrassed by intervention."

"Well," Lincoln said, "draw on me for all the sense I have, and all the information." Still wondering, however, if McClellan was as aware of the weight that had been added as he was of the weight that had been taken away, he returned to the point: "In addition to your present command, the supreme command of the Army will entail a vast labor upon you."

"I can do it all," McClellan told him.

★   ★   ★

Shelby Foote

*Musician sailors take a break with
their instruments on board Admiral
Du Pont's flagship, the Wabash.*

SIX

Scott's Anaconda; The Navy

1861 ★ ★ ★ ★ ★ **A**fter a few hours' sleep the following night, McClellan and his staff got out of their beds at 4 o'clock in the morning, mounted their horses, and, accompanied by a squadron of cavalry, escorted General Scott to the railway station. It was rainy and pitch dark. On the depot platform the gaslight glittered blackly on the officers' rain-suits, so that they seemed clad in lacquered armor.

Touched by this show of respect, as well as by a general order McClellan had issued that day in his praise — "let us do nothing that can cause him to blush for us," it ended; "let no defeat of the army he has so long commanded embitter his last years, but let our victories illuminate the close of a life so grand" — the old warrior was cordial to the man who had made his final weeks in Washington a torment. He sent his regards to the young general's wife and baby, and added that his sensations were "very peculiar" on leaving active duty. Then, the clank of sabers and chink of spur-chains somewhat muffled under the rubberized suits, he received his goodbye salute and boarded the train, which then pulled out.

McClellan returned to his quarters and his bed. Rising for the second time that morning, he found his mind so impressed by the farewell at the depot a few hours ago that he took time to describe it in a letter to his wife. After forwarding Scott's greetings to her and the new baby, he philosophized on what he

★

Known as "Old Fuss and Feathers," Winfield Scott, General-in-Chief of the Union armies, was older than the Constitution and the capital city he was to defend.

had seen: "The sight of this morning was a lesson to me which I hope not soon to forget. I saw there the end of a long, active, and industrious life, the end of the career of the first soldier of his nation; and it was a feeble old man scarce able to walk; hardly anyone there to see him off but his successor. Should I ever become vainglorious and ambitious, remind me of that spectacle."

The old soldier had faded away — had gone, in fact, to live for a time at Delmonico's in New York, where he could get his fill of terrapin; "the best food vouchsafed by Providence to man," he called it, admiring a steaming forkful held six inches above his plate. Yet he had left a great deal more behind him than the memory of that final scene from which his young successor drew a moral. In the '40s, commanding in Mexico, he had conducted, on a live-ammunition training ground, a postgraduate course in the art of war for officers who, having fought against Mexicans, would find a broader scope for their talents when they fought against each other in the '60s. Landing at Vera Cruz, outflanking Cerro Gordo, cutting loose from his base in hostile country to reduce Chapultepec and occupy Mexico City, he had established models for operations that would be repeated, time and again, on a larger scale, so that to list the men who received their baptism of fire under his direction was practically to call the roll of army commanders and generals-in-chief, both North and South, in the war that was building toward a climax at the time of his retirement. All this was much, but he had done still more. He had provided a plan for total war: Scott's Anaconda.

As a Virginian, older than the capital he was defending, he believed he knew the temper of the people across the Potomac and the Ohio. Their love for the Union was as deep as his own, he believed, and in time — provided they could be made to feel the dull reality of war against a more powerful opponent, without being pricked in their hot-blooded pride by the bayonets of a penetrating army — they would see the error of their angry choice and renounce the men who had led them into a wilderness, away from the direction in which their devotion and true interests lay. Out of this belief he evolved his plan, though what was called an anaconda might better have been described as a water serpent.

All down the eastern seaboard, from Chesapeake Bay to the Florida Keys, thence along the shores of the Gulf, counter-clockwise from the Keys to Matamoros, he would establish a deep-water naval blockade to wall the Confederacy off from Europe and whatever aid might come from that direction. Meanwhile, down the length of the Mississippi, from Cairo past New Orleans, he would send an army of 60,000 "rough-vigor fellows" backed by gunboats, thus cutting the Southerners off from the cattle and cereals of Texas, as well as from such foreign help as might be forwarded through the neutral ports of Mexico. Having seized all this he would hold on tight, neither advancing nor yielding ground, and within those constricting coils the South would become in very fact a political and economic wilderness, the awful hug of the serpent producing results which bursting shells and prodding bayonets could never bring about. The flame of rebellion, so difficult to stamp out — as an experienced military leader, Scott was thoroughly aware of all the problems of subduing a hostile and determined people — would die from lack of fuel or be smothered by sheer boredom. Unionist sentiment, unprovoked, would reassert itself. The people would come to their senses and force their hot-headed wrong-minded leaders to sue for peace and readmission to the Union, which they never should have left.

Such was Scott's Anaconda. From the outset, it came in for a considerable measure of ridicule — especially from cartoonists, who confused the metaphor by sketching the old general in a turban, sitting cross-legged as he tried to charm the southern cobra with a flute — as well as violent opposition from such spokesmen as Senator-Colonel Baker, who demanded bold and forward war and would not see that either of these adjectives could be applied to the so-called anaconda plan. Also it was believed to have overrated Unionist sentiment in the South, though whether this was so or not was presently removed to the realm of conjecture; McDowell's march on Manassas, which Scott opposed, applied the goad which the plan would have avoided. It certainly ran against the grain of McClellan's expressed intention to "crush the rebels in one campaign" by an overland march on Richmond. Yet in other respects, of all the plans evolved by many men, right up to the end, it was the first to recognize and utilize the North's tremendous advantage of numbers and material, and it was the first to emphasize the importance of the Mississippi Valley in an over-all view of the war.

Lincoln, at any rate, welcomed it, studied it, and acted on those parts of it which seemed to him most feasible at that stage of the contest. On April 19 — the day the 6th Massachusetts was mobbed in Baltimore and the Friday after the Friday whose dawn saw Sumter under fire in Charleston harbor — he proclaimed a blockade of the southern coast. Proclaiming and enforcing were two different things, however, especially considering the size of the fleet charged with transferring the blockade from dry paper to salt water. At that date the Union navy, scattered over the seven seas, included 42 ships, 555 guns, and 7600 sailors, and though by the end of the year this had been consolidated and increased to 264 ships, 2557 guns, and 22,000 sailors, the magnitude of the task ahead made a navy of almost any size seem small.

The anaconda was required to hug a circumference of about five thousand miles, two-fifths dry land and rivers and the remaining three-fifths shoreline. This 3000-mile coastal portion, belly and crotch of the continent, bisected by the phallic droop of the Florida peninsula, was doubled along much of its length, both in the Atlantic and the Gulf, by intricate mazes of sandbars, lagoons, and outlying islands, which, though less forbidding at first glance than the rocky shores of New England, were obviously at second glance much harder to patrol. Nassau and Havana were less than 700 miles, respectively, from Charleston and New Orleans, while Bermuda was but slightly farther from Wilmington. Such good harbors were few, but each had many entrances and outlets. It would be a slow ship, conned by a clumsy skipper indeed, that could not come and go by the dark of the moon, undetected in making its run to or from the safety of those neutral ports.

Knowing all this, Southerners laughed at the anaconda, much as the northern cartoonists were doing, especially that portion of it covered by the blockade proclamation, and predicted — quite accurately, as it turned out — that when Yankee sailors began patrolling the swampy littoral they would discover that even the mosquitoes had enlisted in the resistance. Besides, there was an economic consideration beyond all this, by which the blockade might be reckoned a positive good from the southern point of view, a reinforcement of one of the most powerful weapons in the Confederate arsenal. Cotton, the raw material of Great Britain's second leading industry, as well as the answer to France's feverish quest for prosperity, was the white gold key that would unlock and swing ajar the door through which foreign intervention would come marching. Remembering the effectiveness of Jefferson's embargo on tobacco, of which the Colonies had not controlled the world supply, the South could expect much greater results from an embargo on cotton, on which she held a world monopoly. Going without tobacco had been unpleasant for Europeans, but they would find it downright impossible to manage without cotton. Unfortunately, there had been a bumper crop the year before; French and English warehouses were bulging with the surplus. But that only lengthened the time factor. When the reserve dwindled and the white stream that fed the jennies and looms and the workers who tended them was shut off, Europe would come knocking at Jefferson Davis's door, offering recognition and the goods of war, the might of the British navy and the use of armies that had blasted Napoleon himself clean off the pages of military history. For all these reasons the South could laugh at and even welcome the proposed blockade, which would strengthen one of her strongest weapons in ratio to its own effectiveness. There was much that was amusing, too, in the contemplation of northern

Cotton, the raw material of Great Britain's second leading industry, as well as the answer to France's feverish quest for prosperity, was the white gold key that would unlock and swing ajar the door through which foreign intervention would come marching.

ships patrolling the southern coast to inforce a southern embargo. Few sailors and no ships at all had come over voluntarily to the Confederate side when the nation split in two. Now, belatedly and paradoxically, they would cross over, under orders from their own Commander in Chief.

At the outset the Confederate government, having almost no regular navy, determined to create an irregular one which would function while the other was being built. The Declaration of Paris, an agreement between the European powers five years back, had defined privateering as illegal; but the United States, remembering the success of independent Yankee vessels against the British merchant marine in the War of 1812 — and not knowing, moreover, when she might be engaged in such a war again — had refused to sign the document. So now the Richmond Congress, recalling such successes, too, authorized the issue of letters of marque to the captains of whatever ships might apply. It was characteristic of the current southern opinion of northern morals that they expected many such applications to come from New England skippers attracted by a chance at easy dollars.

Jefferson Davis launches a toy boat in a barrel in a northern cartoon ridiculing the tiny, makeshift Confederate navy.

These were not forthcoming, but before long about twenty vessels were on the high seas, privateering in the American tradition. Lincoln declared them outright pirates and announced that the crews would be treated as such when captured, with hanging as the penalty after conviction in the courts. Davis, never the man to decline a challenge of any sort, replied that for every Confederate sailor so hanged he would hang a Union soldier of corresponding rank, chosen by lot from among the thousands of prisoners in the Richmond tobacco warehouse.

Thus it stood, threat countering threat, until presently the world was given what appeared to be a chance to see which President had the courage of his convictions. The privateer *Savannah* was taken in June, its crew lodged in a common jail awaiting trial for piracy. Despite the clamor throughout the North in favor of dancing the defendants at a rope end, when the trial was held the New York jury could not agree on a verdict, and thus the crisis passed. Later in the year, however, when the privateer *Jeff Davis* was taken, the crew brought to trial in Philadelphia, convicted of piracy and sentenced to be hanged, Lincoln showed every sign of going ahead: whereupon Davis reinforced his counterthreat by causing lots to be drawn among the Union prisoners. The short-straw men — including that grandson of Paul Revere, captured at Ball's Bluff — were placed in condemned cells to await the action of Abraham Lincoln in reviewing the sentence of the men condemned to death in the City of Brotherly Love.

Lincoln paused and considered; and having reconsidered, he backed down. Though he thus exposed himself to charges of indecision and cowardice, declining to engage in a hanging match with Jefferson Davis, he saved the lives of Union soldiers and Confederate sailors — Americans both — and thereby saved the nation a blot on its record. North and South, however, many persons saw only that Davis had taken the measure of his opponent.

Whatever apparent moral advantage the Confederates gained from this clash of presidential wills, they soon found their bloodless victory offset by three sudden hammer blows struck by the Federal navy — two on the Atlantic coast and one in the Gulf of Mexico: Cape Hatteras and Port Royal, off North and South Carolina, and Ship Island, near New Orleans.

These objectives were the choice of a joint three-man strategy board composed of Army, Navy, and Coast Survey officers appointed to make "a thorough investigation of the coast and harbors, their access and defenses." The fleet was far too small for the enormous job of patrolling the 189 harbor and river openings along the 3549 miles of shoreline between the Potomac and the Rio Grande, and what there was of it was badly in need of ports of refuge, especially along the stormy South Atlantic. Out of this double necessity the blockade gained a new dimension, one in which the army would have a share. Not only could harbor entrances be patrolled; the harbors themselves might be seized, thus reducing the number of points to be guarded and at the same time freeing ships for duty elsewhere. Now, as the summer of the opening year of the war merged into the drawn-out southern fall, it was the task of the strategy board, with its three-headed knowledge of "the coast and harbors, their access and defenses," to select likely targets for the proposed amphibious operations.

The first was modest in scope but effective in execution. Off North Carolina the wide shallows of Pamlico and Albemarle Sounds, inclosed by a barrier of islands and reefs, afforded an ideal anchorage for raiders and blockade runners. Here if anywhere was the place at which the board should point its finger. Off that stormy cape the sea was frequently too rough for a fleet to be able to keep station. The only way to block it was to take it. At Hatteras Inlet, the break in the barrier, the Confederates had built two forts on opposite sides of the passage, Clark and Hatteras. Whoever held these forts held Pamlico Sound, and on August 26 an expedition of fourteen vessels under Flag Officer Silas H. Stringham sailed from Hampton Roads to take them. Among the ships were four transports carrying 860 men under Ben Butler, who thus was given a chance to redeem his blunders at Big Bethel.

This he did, and easily, for the army had almost nothing to do. Stringham, with superior ordnance, stood just outside the range of the rebel guns and for two days threw shells into the forts at will, suffering no hurt himself. Butler's men, put ashore well north of the forts — 300 of them, anyhow; for the surf staved in the landing-boats by the time that many got ashore — marched down the island, wet and hungry, their ammunition ruined by the surf, and arrived in time to watch their general share with Stringham the honor of receiving the surrender of Fort Hatteras, Fort Clark having run up its white flag the day before. Most of the soldiers and three of the ships were left to hold what had been won, while the rest returned to Fortress Monroe with their 615 prisoners. The navy had taken its first Confederate stronghold, and in doing so had reduced its blockade task.

★

The second offensive operation, down in the Gulf in mid-September, was even simpler, requiring not even the token assistance of troops. Here the lower delta of the many-mouthed Mississippi posed a problem much like Hatteras, with raiders and blockade runners entering and leaving the great port of New Orleans almost at will. Though the threat of storms was not as constant, a tropical hurricane was something a man had to see to believe, and sandbars lurked as dangerous as reefs. All in all, the strategy board perceived that here, too, the only way to block the port effectively was to seize it. The navy was by no means prepared to undertake such an assignment just yet, but the board believed it was ready to make a beginning. Ship Island, off the Mississippi coast, would provide an excellent station for patrolling the eastern delta outlets and the passes down out of Lake Pontchartrain, as well as an ideal base from which to launch the attack on New Orleans itself, if and when the opportunity came. So the

Not only were these landsmen still somewhat green about the gills as a result of their experience off Hatteras, but in that storm, along with much else, they had lost nearly all their landing craft. It was to be a job for the naval force alone. In fact, Du Pont preferred it so.

board instructed the navy: Take it. And the navy did, together with its uncompleted fortifications, before the Confederates were prepared to fire a shot in its defense. Thus the Union secured its second foothold along the secession coast.

The third and final operation of the year was far more ambitious than the others, neither of which had given the fleet the large, deep-water harbor it needed in order to maintain a year-round blockade of such busy ports as Wilmington, Charleston, and Savannah. About one-third of the way up the palmetto-studded hundred miles of South Carolina littoral lying between the latter two cities, the strategy board found what it was seeking. Port Royal, the finest natural harbor on the southern coast, would float the navies of the world. Obviously, however, though they had no real need for it themselves, having almost no navy, the Confederates were thoroughly aware of what covetous eyes the Union navy was casting in that direction. If it was to be undertaken, the job must be done in strength, after preparation in great secrecy. Both were provided for; the board took no chances it could avoid. The naval member himself, Captain Samuel F. Du Pont, was appointed to head the expedition of 74 vessels,

★

including transports for a land force of 12,000 men. In late October, sailing under sealed orders, this fleet put out from Hampton Roads, considerable pains
having been taken to conceal its destination.

Almost at once, Du Pont was struck a double blow by fate — in the
form of Confederate intelligence and the weather. He not only lost the advantages of secrecy; he came close to losing his fleet as well. On the day he put out,
the Richmond government alerted its coastal defenses, giving warning that the
force had sailed. Three days later, November 1, the defenders of the fleet's objective received a specific telegram: "The enemy's expedition is intended for
Port Royal." On the same day, the fleet ran into a gale off Hatteras. The wind
approaching hurricane strength, two of the ships went down and the crew of a
third had to heave her guns into the sea to keep from foundering. By dawn of
the following day, November 2, the fleet was so scattered that Du Pont could
sight but one sail from the deck of his flagship, the *Wabash*. He continued
southward, however, and in clear weather two days later dropped anchor off the
bar at Port Royal. Twenty-five of his ships had rejoined by then, together with
reinforcements from the Charleston squadron, and others kept bobbing up
along the horizon. He spent another two days replacing the rebel-destroyed
channel markers, crossing the bar — a dangerous business for the deep-draft
Wabash — completing his attack plan, and finally holding a conference at which
he outlined for his captains the order of battle. At last he was ready, and at
8 o'clock the following morning, November 7, the attack got under way.

He knew what his wooden ships would encounter. At the entrance
to Port Royal Sound the enemy held Fort Beauregard, mounting 20 guns on
Bay Point to the north, and Fort Walker, mounting 23 guns on Hilton Head to
the south. Less than three miles apart, both of these forts were strongly built,
their gunners alerted for a week, awaiting the opportunity Du Pont was about
to offer them. Somewhere beyond them, too, was a Confederate flotilla of three
tugs, mounting one gun each, and a converted river steamer under Commodore
Josiah Tattnall, whom Du Pont knew to be a bold and capable officer, having
messed with him in what was already known as "the old navy." The forts were
Du Pont's main concern, however, and in attempting their reduction he would
have no help from the three brigades of soldiers in the transports. Not only
were these landsmen still somewhat green about the gills as a result of their experience off Hatteras, but in that storm, along with much else, they had lost
nearly all their landing craft. It was to be a job for the naval force alone. In fact,
Du Pont preferred it so. The most he would ask of the army was that it stand by
to help pick up the pieces.

To accomplish the double reduction he had evolved a novel plan
of attack, an order of battle which divided his fighting force into a main
squadron of nine of the heaviest frigates and sloops, ranged in line ahead,

and a flanking squadron of five gunboats. They would enter the sound in parallel columns, the lighter squadron ranged to starboard, and pass midway between the forts, receiving and returning the fire of both. At a point about two miles beyond the entrance, the main force was to round by the south and come back east, moving slowly past Fort Walker, maintaining the heaviest possible fire, then round to the north and head back west, slowing again as it passed Fort Beauregard. The flanking squadron, meanwhile, was to peel off and engage the Confederate flotilla or whatever targets of opportunity the rebels might afford, while the main force kept both forts under fire, widening the elliptical attack so as to bring its guns in closer on every turn.

And so it was. At the signal from the commander on the *Wabash*, leading the way across the sunlit water, the fleet steamed forward, two columns in close order. A flash and a roar shot out from Fort Walker, echoed at once by Beauregard. The ships took up the challenge and the fight was on. As they neared the turning point, Tattnall brought his four makeshift warships down the sound, and from a raking position let go several broadsides at the *Wabash* as soon as she came within range. The gunboats gave him their attention then; whereupon the Confederate, with fourteen Union men-of-war to

Federal shot explodes among Confederates inside Fort Walker. As the fleet, circling in Port Royal Sound, fires on Fort Beauregard (upper right), the flanking squadron (upper left) engages southern gunboats at the mouth of Skull Creek.

his immediate front, discreetly came about and made a swift, flat-bottomed retreat up Skull Creek, three miles northwest of the fort on Hilton Head. He was out of the fight for good, bottled up by the gunboats, which took station off the creek mouth. According to a Savannah newspaper published five days later, Tattnall dipped his pennant three times in jaunty salute to his old messmate, "regretting his inability to return the highflown compliments of Flag Officer Du Pont in a more satisfactory manner."

By then the Federal captain was busy elsewhere, with little time for compliments, highflown or otherwise. As the main column turned south, beginning its first eastward run, each ship opened with its forward pivot against Fort Walker's northern flank, which Du Pont had learned from reconnaissance was its weakest. The cannon being lodged on the parapet — which, if it increased their range, also increased their vulnerability — several were violently dismounted, others lost their crews, and the gunners, taken thus by enfilade from a direction in which they had not expected to fight, were dismayed. A British correspondent on one of the Union ships saw tall columns of dust spring up from the fort to mark the hits the fleet was scoring, and it looked to him "as if we had suddenly raised from the dust a grove of poplars."

Not that the rebel gunnery had been very effective in the first place. The enemy ships, moving along their elliptical course, with constant changes in speed, range, and deflection, were extremely hard to hit. What was more, the defenders had not wasted their scant powder on anything as unprofitable as target practice, and now that it came to bloody work they found that many of the shells would not fit, the powder was inferior, and the crews became exhausted within an hour of opening fire. All of which, sad as it was in Confederate eyes, was really quite beside the point. Fort Walker — to which Fort Beauregard, across the water, was merely adjunct — had been built to be defended only from dead ahead, against a force moving straight in from the sea. When this became apparent, it became apparent, too, that the fight had been lost from the moment Du Pont conceived his plan of attack. The only conditions left to be satisfied were those of honor.

Erratic or deadly, the firing continued, and as the main squadron steamed slowly past Fort Walker, delivering broadsides at point-blank range, the flanking squadron, maintaining its watch over the mouth of the creek up which Tattnall had retreated, added the weight of its guns to the pressure against the vulnerable northern flank, its shells bowling down the line of metal on the parapet. Assailed from both directions by naval crews who worked with coolness and precision — more guns were dismounted; more men fell — the defenders fired even more wildly. The main squadron completed its first pass, closing upon Fort Beauregard, then swept down and around again, coming within less than 600 yards of the fort on Hilton Head, which had but three

★

guns left in working order by the time the ships completed their second run. The *Wabash* was just rounding to the south, leading the way into a third ellipse, when Du Pont received a message that Fort Walker had been abandoned. At 2.20 a naval landing party raised the Union flag above ramparts that were pocked and battered, strewn with wreckage left by men who would not sweat to keep from bleeding, and then had wound up doing both at once. Army transports now put in. By nightfall, troops had occupied the works. Across the way, Fort Beauregard hauled down its flag at sunset, and early next morning the troops crossed over and occupied it too.

The victory was complete, and by it the Federal navy gained an excellent harbor in the very heart-land of secession. Nor was that all. Within the next three days the victors moved up the rivers and inlets and occupied the colonial towns of Beaufort and Port Royal, bringing under their control some of the finest old plantations in the South and thereby affording an opportunity not to be neglected by their abolitionist brethren, who presently arrived and began conducting uplift experiments among the Negro fieldhands. The battle itself had not been without its romantic aspect, for one of the defenders had been Brigadier General Thomas F. Drayton, C.S.A., whose brother, Captain Percival Drayton, U.S.N., commanded one of the attacking frigates; the South Carolina island for which they fought had been their boyhood home.

Satisfying as all this was to supporters of the Union — the loyal brother having won, Federal guns and Federal notions were now in operation within fifty airline miles of Charleston, where secession had had its birth eleven months before — there emerged from the battle another fact which had, for those who understood its implications, more weight than all the other facts combined, heart-warming and romantic though they were. Against stiffer resistance, this third hammer blow had been even more successful than the other two, and nowhere had the fleet failed to seize any objective assigned by the strategy board. Some standard theories were going to have to be revised: the belief that one gun on land was equal to four on water, for example. Steam had changed all that, removing the restrictions of wind and current, and making possible such maneuvers as Du Pont's expanding ellipse. From now on, apparently, the board had only to select its targets, concentrate the might of the fleet, and blast them into submission. Naval power was going to be a dominant factor in this war.

★ ★ ★

★

Shelby Foote

Federals occupy Fairfax Courthouse, in Virginia. The building, less than twenty miles from Washington, served as Confederate headquarters following First Manassas.

S E V E N

Diplomacy; The Build-up

1861 ★ ★ ★ ★ ★ **C**oming as it did in the wake of **defeats along Bull Run** and Wilson's Creek, near opposite ends of the thousand-mile-long fighting line, this triple victory hammered out by the Federal navy did much to revive the flagging martial spirit of the North. There was no corresponding depression in the South, however, the odds in all three of these naval engagements having been too one-sided to give much cause for doubting the proved superiority of Confederate arms. It had been more or less obvious all along that the enemy could concentrate and strike with superior force at almost any point along the perimeter; that had been one of the conditions accepted by Davis when he chose the strategic defensive. When the pressure elsewhere was relieved, when the advantage shifted so that the South would be doing the concentrating and striking, the world would find out whether the North would be able to hold what it had won. Yet now, since that policy involved the dispersal of force to meet attacks from all directions, as the drawn-out fall wore on and the year was rounding toward a close, Southerners began to discover the price they would have to pay, in the hard cash of lost chances, for the advantages that accrued to the defensive.

In late September, after Hatteras and Ship Island had been lost and a third such operation was probably already into the planning stage, Davis went up to Fairfax Courthouse for a conference with the victors of Manassas. While the blasted oaks on the battlefield to their rear turned red in the fine clear weather of early fall, the men who had won that battle lay idle, watching the blue-clad host to their front grow stronger every day. At this stage, Federal troops were joining at the rate of 40,000 a month—about the total effective strength of Johnston's army. Pinkerton, with his tabulated lists compiled by operatives in Richmond, had misled his employer badly. Yet McClellan had been right in his fears that he might be brought to battle before his soldiers were ready: Beauregard was planning an offensive.

Though volunteering had fallen off to such an extent that the men arriving barely replaced those lost by the expiration of short-term enlistments and a liberal granting of furloughs, and though the army was crippled by a shortage of arms and supplies—food as well as munitions—he believed that the northern army, still in something of a state of shock from the whipping it had taken two months back, had perhaps now merely reached that stage of crystallization at which a smartly administered rap would cause it to fly apart again. In reply to the Federal threat to divide and conquer the South by a descent of the Mississippi, Beauregard wanted to make a sudden thrust across the Potomac and divide the Union, east and west, by seizing the strip of territory lying between Pittsburgh and Lake Erie. When the Yankee army came out from behind its Washington intrenchments he would administer the rap that would accomplish its disintegration, then go about his business of division and conquest. The odds were long, he admitted, but they were shorter than they were likely to be at any time hereafter, especially if the Confederates remained passive and continued to allow the growing enemy host time in which to regain its confidence.

Such was his plan, and as Davis listened to it on the first day of October, closeted with the generals at their Fairfax headquarters, within twenty miles of Washington itself, Beauregard expounding and Johnston nodding approval, he could see its advantages, in spite of its abrogation of his claim that "all we ask is to be let alone." Then came the rub. Beauregard declared that he would undertake the movement with 50,000 men, while Johnston held out for 60,000; which meant that Davis would have the problem of finding 10- to 20,000 reinforcements for the invasion.

The Federal navy, having launched its first two amphibious operations, now was preparing a third, whose objective could only be guessed at. Every general in every department along the Atlantic and the Gulf—and, what was worse, every governor of every state that touched salt water; which included all but two of the eleven—not only believed that the blow would be struck, but was convinced that it would be aimed straight at him. They were calling loudly for help, and Davis could foresee the clamor that would follow any request that they forward troops to fatten the army now lying idle in northern Virginia. And with good cause; for in practically every case the political clamor would be followed by a military disaster. Down in North Carolina, for example, the loss of Hatteras had exposed New Bern, and the loss of New Bern would mean the loss of the Weldon railroad, the only supply line between Richmond and the South Atlantic states. Without that line the Virginia army not only could not hope to mount an invasion, it could not even be maintained in its present position beyond ten days. On the Gulf the situation was almost as critical. The army being assembled and drilled at Pensacola might be considered available, but the recent seizure of Ship Island had exposed the nation's tender underbelly to assault, and that army was all that stood in a position to blunt the point of such a stab. Wherever Davis looked, the situation was such that to strip one area for the removal of troops to another would be to exchange possible success for probable disaster.

Beauregard urged in vain that the length of the odds was an argument for, not against, the risk; that desperate men must take desperate chances,

---

Wherever Davis looked, the situation was such that to strip one area for the removal of troops to another would be to exchange possible success for probable disaster.

---

and that whatever was lost in the interim could be retaken after a victory on northern soil. Davis shook his head. No reinforcements could be sent, he said, without "a total disregard for the safety of other threatened positions."

The Creole could only shrug, while Johnston sat resigned, not being exactly a forward, cut-and-slash sort of commander in the first place. That ended all talk of a fall offensive, either along the Virginia line or elsewhere. For this year at least, the nation was committed to the dispersed defensive, and Davis took the cars back to Richmond.

He had troubles enough to vex him there, what with the day-to-day frets of office, the long nights rendered sleepless by neuralgia, and the fire-eaters shouting angrily that he had no policy that could even hinder, let alone halt, the southward crunch of the gigantic war machine the North was building unmolested. The cabinet he had assembled with such concern for political expediency had already begun to come apart at the seams. The brilliant and unpredictable Toombs, after hesitating to recommend the firing of the opening shot at Sumter, had bridled, once the shot had been fired, at being desk-bound while other men were learning the glad companionship of service in the field. On the day of Manassas, the issue being still in doubt in Richmond, where all that was known was that the guns were booming, he could abide it no longer. He submitted his resignation, as of that day, and left his post as head of the State Department to enter the army as a Georgia brigadier. Within another two months War Secretary Leroy P. Walker had done likewise, though for quite different reasons. Instead of feeling left out or insufficiently employed, the Alabamian had been employed beyond his capabilities, and he knew it. Swamped with work, trussed up in yards of red tape, he too departed for the field, where a man had only the comparatively simple frets of being killed or mangled. They would be missed, especially Toombs, but their going gave Davis a double—or in fact, as he worked it out, a triple—opportunity.

As Attorney General, Judah P. Benjamin was largely wasting his talents, since the Justice Department no more had courts than the Postal Department, in the early months, had stamps. The War Office, which Walker had left in such a snarl, seemed the perfect field for Benjamin's administrative abilities. Accordingly, Davis shifted him there. This still left two vacancies, and in filling them the President corrected another shortcoming. The all-important border states had come into the Confederacy in April, and all this time had been without representation in the cabinet, there having been no vacancy. Now that there were two such, Davis filled them with men of distinction from Virginia and North Carolina: Robert M. T. Hunter of the former and Thomas Bragg of the latter. The Virginian went in as head of the State Department and the North Carolinian was given Benjamin's post as Attorney General. How Davis would get along with them remained to be seen. Like most of the old cabinet members, neither of the new ones had been intimate friends of his in private life before the war; nor were they now.

At any rate he had his family with him, established at last in what was called the White House of the Confederacy, not because it was white (it wasn't; it was gray) but because the President's residence had been called that under the old flag: a handsome, high-ceilinged mansion on the brow of a hill at the eastern end of Clay Street, with a garden to the rear, downhill, shaded by poplars and sycamores and the horse-chestnuts his wife loved. Though the Virginia ladies looked askance and called her "a western belle" behind their fans, Mrs Davis, already heavy with the child she had conceived in Montgomery and would bear in Richmond in December, assumed her social duties with grace and charm. She was a credit to her position and a comfort to her husband. Yet even with her there to minister to his mental and bodily ills, the long hours and the constant strain were telling on his health and on his temper, both highly frangible in the first place.

Twenty years of public life had not thickened his skin against the pricks of criticism, and the past seven months had even thinned it. At times he was like a flayed man in a sandstorm. His wife could overlook the sidelong

★

Varina Howell Davis (left) was the graceful and charming mistress of the presidential residence, the so-called White House of the Confederacy (below), in Richmond.

glances of the FFVs, but to Davis any facial tic of disagreement became at once a frown of disapproval. He had lost none of the gracious manner by which he could charm an opponent into glad agreement, yet now he scorned to employ it, and turned snappishly upon any man who crossed him. Smarting under the goads of office, he fell out with whoever did not yield to him in all things, and any difference was immediately made personal.

It had been thus even in the case of the two generals he had counseled with at Fairfax. Though nothing in their words or manner had shown this at the conference itself — all three being gentlemen and patriots who, in any given situation for which they had had time to steel their tempers, could place the national good above personal bias — Davis had shared a sort of running quarrel-by-courier with both of the ranking heroes of Manassas. Beauregard with his bloodhound eyes and swarthy complexion, his hair brushed forward at the temples, Napoleonic in aspect and conception, eager for glory, Gallic and expansive, and Johnston with his prim, high-colored, wedge-shaped face, his balding head, his gray-shot sideburns and goatee, Virginia-proud, Virginia-genial when he wanted to be, cunctative as Fabius Maximus yet jaunty as a gamecock: these two had known the quick wrath and the withering scorn of the intellectual Davis in dispatches that were alternately hot or icy, but which in either case, when designed to sting, performed that function all too well. Gone was the glad comradeship they had shared on the field of Manassas, born of relief and exultation in that July twilight while the Union flood ran backward up the roads to Washington. Since then, both men had fallen from presidential favor.

Beauregard fell first. The man who had shown much modesty on his arrival at Richmond, with the laurels of Sumter still green on his brow, became a different man entirely when he took up his pen in the seclusion of his tent. After Manassas, talk had grown rife that the President had prevented any pursuit of the routed enemy: so rife, indeed, that Davis took the unusual step of asking his generals to deny the rumor officially. This Beauregard was glad to do, and promptly. But in his report on the battle, which unfortunately got to the newspapers before it reached the presidential desk, he reverted to his original scheme for combining the armies to crush the Union forces in detail — the plan which had been outlined by one of his aides at the first Confederate war council, held at the Spotswood a week before the battle — with the implication that its having been rejected was the reason why the southern army was not in the northern capital now.

Davis would not let this pass. "With much surprise, I found that the newspaper statements were sustained by the text of your report," he wrote, and took the general to task. His last letter to the Louisianian had begun "My dear General" and ended "Very truly, your friend." This one opened with a frigid "Sir" and closed with an ambiguous "Very respectfully, yours &c."

The breach widened as the general's friends took up the cudgel. At last, in early November, Beauregard himself aired the grievance in a letter to the Richmond *Whig.* Headed "within hearing of the enemy's guns," it referred to the "unfortunate controversy now going on," and said in part: "I entreat my friends not to trouble themselves about refuting the slanders and calumnies aimed at me.... If certain minds cannot understand the difference between *patriotism*, the highest civic virtue, and *office-seeking*, the lowest civic occupation, I pity them from the bottom of my heart." However, the reaction was quite different from what he had anticipated. In reference to the "unique" heading, for example, a rival paper asked:

Practically overnight his dark hair was shot with gray: a phenomenon for which the different factions offered different explanations. Friends said that this was the result of overwork and heavy responsibility. Others attributed it to the blockade, which had cut him off from accustomed shipments of French hair dye.

"Are we expected to give special credit to the general's lucubrations by reason of a fact certainly not very unusual in military operations?" The public, too, was disenchanted; a star had lost its luster. If Davis himself had chosen the words and directed the actions, the general could not have played more neatly into his hands.

The Creole was unhappy anyhow. He felt cramped, no more than a supernumerary, now that his army was merely a corps in Johnston's command. Practically overnight his dark hair was shot with gray: a phenomenon for which the different factions offered different explanations. Friends said that this was the result of overwork and heavy responsibility. Others attributed it to the blockade, which had cut him off from accustomed shipments of French hair dye. Whatever caused his graying, before the end of the year it was plain that he would have to go. Davis was considering sending him West, where he would find problems of such complexity that even his active mind would be kept busy and there would be ample opportunity for him to exercise his talents, both with the sword and the pen.

★

Outraged when he was not named the senior general in the Confederate army, Joseph E. Johnston complained bitterly to President Davis.

Trouble with Johnston had begun even sooner—all the way back in their West Point days, some said, when he and Davis were alleged to have had a fist fight over the favors of Benny Haven's daughter. Johnston won both the fight and the girl, rumor added; which might or might not have been true. At any rate, whatever had gone before, anger flared in considerable heat soon after the last day of August, when Davis forwarded to the Senate the names of five men to be given the rank of full general, lately provided for by law. The Senate confirmed them promptly, and in the order proposed. Adjutant-General Samuel Cooper headed the list, a sixty-six-year-old New Yorker who had married South and crossed over from the old army, in which he had held the same position. Next came Albert Sidney Johnston, still on the way from California after resigning his U.S. commission, a Kentucky-born Texan whom Davis and many others considered the first soldier of the Confederacy. Third was Robert E. Lee, mobilizer and former commander of all the Virginia forces, now campaigning in the Alleghenies, charged with regaining what had been lost out there. Near the bottom of the list came Joseph E. Johnston himself, followed only by P. G. T. Beauregard, who came fifth.

When notice of these promotions reached Johnston he was outraged in his sense of equity and wounded in his pride. In the old army he had outranked them all, having been appointed Quartermaster-General, with a staff commission as a brigadier, while they were only colonels. He saw no justice in Davis' assumption that seniority for line command must be based exclusively on

★

line service, in which both Lee and the other Johnston had held their commissions. All he saw was that he had been passed over.

Accordingly, while his wrath still smoked, he sat down and wrote a six-page letter of protest addressed to Jefferson Davis as the author of his woes. After expressing his "surprise and mortification," he wrote: "I now and here declare my claims, that notwithstanding these nominations by the President and their confirmation by Congress I still rightfully hold the rank of first general of the Armies of the Southern Confederacy." The order of names on the list, he added, "seeks to tarnish my fair fame as a soldier and a man, earned by more than thirty years of laborious and perilous service. I had but this, the scars of many wounds, all honorably taken in my front and in the front of battle, and my father's Revolutionary sword. It was delivered to me from his venerated hand, without a stain of dishonor. Its blade is still unblemished as when it passed from his hand to mine"; and much else, in much the same vein of outraged virtue. He waited two days before sending it. Then, finding his anger still uncooled, and remaining convinced of the trenchancy of his arguments and the fitness of the words he had used to advance them, he forwarded the letter unrevised.

Davis read it with a wrath that quickly rose to match the sender's. This Virginian, rattling his father's sword between lines that spoke of his "fair fame" and his wounded front, outdid even Beauregard. In composing his reply, however, Davis employed not a foil but a cutlass. Rejecting the nimble parry and riposte of rhetoric and logic, at both of which he was a master, he delivered instead one quick slash of scorn:

> *Sir: I have just received and read your letter of the*
>
> *12th instant. Its language is, as you say, unusual; its*
>
> *arguments and statements utterly one sided, and*
>
> *its insinuations as unfounded as they are unbecoming.*
>
> *I am, &c.*
>
> *Jeff'n Davis.*

Knowing Johnston he knew the effect this letter would have. He knew that it would never be forgotten or forgiven and that it must necessarily underlie a relationship involving the fortune, if not the very being, of their new nation. In writing and sending this reply it was therefore as if he deliberately threw off-center a vital gear in a machine which had been delivered into his care and was his whole concern. Yet his reasons, his motivations, were basic. Loving his country he was willing to give it all he owned, including his life; but he would not sacrifice his prerogative or his pride, since in his mind that would have been to sacrifice not only his life but his existence. There was a difference. It was not only that he would not. He could not. Without his prerogative, he would not be President; without his pride, he would not even be Davis.

Men interpreted him as they saw him, and for the most part they considered him argumentative in the extreme, irascible, and a seeker after discord. A Richmond editor later wrote, for all to read, that Davis was "ready for any quarrel with any and everybody, at any time and all times; and the suspicion goes that rather than not have a row on hand with the enemy, he would make one with the best friend he had on earth."

Since Davis seldom chose to explain his actions — such explanations not fitting his conception of the dignity of his office — all too often the editor's charge seemed true. It appeared to be quite literally true in one case which came up about this time. He received from a general in the field a confidential report that a subordinate must be dismissed. This officer was an old friend of Davis', and when he received the presidential order of dismissal he came to Richmond to plead his case before the man who had signed it. "You know me," he said. "How could I ever hold my head up under the implied censure from you, my old friend?" Davis would give him no explanation. Choosing rather to alienate a friend than to betray a confidence, or even infer that there was a confidence he could not betray, he told him: "You have, I believe, your orders. I can suggest nothing but obedience." And neither the friend nor the editor, nor for that matter the parlor gossips in Richmond, ever learned why this was done; nor that Davis came home that evening, suffering from the dyspepsia which was with him a symptom of nervous upset, and went to his room without eating.

★ ★ ★ *I*n this dark autumn, while Beauregard and Johnston chafed and politicians grew bitter at having to accept disproof of their prediction that the war would be a ninety-day excursion, Davis was disappointed by another general from whom he had expected much. Robert E. Lee's failure, however, came not because he was self-seeking or insubordinate — Lee was never either — but seemingly because he was incompetent in the field. The harshness of this judgment was emphasized by the contrast between what was done and what had been expected.

When Garnett fell in western Virginia and his army scattered before the skillful combinations of McClellan, it became necessary for Davis to send someone out there to put the pieces back together. Lee was the obvious choice. A man of considerable handsomeness and moral grandeur, hero of the Mexican War, he was Virginia's first soldier. Though it was not widely known that he had been tendered command of the U.S. forces before his resignation to go with his state, it was a matter of general knowledge that his rapid mobi-

*Virginians opposed to secession rally at the
Custom House in Wheeling to disavow the
Confederacy and form a Unionist government.*

lization of Virginia's troops had made possible the victory at Manassas. One week after that battle he started west, taking with him the expectations of the President and the southern people.

Federal military successes in the region had reinforced an earlier political maneuver. Back in April, when the Richmond convention voted for secession, the western members crossed the mountains and assembled in Wheeling, where — on grounds that by voting for secession the other members had committed treason and thereby placed themselves outside the law — they drew up a new constitution, elected a new governor, and petitioned Washington for recognition as the lawful government of the state. Lincoln, of course, welcomed them, and presently their representatives were occupying the Virginia seats in Congress and laying the groundwork for the creation of the loyal state of West Virginia. Nothing was more galling to Confederate Virginians than the presence of these men in Washington, and one of the things expected of Lee was that he would abolish the rump government which had sent them there.

★

Strategically, too, the region was of great importance. Along its far edge ran the Ohio River, which not only was the traditional natural barrier of the new nation, but also flowed down toward the heart of Kentucky. Through its northern counties ran two vital supply lines, the Baltimore & Ohio Railroad and the Chesapeake & Ohio Canal. These severed, Washington would have to find a roundabout route for drawing men and supplies from the West. Still more important, with only a one-hundred-mile neck of land dividing the northward jut of its tiny panhandle from the shores of Lake Erie, it was the best location from which to launch an offensive such as the one proposed by Beauregard at Fairfax. That narrow isthmus also divided the Union, east and west; to seize it would be to split the North in two. When Lee left Richmond, all these opportunities lay before him in the western mountains, and no one went on record then as doubting that he would accomplish everything to which he put his hand.

What the public did not know was that he did not go out there to command but to advise, to coördinate the operations of four small independent "armies" whose commanders included one professional soldier, one scholarly ex-diplomat, and two high-tempered politicians. The campaign was to be conducted seventy miles from the nearest railhead, in an area whose population was largely hostile and whose principal "crop" was mountain laurel, so that supplies had to be brought up over roads made bottomless by rain that seldom slacked. "It rained thirty-*two* days in August," one veteran asserted. The troops were hungry and ragged, cowed by the defeats of the past month, half of them down with measles or mumps and the other half lacking confidence in their leaders. It was here in the mountains that Lee encountered for the first time a new type of animal: the disaffected southern volunteer. "They are worse than children," he declared, "for the latter can be forced."

Nevertheless, with such material and under such conditions, he now tried to work with the first pair in his highly diversified quartet of brigadiers. The soldier, W. W. Loring, who had been there only a week, resented Lee's arrival as a sign that the government did not trust him, and the diplomat, Henry R. Jackson, though willing, was inexperienced; with the result that when Lee attempted to trap the Federals on Cheat Mountain by an involved convergence of five columns from the two commands, the soldier balked, the diplomat blundered, and nothing was accomplished except to warn the Union troops of the movement, which had to be called off. Failing here, Lee looked south, where the two politicians were independently arrayed.

They were John B. Floyd and Henry A. Wise, both one-time governors of Virginia, the latter having occupied that office during the John Brown raid and the former having gone on to become Secretary of War in Buchanan's cabinet. Floyd had shown a tendency to grow flustered under pressure, and Wise had indicated what manner of soldier he was by ordering a battery com-

*In 1838, thirty-one-year-old Robert E.
Lee posed for this portrait clad in the dress
uniform of a lieutenant of engineers.*

mander to open fire in woods so thick that he could see no target and could therefore do no execution. "Damn the execution, sir!" Wise replied when the artillerist protested. "It's the *sound* that we want."

These shortcomings were nothing, though, compared to the relationship that Lee discovered existing between the commanders when he arrived. With an eye for past rivalries, and for possible future ones as well, the two ex-governors seemed more intent on destroying each other than they were on injuring the enemy to their front. Wise had raised an independent Legion, and when Floyd, who outranked him, came into the district, he telegraphed Richmond: "I solemnly protest that my force is not safe under his control." Floyd,

★

enjoying the advantages of such rank, countered by offering to swap Wise's Legion for any three regiments of infantry, sight unseen. It was obvious that neither of these generals, intent as they were on mutual destruction—for which Floyd was perhaps the better equipped, having three newspaper editors on his staff—would be anxious, or maybe even willing, to coöperate in any venture which might bring credit to his adversary.

Yet Lee did what he could. He designed another combined operation, this time up the Kanawha Valley, and finally got the two commands in motion: whereupon, at the critical moment, with the enemy before them, the rivals took up separate positions, twelve miles apart, and, each declaring his own position superior, refused to march to join the other. Lee, whose primary reaction to the situation was embarrassment, was spared the ultimate necessity for sternness, however, when a War Department courier arrived with a dispatch instructing Wise to report immediately to Richmond. Wise pondered mutiny, but then, advised by Lee, decided against it and left, muttering imprecations.

With his problem thus reduced at least by half, Lee assembled the forces and took up a strong defensive position, planning destruction for the Federals. He hoped they would attack; if not, then he would launch an attack himself. For three days he waited. On the fourth he found the woods in front of him vacant, the enemy having pulled back out of reach, unobserved. All Lee could do, with winter closing in, was pull back, too. The three-month campaign was over, and he followed Wise to Richmond.

It was over and he had accomplished none of those things the public had expected. He had kept the advancing Federals off the Virginia Central and the Virginia & Tennessee Railroads, but this was generally ignored in the shadow of the darker fact that, with all those bright prospects before him, he had not even fought a battle. A Richmond journalist reviewed the operation thus: "The most remarkable circumstance of this campaign was, that it was conducted by a general who had never fought a battle, who had a pious horror of guerillas, and whose extreme tenderness of blood induced him to depend exclusively upon the resources of strategy to essay the achievement without the cost of life."

Lee had already written his wife, "I am sorry . . . that the movements of our armies cannot keep pace with the expectations of the editors. . . . I know they can arrange things satisfactory to themselves on paper. I wish they could do so in the field." And yet there was justice in the charge. Lee *had* been tender of bloodshed, designing complicated envelopments to avoid it—none of which had worked. Above all, he had shown himself incapable of jamming discipline down insubordinate throats. Besides, the journalist was reflecting general opinion. The public saw Lee now as a theorist, an engineer, a desk soldier, one who must fight by the book if he fought at all, and those who had watched with pride as he set out, expecting satisfaction for their hopes, now prepared looks of scorn for his return.

★

They did not use them to his face, however. Three months of adversity in the mountains had given him an austerity that would not permit familiarity, not even the familiarity of scorn. At fifty-four he had grown a beard; it came out gray, and people looked at him in awe. But beyond the influence of his presence, they sneered and called him Granny Lee and Evacuating Lee and wondered what use could be made of a soldier who would not fight.

Davis found a use for him as soon as he returned in early November. Having learned in private the details of the campaign — details which the public did not know, since Lee's delicacy, even toward men whose bickering had wrecked his reputation, would not allow him to include them in a report for the record — the President sent him to the South Atlantic coast, where his engineering abilities would be useful in improving the defenses. Hatteras Inlet and Ship Island had been lost, and a third blow seemed about to land. It landed, in fact, the day Lee got there. He arrived just in time to hear the guns at Port Royal and meet the fugitives streaming rearward from that fight. The Virginian could scarcely be blamed for this, yet a South Carolina matron wrote of him in her diary next day: "*Preux chevalier*, booted and bridled and gallant rode he, but so far his bonnie face had only brought us ill luck."

He believed more in work, however, than in luck. Having studied the situation, he strengthened some forts, abandoned others, and redrew the defenses, shifting them back from the sounds and rivers so that the invaders would have to fight beyond range of their gunboats. This called for digging, which Lee ordered done, and this in turn brought a storm of protest. His soldiers, especially the native South Carolinians, found the order doubly onerous. Digging wasn't fit work for a white man, they complained, and a brave man wouldn't hide behind earthworks in the first place. He put them at it anyhow, and as they dug they coined a new name for him: King of Spades.

★ ★ ★   **G**ranny Lee, Evacuating Lee, the King of Spades, was one of several ranking Confederates who found their loyalty to Davis repaid in kind. Risking, sometimes losing, the affection and confidence of large segments of the people for their sakes, Davis sustained them through adversity and unpopularity, whether the public reaction seemed likely to reach an end or not. Obviously this had its drawbacks. Then and down the years, depending on the critic's estimate of the bolstered individual, it was the quality for which he was at once most highly praised and most deeply blamed. Yet one advantage it clearly had for southern leaders, with a value greatly enhanced by the fact that it was seldom available to their opposite northern numbers: No man, knowing that Davis trusted him and knowing what that trust entailed, ever had to glance back over his shoulder, wondering whether the government — meaning Davis — would support him against the clamor of the disgruntled or sacrifice him on grounds of political expediency. And if this was clear to the generals thus sustained, it was even clearer to the politicians, who knew that Davis would do his duty as he saw it. When legislation which they knew was bad for the country came before them, they did not hesitate to pass the measure if it was popular with the folks back home, knowing that Davis would exercise his veto. (He employed it thirty-nine times in the course of the war, while his opponent used it thrice, and only in one case was it overridden.) Thus in dignified silence he shouldered the blame for men who called him obstinate and argumentative and did their worst to swell the chorus of abuse.

His tenure was no longer merely provisional. On the first Wednesday in November he and Stephens were elected, without opposition, to six-year terms of office. Inauguration ceremonies were scheduled for Washington's birthday, which seemed a fitting date for the formal launching of the permanent government established by the Second American Revolution. That this government *was* permanent, in fact as well as name, Davis had no doubt. "If we husband our means and make a judicious use of our resources," he assured the Provisional Congress at its final session, November 18, "it would be difficult to fix a limit to the period during which we could conduct a war against the adversary whom we now encounter."

For that adversary, whose leader styled the southern revolution a "rebellion" and whose people now were submitting meekly to indignities no American had ever encountered without fight, he expressed contempt. "If instead of being a dissolution of a league, it were indeed a rebellion in which we are engaged, we might find ample vindication for the course we have adopted in the scenes which are now being enacted in the United States. Our people now look with contemptuous astonishment on those with whom they had been so recently associated. They shrink with aversion from the bare idea of renewing such a connection. When they see a President making war without the assent of Congress; when they behold judges threatened because they maintain the writ of *habeas corpus* so sacred to freedom; when they see justice and law trampled under the armed heel of military authority, and upright men and innocent women dragged to distant dungeons upon the mere edict of a despot; when they find all this tolerated and applauded by a people who had been in the full enjoyment of freedom but a few months ago — they believe that there must be some radical incompatibility between such a people and themselves. With such a people we may be content to live at peace, but the separation is final, and for the independence we have asserted we will accept no alternative."

Yet even as he spoke, thus stigmatizing his opponent across the Potomac, Davis was faced with the necessity for emulating his "tyrannous" example. Two days after the first-Wednesday election an insurrection exploded in the loyalist mountain region of East Tennessee. Bridges were burned and armed men assem-

William Brownlow, leader of the anti-secession movement in East Tennessee, nearly became a martyr for the Union cause.

bled to assist the expected advance of a Union army through Cumberland Gap.

Though undeveloped industrially, the area was of considerable economic value as a grain and cattle country, offsetting the one-crop cotton agronomy farther south, and of even greater strategic importance because of the Virginia & Tennessee Railroad running through Knoxville and Chattanooga, westward to Memphis and the Transmississippi. The insurrection confronted Davis with a problem much like the one that had confronted Lincoln in Maryland immediately after Sumter, and Davis met it with measures even sterner. Troops were sent at once from Memphis and Pensacola. Resistance was quashed and a considerable number of Unionists arrested. Habeas corpus, "so sacred to freedom," went by the board. When the Confederate commander in Knoxville asked what he should do with these men, Davis had the Secretary of War reply that those insurrectionists not actually known to be bridge burners were to be held as prisoners of war. As for the burners themselves, they were "to be tried summarily by drumhead court martial, and, if found guilty, executed on the spot by hanging. It would be well," the Secretary added, "to leave their bodies hanging in the vicinity of the burned bridges."

Five were so hanged, and others were held, including that William G. Brownlow who earlier had said that he would fight secession on the ice in hell. Admittedly the leader of regional resistance, he was editor of the Knoxville *Whig* and formerly had been a Methodist circuit rider; wherefore he was called Parson. An honest, fearless, vociferous man who neither smoked nor drank nor swore, he had courted only one girl in his life "and her I married." Though he was mysteriously absent from home on the night of the burnings, his actual complicity could not be established. He was held in arrest—for a time, at least, until his presence proved embarrassing in the light of Davis' complaint about "upright men . . . dragged to distant dungeons" in the North. Again through the Secretary of War, under the theory that it was better for "the most dangerous enemy" to escape than for the honor and good faith of the Confederate government to be "impugned or even suspected," Davis directed that the parson-editor be released to enter the Union lines. Though he was thus denied the chance to recite the speech he had memorized for delivery on the gallows, Brownlow went rejoicing. "Glory to God in the highest," he exclaimed as he crossed over, "and on earth peace, good will toward all men, except a few hell-born and hell-bound rebels in Knoxville."

Under his reek of fire and brimstone there was much that was amusing about Brownlow. But there was nothing laughable about what he represented. Least of all was there anything comical about the situation he and his followers had created in the mountains of Tennessee. Now it had come to this, that Americans danced at rope ends as a consequence of actions proceeding from their political convictions. The harshest irony of all was that they were hanged by the direction of Jefferson Davis, who loved liberty and justice above all things, and who as a grown man, in a time of sickness, halted a reading of the child's story "Babes in the Woods" (it was characteristic that he had never heard it) because he would not endure the horror of the tale. The operation on his high-strung nature of such incidents as these in Tennessee caused him to remark long afterward, concerning his northern opponent's fondness for anecdotes and frontier humor, that he could not "conceive how a man so oppressed with care as Mr Lincoln was could have any relish for such pleasantries."

He was afflicted, however, by troubles both nearer and farther than the stern, unpleasant necessity for jailing, banishing, and hanging insurrectionists in eastern Tennessee. Fire-eaters in Richmond and the Deep South, their claim to the spoils of higher offices denied, their policy of bold aggression rejected, were everywhere disaffected. Vocal in their disaffection, they had now begun to raise a multivoiced outcry like the frantic babble of a miscued chorus. Charging that Davis had "no policy whatever," they represented him as "standing in a corner telling his beads and relying on a miracle to save the country." As caricature, the likeness was not too far-fetched, and the fact that the no-policy charge was true, or nearly true, did not make the barbs of criticism sting one whit the less.

His critics would have had him strip the troops from threatened points and send them marching forthwith against the North, staking everything on one assault. To Davis, this not only seemed inconsistent with his repeated claim that the South was merely defending herself against aggression, it seemed unnecessarily risky. That way the war might be quickly won, as Beauregard had pointed out; but it also might be quickly lost that way. Davis preferred to watch and wait. He believed that time was with him and he planned accordingly, not yet by any means aware that what he was waiting for would require a miracle. At this stage, in Davis' mind at any rate, nothing seemed more likely, more inevitable, than foreign intervention; as had been shown by his first action in attempting to secure it.

★ ★ ★ **B**ack in the Montgomery days, a month before Sumter, Barnwell Rhett, chairman of the foreign affairs committee, reported a bill to Congress providing for the dispatch of a three-man mission to secure the recognition of the Confederacy by the European powers. Rhett had certain notions as to what these men should do over there, but he could not give instructions to such emissaries; the making of treaties rested with the President, who seemed to believe that nothing more would be needed than a polite call on the various proper statesmen across the water, whereupon those dignitaries would spread their arms to welcome a new sister bringing a dowry of precious cotton into the family of nations. This belief was emphasized by the fact that the man appointed to head the mission was William L. Yancey, the fieriest fire-eater of them all. For fifteen years the southern answer to the most outspoken of northern abolitionists, the Georgia-born Alabamian extended his defense of the "peculiar institution" to include a proposed reopening of the African slave trade — with the result that his name was anathema to every liberal on earth. In selecting Yancey to represent her, it was as if the South said plainly to all Europe: "To get cotton you must swallow slavery."

*A*rdent secessionist Robert Barnwell Rhett headed the Confederate legislature's foreign affairs committee.

Nothing in his personality had shown that he would be armed with patience against discouragement or with coolness against rebuff, or indeed that he was in any way suited to a diplomatic post. Discouragement was not expected, however, let alone rebuff. Besides, Yancey having declined the minor cabinet job of Attorney General, the appointment solved the problem of what to do with him. Since that February evening on the gallery of the Exchange Hotel, when he presented "the man and the hour" to the crowd, no fitting use for his talents had been found. Now there was this — though some de-

William L. Yancey was chosen to lead the South's first diplomatic mission to seek recognition of the Confederacy in Europe.

clared that he was being hustled off the scene as a possible rival before the election of a permanent President came round.

However that might have been, when he and his associates, Pierre A. Rost and A. Dudley Mann, received their instructions from the State Department, something came over Yancey that seemed to come over all fire-eaters when they were abruptly saddled with the responsibility for using more than their lungs and tongues—something akin to the sinking sensation that came over Roger Pryor, for example, when he was offered the honor of firing the first shot of the war. Returning from the conference, Yancey went to Rhett and told him of the instructions. They had agreed at the outset that the power to make commercial treaties was necessary to the success of the mission. However, the commissioners had not been given such power. All they were to do was explain the conflict in terms of the rightness of the southern cause, point out the Confederacy's devotion to low tariffs and free trade, and make a "delicate allusion" to the probable stoppage of cotton shipments if the war continued without European intervention. Hearing this, Rhett shared his friend's dismay. "Then," he told Yancey, "if you will take my advice as your friend, do not accept the appointment. For if you have nothing to propose and nothing to treat about, you must necessarily fail. Demand of the President the powers essential to your mission, or stay at home."

★

Whatever his qualms and misgivings, Yancey did not take his friend's advice. Sailing on the eve of Sumter, the commissioners reached England in late April to discover that the nation they represented was in the process of being increased from seven states to eleven, doubled in size east of the Mississippi and more than doubled in wealth and population. Soon afterwards, May 3, they secured an interview with Lord John Russell, Secretary of State for Foreign Affairs, who had replied to their request for an audience that he would be pleased to hear them, but that "under present circumstances, I shall have but little to say."

The interview was as one-sided as his lordship predicted. Having heard the envoys out, he replied — without committing his government in the slightest — that the Confederacy's request for recognition would be placed before the Cabinet at an early date. Six days later there was a second, briefer meeting; and that was all. In Paris, Napoleon III was more genial and less forthright, though he did make it clear in the end that, however much he wished to intervene, France could not act without England. So Yancey and Mann, leaving Rost to watch Napoleon, returned to London to try again.

Their hopes were higher now, and with good cause. When Lincoln announced a blockade of the southern coast, Britain — in accordance with international law, since obviously no nation would blockade its own ports — issued in mid-May a proclamation of neutrality, granting the Confederacy the rights of a belligerent, and the other European powers followed suit. That was much, and when more followed, Manassas enhancing the dignity of southern arms, Yancey thought the time was ripe for recognition. Accordingly, another note was sent to Russell, requesting another interview. The reply came back: "Earl Russell presents his compliments to Mr W. L. Yancey, Mr A. Dudley Mann, and would be obliged to them if they would put in writing any communications they wish to make to him."

This was something of a shock; yet they smothered their anger and complied, writing at length and basing their claims for recognition on recent Confederate triumphs. The reply to this was a bare acknowledgment of receipt; which in turn was another shock, for they knew that an English gentleman was never rude except on purpose. Again they swallowed their pride, however, and, Rost having recrossed the channel to lend what weight he could, continued to send letters until early December, when the Foreign Secretary added the last straw: "Lord Russell presents his compliments to Mr Yancey, Mr Rost and Mr Mann. He has had the honour to receive their letters of the 27th and 30th of November, but in the present state of affairs he must decline to enter into any official communication with them."

That broke the camel's back, for Yancey anyhow, whose pride had been subjected to a good deal more than it could bear. He resigned and sailed for home. Arriving he went straight to Rhett, whose advice he had not taken.

"You were right, sir," he declared. "I went on a fool's errand."

Davis might continue to comfort despair with hope; Yancey himself had none. "While the war which is waged to take from us the right of self-government can never attain that end," Davis asserted at the final session of the Provisional Congress—knowing the "delicate allusion" would be heard across the Atlantic—"it remains to be seen how far it may work a revolution in the industrial system of the world, which may carry suffering to other lands as well as our own." It did not remain to be seen as far as Yancey was concerned. He had been there; he had seen already. He put no faith in anything that might happen in those nations whose statesmen had galled his pride.

> *"The sentiment of Europe is anti-slavery, and that portion of public opinion which forms, and is represented by, the government of Great Britain, is abolition. They will never recognize our independence until our conquering sword hangs dripping over the prostrate heads of the North...."*
>
> — William L. Yancey

Speaking in New Orleans in the spring, soon after his return, he told the people outright what he had told Davis earlier in private: "You have no friends in Europe.... The sentiment of Europe is anti-slavery, and that portion of public opinion which forms, and is represented by, the government of Great Britain, is abolition. They will never recognize our independence until our conquering sword hangs dripping over the prostrate heads of the North.... It is an error to say, 'Cotton is King.' It is not. It is a great and influential factor in commerce, but not its dictator. The nations of Europe will never raise the blockade until it suits their interests."

Thus Yancey, who had failed. How much his words were influenced by the fact that he had failed, his pride having been injured in the process, Davis could not know. At any rate, having spoken from the outset scarcely a public word that was not designed for foreign as well as domestic ears, the southern President had banked too heavily on European intervention to turn back now. The pinch of a cotton shortage not yet having been felt, the jennies and looms were running full-speed in England and France, and whether such a

★

pinch, even if it eventually came, would "work a revolution," as Davis remarked in his mid-November speech, "remain[ed] to be seen."

Nor for that matter could he know how much of this initial failure had been due to ineptness. Yancey was many things, including a brilliant orator, but he was obviously no diplomat. Even before the final rebuff, which prompted his departure, Davis had moved to replace him, and the other two commissioners as well. Yancey would be recalled, his talents given a fitter scope, and Mann and Rost "disunited," one being sent to Spain and one to Belgium, their places to be taken at London and Paris by men whose gifts and reputations were more in keeping with the weight of their assignments: James M. Mason and John Slidell, former U.S. senators from Virginia and Louisiana.

The Virginian was the more prominent of the two. Grandson of George Mason of Gunston Hall (framer of the Bill of Rights) and withal an able statesman on his own, at sixty-three he had rather a ferocious aspect, with "burning" eyes and a broad, fleshy nose, a mouth drawn down at the corners, and brown, gray-shot hair bushed out around a large, pale, smooth-shaven face. His name, like Yancey's, was anathema to abolitionists, for he was the author of the Fugitive Slave Law and also of a public letter eulogizing Preston Brooks for caning their common adversary Sumner. Though he had got both his schooling and his wife in Philadelphia, Mason was an ardent secessionist and disapproved in general of things northern. He had been to New England once, to dedicate a monument, and found it quite distasteful. Invited to return, he replied that he would never visit that shore again, "except as an ambassador." Which was what he was now, in effect: on his way to the Court of St James's, however, not to the northern republic.

His companion Slidell was five years older and looked it, with narrowed eyes and a knife-blade nose, his mouth twisted bitterly awry and his pink scalp shining through lank white locks that clamped the upper half of his face like a pair of parentheses. He was New-York-born, the son of a candle-maker who had risen, but he had removed to New Orleans as a young man to escape the consequences of debt and a duel with a theatrical manager over the affections of an actress. Importing the methods of Tammany Hall, he prospered in Louisiana politics. Though not without attendant scandal, he won himself a fortune in sugar, a Creole bride, three terms in Congress — one in the House and two in the Senate — and an appointment as Minister to Mexico on the eve of war with that nation, which event prevented his actual service in that capacity. He was aptly named, being noted for his slyness. At the outbreak of hostilities, back in the spring, an English journalist called him "a man of iron will and strong passions, who loves the excitement of combinations and who in his dungeon, or whatever else it may be, would conspire with the mice against the cat rather than not conspire at all." Possessing such qualities,

*The capture of Confederate emissaries
James Mason (left) and John Slidell nearly
led the North to war with Great Britain.*

together with the ability to converse in French, New-Orleans-style, and also in
Spanish, Empress Eugénie's native tongue, Slidell seemed as particularly well
suited for the atmosphere of the City of Light as Mason, with his rectitude
and cavalier descent, was for London.

Davis and the nation expected much from this second attempt at winning foreign recognition and assistance. By early October the two were in
Charleston with their secretaries and Slidell's wife and daughters, awaiting a
chance to run the blockade. At first they intended to take the Confederate cruiser
Nashville, being outfitted there as a commerce raider. That would have been to arrive in a style which the British, as a naval people, could appreciate. Unwilling to
wait, however, they booked passage instead on a small private steamer, the *Gordon*,
and at 1 o'clock in the morning, October 12, slipped out of the harbor and crossed
the bar in a driving rain, bound for Nassau. From there, having found no steamer
connection with England, the *Gordon* sailed for St Thomas, a regular port for
transatlantic packets. Running low on coal, her captain put into Cárdenas, on the
north coast of Cuba, whence the commissioners made their way overland to Havana. November 7 they boarded the British mail steamer *Trent*, which cleared for
Southampton that same day. Thus, the blockade having been run without inci-

dent, themselves securely quartered on a ship that flew the ensign of the mightiest naval power in the world, the risky leg of the journey was behind them.

So they thought until noon of the following day, when the *Trent*, steaming through the Bahama Passage, 240 miles out of Havana, sighted an armed sloop athwart her course at a point where the channel narrowed to fifteen miles. The *Trent* broke out her colors and continued on her way; whereupon the sloop ran up the union jack — and put a shot across her bow. After a second shot, which was closer, the *Trent* stopped engines.

"What do you mean by heaving my vessel to in this way?" the British captain shouted through a trumpet.

For answer the sloop put out two boats, which as they drew nearer were seen to be loaded with sailors, armed marines, and a naval officer who identified himself as he came aboard: Lieutenant D. MacNeill Fairfax of the screw sloop *San Jacinto*, Captain Charles Wilkes, U.S.N., commanding. Having information that Confederate Commissioners James M. Mason and John Slidell were aboard, he demanded the passenger list. At this, Slidell came forward. "I am Mr Slidell. Do you want to see me?" Mason stepped up, too, but no introduction was necessary, he and the lieutenant having met some years ago. (For that matter, Slidell and Captain Wilkes, waiting now aboard the sloop, had been boyhood friends in the old First Ward, back in their New York days, though they had had a falling out before Slidell's departure.) Their identities thus established, together with those of their secretaries, Lieutenant Fairfax informed the British captain, who all this time had scarcely ceased objecting, that he was seizing the four men for return to the United States and trial as traitors. When the captain continued to object — "Pirates! Villains!" some of the passengers were crying; "Throw the damned fellow overboard!" — the lieutenant indicated the *San Jacinto*, whose guns were bearing on the unarmed *Trent*. The captain yielded, still protesting; Mason and Slidell and their secretaries were taken over the side.

"Goodbye, my dear," the Louisianian told his wife on parting. "We shall meet in Paris in sixty days."

The two ships drew apart and continued on their separate courses, northward and northeastward toward their two countries, bearing their respective emotional cargoes of exultation and outrage: cargoes in each case large enough, and fervent enough, to be shared by all the people who, off on those different points of the compass, awaited their arrival all unknowing.

★ ★ ★ *D*avis in Richmond was scantly braced for such a smile of fortune. After so many disappointments, he hardly presumed even to hope for such news as this which now was coming his way across the water. Here was a ready-made, bona fide international incident, brought about not by the machinations of cloak-and-dagger agents sent out by the Confederate secret service, but by a responsible northern naval officer who had taken unto himself the interpretation of law on the high seas and who in his rashness had inforced that interpretation against the flag which admittedly ruled those seas.

The news would be no less welcome for being unexpected; Davis was badly in need of encouragement at this point. At the outset he had predicted a long war. Now he was showing the erosive effects of living with the fulfillment of his prediction. He was thinner, almost emaciated; "gaunted" was the southern word. His features were sharper, the cheeks more hollow, the blind left eye with its stone-gray pupil in contrast to the lustrous gleam of the other — a "wizard physiognomy," indeed. The lips were compressed and the square jaw was even more firmly set to express determination, as if this quality might prove contagious to those around him. Under the wide brim of a planter's hat, his face had lost all signs of youth. It had become austere, a symbol; so that a North Carolina soldier, seeing him thus on the street one day, walking unaccompanied as was his custom, stopped him and asked doubtfully, "Sir, mister, be'ent you Jefferson Davis?" And when Davis, employing the careful courtesy which was habitual, admitted his identity: "Sir, that is my name" — "I thought so," the soldier said. "You look so much like a Confederate postage stamp."

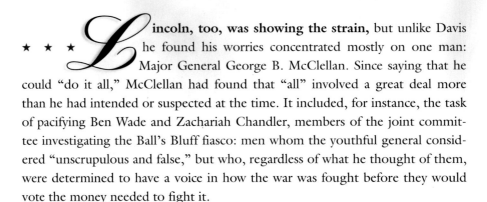

★ ★ ★   **L**incoln, too, was showing the strain, but unlike Davis he found his worries concentrated mostly on one man: Major General George B. McClellan. Since saying that he could "do it all," McClellan had found that "all" involved a great deal more than he had intended or suspected at the time. It included, for instance, the task of pacifying Ben Wade and Zachariah Chandler, members of the joint committee investigating the Ball's Bluff fiasco: men whom the youthful general considered "unscrupulous and false," but who, regardless of what he thought of them, were determined to have a voice in how the war was fought before they would vote the money needed to fight it.

They did not like the way it was being fought at present; or, rather, the way it was not being fought at all. Above Harpers Ferry the Confederates had cut the B & O, one of the main arteries of supply, while down the Potomac they had established batteries denying the capital access to the sea. "For God's sake," Wade cried, infuriated by such effrontery, "at least push back the defiant traitors!" It did no good to explain that such outposts would crumble of their own accord, once the main attack was launched, and that meanwhile, undeterred by incidentals, the proper course was to concentrate on building up the force with which to launch it. The congressmen saw only that the rebels were holding such positions unmolested. Or if McClellan's thesis was true, as to what the rebel reaction would be, they wanted to see it demonstrated. They had had enough of delay.

A Massachusetts Adams declared in August, "We have now gone through three stages of this great political disease. The first was the cold fit, when it seemed as if nothing would start the country. The second was the hot one, when it seemed almost in the highest continual delirium. The third is the process of waking to the awful reality before it. I do not venture to predict what the next will be."

McClellan had already ventured a prediction: "I shall . . . crush the rebels in one campaign." That was still his intention. Yet now, with the war still in the waking stage, all that he was truly sure of was that he did not want this phase to end as the first two had done, at Sumter and Bull Run. In spite of which, to his dismay — with those examples of unpreparedness stark before him — he was being prodded by rash counselors to commit the selfsame errors. Adams had seen the nation struggling for its life as if in the throes of breakbone fever; the war was "this great political disease," attacking the whole organism. But McClellan, who was a soldier, not a politician or a diplomat, could not or would not see that the contest was political as well as military, that the two had merged, that men like Wade and Chandler were as much a part of it as men like Johnston and Beauregard — or McClellan himself, for that matter. Given the time, he believed he could get over or around the enemy intrenched across the Potomac; he could "crush" them. He could never get over or around men like Wade and Chandler, let alone crush them, and he knew it. And knowing it he turned bitter. He turned peevish.

"The people think me all-powerful," he wrote in one of the nightly letters to his wife. "Never was there a greater mistake. I am thwarted and deceived . . . at every turn." At first it was the politicians: "I can't tell you how disgusted I am becoming with these wretched politicians." Next it was the Administration itself: "I am becoming daily more disgusted with this Administration — perfectly sick of it. If I could with honor resign I would quit the whole concern tomorrow." "It is sickening in the extreme, and makes me feel heavy at heart, when I see the weakness and unfitness of the poor beings who control the destinies of this great country." "I was obliged to attend a meeting of the cabinet at 8 p.m., and was bored and annoyed. There are some of the greatest geese in the cabinet I have ever seen — enough to tax the patience of Job."

So far, the President was not included in the indictment. McClellan wrote, "I enclose a card just received from 'A. Lincoln'; it shows too much deference to be seen outside." Having come to know Lincoln better, he found he liked him, or at any rate thought him amusing. One day as he was writing he had callers, and when he resumed his letter he wrote, "I have just been interrupted here by the President and Secretary Seward, who had nothing very particular to say, except some stories to tell, which were, as usual, very pertinent, and some pretty good. I never in my life met anyone so full of anecdote as our friend."

It was not all anecdote. One day a division commander came to see the general and found Lincoln with him, poring over a map of Virginia and making operational suggestions, to which McClellan listened respectfully but with obvious amusement. At last the amateur strategist left. Returning from seeing him to the door, McClellan looked back over his shoulder and smiled. "Isn't he a rare bird?" he said.

Lincoln had been boning on the science of war, borrowing military treatises from the Library of Congress and reading them in the small hours of the night. He took a particular pleasure in discussing strategy with his young general-in-chief, who had been so good at such studies himself. McClellan saw no harm in all this. He viewed Lincoln's efforts with that air of amused tolerance reserved by professionals for amateurs, and the visits afforded relaxation from the daily round. Besides, such studies and discussions were leading the President toward a better comprehension of the military problem: especially of the necessity for protecting the commanding general from the interference of politicians.

"I intend to be careful and do as well as possible," McClellan said earnestly one night as they parted after such a conference. "Don't let them hurry me, is all I ask."

"You shall have your own way in the matter, I assure you," Lincoln told him.

Whereupon—as if, having gotten what he wanted in the way of assurance, he could move on now to other things; or perhaps because his tolerance or his capacity for amusement was exhausted—McClellan changed his tone. Now he wrote, "I have not been at home for some three hours, but am concealed at Stanton's to dodge all enemies in the shape of 'browsing' presidents, etc."

The friend affording sanctuary was Edwin M. Stanton, the attorney who had snubbed Lincoln four years ago when the gangling Springfield lawyer came to Cincinnati to assist in a patents case. Irascible and sharp-tongued, a leading Democrat, Stanton was even more important now. Having served as Attorney General during Buchanan's last four months, he had gone on to become chief legal adviser to the present Secretary of War. His first impression of "that long-armed creature" had not changed, but now at least he took the trouble to exercise his wit at his expense. Du Chaillu, for example, had not needed to go all the way to the Congo in search of the missing link; there was an excellent specimen here in Washington. "The original gorilla," he called Lincoln, and McClellan took up the phrase in letters to his wife. They laughed together at a perspiration splotch on the back of Lincoln's shirt, Stanton remarking that it resembled a map of Africa.

If he noticed this at all, Lincoln took it calmly. He was accustomed to being laughed at, and had even been known to encourage laughter at his own expense. Such friends as he cared about had a deep appreciation of humility, and he could afford to let the others go. Attracted, however, as so many were, by McClellan's forthright air of youthful manliness, he did not want to lose him as a friend. Then one mid-November night he drew the rebuke humility must always draw from pride. He and Seward, accompanied by Lincoln's young secretary John Hay, went over to McClellan's house. When the servant told them the general was attending a wedding but would be back presently, they said they would wait. They had waited about an hour when McClellan returned. The servant told him the President and the Secretary of State were there, but he seemed bemused as he went past the door of the room where they were waiting. They waited another half hour, then once more sent the servant to inform the general that they were there. The answer came — "coolly," Hay recorded — that McClellan had gone to bed.

On the way home, when the secretary broke out angrily against what he called the "insolence of epaulets," Lincoln, though he was saddened by this final indication that he had lost a friend, quietly remarked that this was

*Allan Pinkerton (left), McClellan's
primary source of military intelligence, discusses
his latest information with the general.*

no time for concern over points of etiquette and personal dignity. "I will hold McClellan's horse if he will only bring us success," he said soon afterward. But Hay observed with satisfaction that from then on, when the President wanted to see McClellan, he summoned him to the White House.

The Young Napoleon had changed. "We shall strike them there," he used to say, gesturing toward the eastern end of the rebel lines at Centreville when he rode out on inspection. After inching some troops forward "by way of getting elbow-room," he gaily told his wife: "The more room I get the more I want, until by and by I suppose I shall be so insatiable as to think I cannot do with less than the whole state of Virginia." He did not talk that way now, or write that way either. That was in the past. Bored, annoyed, disgusted, sick, thwarted and deceived at every turn, he no longer gestured aggressively toward the Centreville-Manassas lines. According to Pinkerton, 90,000 gray-clad soldiers, superbly equipped and thirsty for blood, with one Manassas victory already blazoned on their battleflags, were behind those earthworks praying for McClellan's army to advance and be wrecked, like McDowell's, on those same plains. All that stood between the army and catastrophe was Little Mac, resisting the unscrupulous men who would hurl it into the furnace of combat before the mold had set.

By now, though, more than the frock-coated congressmen were urging him forward against his will. While the clear bright days of autumn declined and the hard roads leading southward were about to dissolve into mud, the public was getting restless, too, wondering at the army's inaction. The soldiers loved and trusted him as much as ever; Our George, they called him still. But to the public he seemed overcautious, like a finicky dandy hesitating to blood a bright new sword, either because he did not want to spoil its glitter, or else because he did not trust its temper. Horace Greeley, the journalistic barometer, had recovered from his fright and recommended his Forward-to-Richmond chant. Other voices swelled the chorus, while shriller cries came through its pulse to accuse the young commander of vacillation. McClellan was reduced to finding consolation in the approval of his horse, Dan Webster: writing, "He, at least, had full confidence in his master."

* * * *Affairs were progressing no better in the West.* Politically, though the storm still raged from point to point and fugitive secessionist legislatures were assembling, Missouri and Kentucky had been secured to the Union. Militarily, however, little had been done since Wilson's Creek and Frémont's feverish southward march into the vacuum created by that explosion. Assuming the supreme command on the day the Pathfinder received Lincoln's order deposing him, McClellan promptly reorganized that vast, conglomerate area into two departments.

The first, Frémont's old Department of the West, to which was added

*H*enry W. Halleck's habit of scratching his elbows while thinking led one detractor to claim that Halleck's elbows were the seat of his mental powers.

that part of Kentucky west of the Cumberland River, was under Henry W. Halleck; while the second, the Department of the Ohio, including the rest of Kentucky and Tennessee, had Don Carlos Buell for commander. Both were responsible to McClellan, but neither was accountable to the other. Each in fact saw the other as his rival for the future command of the whole. And therein lay the seeds of much mischief. Admittedly, ambition and rivalry were the stimuli that made the military organism tick. But in this case, with McClellan racked by problems of his own in Washington, the result was that there was not only little coördination of effort between theaters, East and West; there was also little coöperation between the armies resting flank to flank on opposite banks of the Cumberland.

A major general at forty-six, three years older and one rank higher than his rival, Halleck had the advantage at the outset. Buell was generally considered one of the best officers in the service, particularly as an organizer and disciplinarian; yet Halleck was not only senior in age and grade, he was by far the more distinguished in previous accomplishments. Author of *Elements of Military Art and Science*, a highly respected volume issued fifteen years before, translator of Jomini's *Napoleon*, authority on international law, on which he had published a treatise just before the war began, he was called Old Brains by his fellow officers, not altogether jokingly. In the shadow of all this, even as a result of it, Buell had one not inconsiderable advantage: Halleck had been McClellan's rival for the post of general-in-chief — old Winfield Scott had favored him, for one — and Little Mac, perhaps somewhat influenced by this, considered Buell the superior in practical ability as a soldier in the field. That was arbitrary, though, or anyhow problematical, since the two West Pointers had been promoted equally for gallantry in the Mexican War and had had no such opportunity for distinction since.

In another direction, there was little room for doubt. Both were more impressive in the abstract than prepossessing in the flesh; but here the advantage clearly passed to the junior, if only by default. Of average height, inclined toward fat and flabbiness, Halleck had an unmilitary aspect. Balding, he wore gray mutton-chop side whiskers and looked considerably older than his years. The olive-tinted flesh of his face hung so loosely that it quivered when he moved, particularly his double chin, and he had a strangely repellent habit of crossing his arms on his lower chest to scratch his elbows when he was worried or plunged in thought. In manner he was irritable and sometimes harsh, not inclined to allow for the smaller brains of lesser men. Interviewed, he would hold his head sideways and stare fishily, directing one goggle eye toward a point somewhere beyond his interviewer. This caused one disconcerted officer to remark that conversing with Halleck was like talking to someone over your shoulder.

No one ever said this about Buell. His glance was piercing and direct: too much so, perhaps, for he was even harsher in manner than Halleck. Dark-skinned, with a scraggly, gray-shot beard, close-set eyes, and a hawk-beak nose, Buell maintained an icy reserve, engaged in no small talk, and brooked no difference of opinion from subordinates. Despite his operatic name, Don Carlos, there was nothing flamboyant in his nature. Like McClellan he was an excellent disciplinarian, robust of physique, and a hard, methodical worker round the clock; but he had scarcely a vestige of McClellan's charm, none of his glamor, and therefore none of his popularity, either. He never expressed the least regret at this, however. Apparently he never believed that popularity could be a useful factor in turning farmboys into soldiers. Or if so, not by him; he never sought it.

Instructions given the two commanders on setting out were similar as to policy. Both were told to hold firmly onto all that had been gained in Missouri and Kentucky, meanwhile impressing on the people of the area that the army's purpose was the restoration of the Union, not the abolition of slavery, which was not even incidentally on the agenda. In addition, Halleck was to assemble his troops "on or near the Mississippi, prepared for such ulterior operations as the public interests may demand," while Buell massed for an advance into the loyalist mountain region of eastern Tennessee. The former plan had reference to Frémont's dream of a lopping descent of the Father of Waters. The latter was Lincoln's fondest project. He hoped that Buell would accomplish there what McClellan had accomplished in western Virginia under similar conditions, the people having voted five-to-one against secession back in June. Nothing vexed the President more than the fact that this Union stronghold was in south-

★

ern hands. "My distress," he wrote, "is that our friends in East Tennessee are being hanged and driven to despair, and even more, I fear, are thinking of taking rebel arms for the sake of personal protection." Besides, he saw great strategic profit in an advance through Cumberland Gap, since taking Knoxville would cut the northernmost east-west Confederate railroad, thus coming between the secessionists and what Lincoln called their "hog and hominy."

Buell, who had helped to frame his own instructions, saw it that way, too, on setting out. Soon after he reached Louisville, however, peering southeast across the barrens in the direction of the Gap, which he saw now as a natural fortress straddled athwart his path, he changed his mind. For him, as for McClellan — whom he addressed as "My dear Friend" in official dispatches — obstacles loomed more starkly at close range. Features that seemed innocuous on a two-dimensional map could dominate a three-dimensional landscape. Even the absence of some feature, whether natural or man-made, could prove ruinous: as for instance a railroad. From his base on the Ohio he observed that there were no railroads by which he could haul supplies to feed and equip an army moving directly upon East Tennessee. He would have to depend on a wagon train, grinding weary distances over wretched roads and vulnerable to raiders throughout its length. The more he looked the more impossible it seemed, until presently he abandoned it altogether.

Don Carlos Buell, commanding the Union Department of the Ohio, proved too pedantic and cautious to be a good leader.

He did not abandon his offensive plans, however. Buell was nothing if not thorough. Turning his mind's eye westward along a sixty-degree arc, he perceived that Nashville, the Tennessee capital on the Cumberland, a manufacturing center and a transportation nexus, was not only closer than Knoxville, it was even a bit closer than Cumberland Gap. The way led through a land far richer in supplies, with no natural fortress at the end, and best of all there was a railroad all the way. Nashville taken, the Confederates defending East Tennessee would be outflanked; when they fell back he could march in unopposed. This might take a bit longer, but it was surer. As for the Unionists awaiting his advance into the mountains, Buell believed their constancy would "sustain them until the hour of deliverance." Thus he wrote in mid-December, by which time five had already been "sustained" by the necks after drumhead trials for arson.

Before occupying Nashville he would have to cross the Cumberland River, but he did not consider this a drawback. He counted it a positive advantage, since it meant that he could secure the coöperation of Union gunboats on that stream. This in turn meant securing the coöperation of Halleck, and now that his mind had turned that way, Buell went on to essay grand strategy. He proposed nothing less than an all-out concerted drive by both Kentucky armies, with Nashville as the objective: Halleck to advance from the northwest in "two flotilla columns up the Tennessee and the Cumberland," and himself from the northeast, down the railroad. The result would be to penetrate, and thereby outflank, the whole Confederate line; whereupon the Federals could occupy not only East Tennessee, his original objective, but the entire state, along with whatever parts of Kentucky remained in enemy hands. In his enthusiasm, which somewhat resembled the elation of a poet just delivered of an ode, he wrote McClellan of his plan, remarking incidentally that he feared no advance by the rebels at Bowling Green ("I should almost as soon expect to see the Army of the Potomac marching up the road") and closing with a light-hearted request for a few high-ranking officers, "not my seniors," to assist him in carrying out his plan: "If you have any unoccupied brigadiers...send six or eight, even though they should be no better than marked poles."

Far from being elated, or even amused, McClellan was chagrined and upset by the proposal. He saw the soundness of this substitute plan—which, moreover, had the sort of strategic brilliance he admired—yet he hated to lose the advantages of the first. Invading eastern Tennessee, Buell's army would not only sever one of the arteries supplying the Confederates in northern Virginia; it would also be poised on their flank, and could then be angled forward to maneuver them out of their intrenched position and assist in the taking of Richmond. For this reason, as well as the political ones, McClellan replied that he still considered "a prompt movement on eastern Tennessee imperative," but "if there are causes which render this course impossible," he regretfully allowed, "we must submit to the necessity." All the same, he did not submit without frequent backward glances. By the end of November he was hoping Buell would attempt both movements, one on East Tennessee, "with say 15,000 men," and one on Nashville "with, say, 50,000 men." He added, by way of encouragement, "I will at once take the necessary steps to carry out your views as to the rivers."

This meant that he would urge Halleck to undertake the advance from western Kentucky. When he did so, in a telegram sent December 5, Halleck replied from St Louis the following day: "I assure you, General, this cannot be done with safety at present. Some weeks hence I hope to have a large disposable force for other points; but now, destitute as we are of arms, organization, and

★

discipline, it seems to me madness to remove any of our troops from this State."

In all conscience, McClellan had to admit that Old Brains had his hands full already. Charged with restoring order to the chaos Frémont left—"a system of reckless expenditure and fraud, perhaps unheard of before in the history of the world," his instructions warned him—he had to attend at once to the guerilla bands marauding in his rear, to Price and McCulloch, reported marching against his front, as well as to the enormous task of preparing for the descent of the Mississippi. As if all this was not enough, he was having to deal at the same time with a mentally upset brigadier, red-haired Tecumseh Sherman, who was bombarding headquarters with reports of rebel advances from all directions. "Look well to Jefferson City and the North Missouri Railroad," Sherman would wire; "Price aims at both."

Succeeding Anderson when the Sumter hero's health broke, Sherman earnestly told the Secretary of War that 200,000 troops would be needed to put down the rebellion in the Mississippi Valley alone, and when this "evidence of insanity" was reinforced by other alarming symptoms reported in the papers—a brooding melancholy broken only by intermittent fits of rage and fright—he was relieved of his command. Superseded by Buell, he was sent to serve under Halleck in Missouri, where his fidgety manner and tocsin-shrill dispatches presently served to verify the suspicions which had followed him from Kentucky. He appeared thoroughly demoralized: "stampeded," Halleck called it, but McClellan put it simpler, saying, "Sherman's gone in the head." In hopes that a few weeks' rest would restore his faculties, Halleck gave an indefinite leave of absence to the distraught Ohioan, whose wife then came down and took him home.

★ ★ ★ *N*ot all of Halleck's personnel problems could be handled so easily. As a sort of counterbalance to the highly nervous Sherman, he had another brigadier who seemed to have no nerves at all. The trouble with U. S. Grant was that, for all Halleck knew, he might have no brains either.

There were indications of such a lack. Grant was a West Pointer and had been commended for bravery in Mexico, but since then his reputation had gone downhill. Stationed out in California, he had had to resign his captain's commission because of an overfondness for the bottle, and in the seven following years he had been signally unsuccessful as a civilian. Commissioned a colonel of Illinois volunteers, he had won promotion to brigadier by a political fluke, his congressman claiming it for him as a due share of the spoils. Since then he had done well enough in a straightforward, soldierly way; he had not panicked under pressure, and best of all he had worked with what he had instead of calling for help in each emergency. Aware of his unsavory past, however, Halleck could never be sure when a relapse might come, exposing the basic instability of Grant's character and leaving the army commander to take the blame for having reposed the nation's trust in such a man.

Despite his seedy appearance (he was five feet eight inches tall and weighed 135 pounds; one eye was set a trifle lower than the other, giving his face a somewhat out-of-balance look; he walked with a round-shouldered slouch, pitching forward on his toes, and paid as scant attention to the grooming of his beard as he did to the cut and condition of his clothes) Grant had proved himself a fighter. But that could have its drawbacks when it included, as it seemed to do in this case, a large element of rashness. Halleck did not want to be embarrassed by Grant, the way Frémont had been embarrassed by the ill-fated Lyon: with whom, for that matter, in spite of his lack of surface fire, the thirty-nine-year-old Illinois brigadier had shown a disturbing degree of kinship. Wilson's Creek had come within three weeks of Bull Run, and had been fought to the same pattern. Then on the eve of Halleck's arrival, within three weeks of Ball's Bluff, came Belmont. Even apart from the balanced chronology, East and West, the resemblance was much too close for comfort.

Though Bishop Polk had won the race for Columbus, Grant had been by no means willing to admit that this gave the Confederates any permanent claim to the place. Within the week, having occupied Paducah, he had written Frémont: "If it were discretionary with me, with a little addition to my present force I would take Columbus." The Pathfinder made no reply to this, but when he took the field at last, marching against the victors of Wilson's Creek, he had his adjutant order Grant to feint against Polk to prevent that general from reinforcing Price. In doing this Grant was to make a show of aggression along both sides of the Mississippi, keeping his troops "constantly moving back and forward...without, however, attacking the enemy." Also in accordance with orders, on November 3 — the day Frémont left Springfield, relieved of command, and Winfield Scott left Washington, retired — Grant sent a column southward, west of the river, to assist in an attempt to bag or destroy a force under M. Jeff Thompson, reported down near the Missouri boot-heel, in the St Francis River area. Two days later a dispatch informed him that Polk was definitely sending reinforcements to Price. Marching "back and forward" not having sufficed to immobilize the bishop, Grant now was ordered to make a demonstration against Columbus itself.

Accordingly, on the 6th he loaded five infantry regiments, supported by two cavalry troops and a six-gun battery, onto four transports — 3114 men in all — and steamed down the river, protected by two gunboats. Nine miles below Cairo, tied up for the night against the eastern bank, he received a report that Polk had ordered a strong column to cut off and destroy the troops Grant had sent to do the same to Thompson. The message arrived at 2 o'clock in the morning, and within the hour Grant made his decision. Instead of a mere demonstra-

*Brigadier General Ulysses S. Grant
posed in his new dress uniform for this
portrait taken in October 1861.*

tion, he would launch a direct, all-out attack on Belmont, the steamboat landing
opposite Columbus, where the enemy column was reported to be assembling.

At dawn the downstream approach got under way, the troops experiencing the qualms and elation of facing their first test under fire. Their emotions
perhaps would have been less mixed, though probably no less violent, if they
had known that none of the conditions their commander assumed existing at or
near Columbus was true. Polk had no intention of reinforcing Price, nor was he

During the Battle of Belmont, Grant's endangered troops put the torch to a captured rebel camp, denying its supplies to the Confederates.

preparing a column to bag the force that supposed itself to be pursuing Thompson, who for that matter had retired from the field by now. Far from being a staging area, Belmont was only an observation post, a low-lying, three-shack hamlet dominated by the guns on the tall bluff across the river and manned by one regiment of infantry—half of which was on the sick list—one battery of artillery, and a scratch collection of cavalry. Unaware that the drama in which they were taking part was in fact an Intelligence comedy of errors, Grant's men came off their transports at 8 o'clock, three miles above Belmont, their debarkation concealed by a skirt of timber. While the gunboats continued downstream to engage the batteries on the Columbus bluff, the troops formed a line of battle and marched southward toward the landing, skirmishers out. Presently, the guns of the naval engagement booming hollow across the water to their left, they came under heavy musket fire from out in front.

By now there was more to oppose them than one half-sick infantry regiment. Polk, having learned of the attack, had reinforced the Belmont garrison with four regiments under Brigadier General Gideon Pillow, the Tennessean who had preceded him in command. Ferried across the river, they hurried northward from the landing, scorning the protection of previously constructed fortifications, and took position in the path of Grant's advance. It was hard, stand-up fighting, the forces being about equal, five regiments on each side, each force being supported by a battery of light artillery. The Federals had the initiative, however, and also they had Grant, who was something rare in that or any war: a man who could actually learn from experience. Three months before, he had made a similar advance against an enemy position reported held by Colonel Thomas Harris and his command, and as Grant drew closer, mounting the ridge that masked the camp, "my heart kept getting higher and higher until it felt to me as though it was in my throat." He kept his men going, he said, because "I had not the moral courage to halt and consider what to do." Then, topping the rise, he found the camp deserted, the enemy gone. "My heart resumed its place. It occurred to me at once that Harris had been as much afraid of me as I had been of him. This was a view of the question I had never taken before; but I never forgot it afterwards."

★

He did not forget it now. Leaving five companies near the transports as rear guard, he put the rest in line and pushed straight forward, his six guns barking busily all the while. Under such pressure, the Confederates gave ground stubbornly — until, after about two hours of fighting, the Federals roaring down upon them in the vicinity of the camp, they broke, giving way completely, and took off for the rear in headlong panic. Here, on a narrow mud-flat left by the falling river and protected by a steep low bank, they found shelter from the humming bullets. "Don't land! Don't land!" they called out to reinforcements arriving by boat from Columbus. "We are whipped! Go back!"

They spoke too soon. Grant's men, having overrun the camp, had stopped to loot, and their officers, elated by the rout, "galloped about from one cluster of men to another," according to Grant, "and at every halt delivered a short eulogy upon the Union cause and the achievements of the command." Like the whipped men under the river bank, they thought the battle was over. This was by no means the case, as they presently discovered. Now that their own men were out of the way, the artillerists on the Columbus bluff could bring their guns to bear: particularly one big rifled Whitworth, which began to rake the captured campsite. What was more, the reinforcements arriving by boat ignored the cries, "Don't land! Go back!" and coming up during the lull, formed a line of battle, preparing to attack. Disgusted, Grant ordered the camp set afire to discourage the looters and orators, and did what he could to reassemble his command. Meanwhile other Confederate reinforcements were pouring ashore to the north, between Belmont and the transports. When an aide rode up, exclaiming, "General, we are surrounded!" — "Well," Grant said, "we must cut our way out as we cut our way in."

All this time, Grant's faulty intelligence having made the Federal plans impenetrable, Polk had refused to believe that the action across the river was anything more than a feint to distract his attention from the main effort, which he believed would come from the Kentucky side. Columbus was a prize worth bleeding for, but it made no sense, as far as he could see, for the enemy to launch a serious attack against Belmont, a place not only worthless in its own right, but obviously untenable, even if taken, under the frown of the batteries on the bluff across the river. Therefore, after sending the four regiments at the outset, he had refused to be distracted. Now, though, the attack from the east not having developed and Pillow having been flung back to the landing, Polk sent Brigadier General B. F. Cheatham with three more regiments and crossed the river himself to see how they fared. With 5000 angry, vengeful Confederates on the field, including those who had rallied after cowering under the bank, Grant's elated but disorganized 3000 were going to find it considerably harder to "cut our way out," no matter how bravely the words were spoken, than they had found it to "cut our way in."

★

In the end, however, that was what they did, though at the cost of abandoning most of their captured material, including four guns, as well as many of the non-walking wounded and one thousand rifles, which the defenders afterwards garnered from the field. Grant had held back no reserves to throw into the battle at critical moments, but he performed more or less as a reserve himself, riding from point to point along his line to direct and animate his troops. Except for one regiment, which was cut off in the fighting and marched upstream to be picked up later, he was the last man aboard the final transport.

The skipper had already pushed off, but looking back he recognized the general on horseback and ran a plank out for him. (Polk saw him, too, though without recognition. From the nearby skirt of timber which had screened the debarkation, the bishop, seeing the horseman, said to his staff, "There is a Yankee; you may try your marksmanship on him if you wish." But

With 5000 angry, vengeful Confederates on the field . . . Grant's elated but disorganized 3000 were going to find it considerably harder to "cut our way out," no matter how bravely the words were spoken, than they had found it to "cut our way in."

no one did.) Grant had already had one mount shot from under him today, and when he chose another he chose well. The horse — which, Grant said, "seemed to take in the situation" — put its forefeet over the lip of the bank, tucked its hind legs under its rump, and "without hesitation or urging," slid down the incline and trotted up the gangplank.

That ended the Battle of Belmont, and though the casualties were about equal — something over 600 on each side, killed, wounded, and captured — it followed in general the pattern of all the battles fought that year, the attackers achieving initial success, the defenders giving way to early panic, until suddenly the roles were reversed and the rebels were left in control of the field, crowing over Yankee cowardice. At Belmont as at Bull Run — and especially as at Ball's Bluff, which it so much resembled, the repulsed troops having narrowly missed annihilation at the end — there were indications of blundering and ineptness. "The victory is complete," Grant asserted in dispatches, but two days after the battle the Chicago *Tribune* editorialized: "The disastrous termination of the Cairo expedition to Columbus is another severe lesson on the management of this contest with the rebels. Our troops have suffered a bad defeat. . . . The rebels have been elated and emboldened while our troops have been depressed, if not discouraged." The following day, in printing the casualty lists, the editor added: "It may be said of these victims, 'They have fallen, and to what end?' "

To what end, indeed. And now began the talk of Grant the butcher. This was no victory; not a single tactical advantage had been won; he just went out and came back, losing about as many as he killed. Yet certain facts were there for whoever would see them. He had moved instead of waiting for fair weather, had kept his head when things went all against him, and had brought his soldiers back to base with some real fighting experience under their belts. They were having none of the butcher talk. They had watched him alongside them where bullets flew the thickest and had cheered him riding his trick horse up the gangplank, the last man to leave the field. What was more, they knew the expedition had been designed in the first place to save the lives of their friends in the supposedly threatened column out after Thompson, and they knew now that if ever *they* were thought to be so trapped, Grant himself would come to get them out. Best of all, they had met the rebels in a stand-up fight which proved, for one thing, that blue-bellied Yankees were not the only ones who would panic and scatter and take off for defilade, crying, "We are whipped! Go back!"

Appointed to the western command two days after the battle, Halleck, who had been a civilian as well as a soldier, could see both points of view as to Belmont and the general who fought it. However, in spite of his qualms about Grant's rashness and the chances for being embarrassed by it, he was mainly glad to have him. Experienced leaders were all too few in the West. "It is said, General," he told McClellan, "that you have as many regular officers on your personal staff as I have in this whole Department." He had, in fact, hardly an army at all, he protested, "but rather a military rabble," and upon arriving he wired Washington: "Affairs in complete chaos. Troops unpaid; without clothing or arms. Many never properly mustered into service and some utterly demoralized. Hospitals overflowing with sick."

Burdened as he was with such problems — far too little of what he wanted, far too much of what he didn't — it was no wonder that he declined to aid his rival Buell by advancing southeast up the rivers, saying quite plainly: "It seems to me madness." Nor was it any wonder that Buell, similarly laden and thus denied assistance, saw no chance of advancing in any direction, either toward Knoxville, as Lincoln and McClellan kept urging, or toward Nashville, as he himself preferred. Both generals promised results as soon as conditions permitted. Meanwhile they did what they could to improve what they had inherited from Frémont and from Sherman.

★

To this task they brought their skill as organizers, disciplinarians, and administrators, building a war machine for the West comparable to the one McClellan was forging in the East. Not even their worst enemies denied their considerable talents along these lines, Jefferson Davis remarking before the year's end: "The Federal forces are not hereafter, as heretofore, to be commanded by path-finders and holiday soldiers, but by men of military education and experience in war."

★ ★ ★ *M*cClellan drew from this what solace he could, knowing it was much. Meanwhile, preparing for the great day if the great day ever came, he continued to drill and train his army, staging large and ever larger reviews, until at last, near Bailey's Crossroads, November 20, he put on the largest one of all.

Seven full divisions — 70,000 riflemen and cannoneers and troopers, equipped to the limit of the nation's purchasing and manufacturing power — swung in cadenced glitter past the reviewing stand, where ladies fluttered handkerchiefs and politicians swelled their chests with pride, covering their hearts with their hats as the colors rippled by. And yet, while the dust settled, while the troops filed off to their encampments and the civilians rode in their carriages back to Washington, there was a feeling that all this panoply, grand and enjoyable as it was, did not make up for the Quaker-gun humiliation of Munson's Hill or erase the shame of Bull Run, which still rankled. Nor, for that matter, did it reopen the Potomac or chase the rebels off the B & O. In fact, looking back on the daylong surge of armed might past the grandstand, the politicians were reinforced in their opinion that so fine an army should be used for something sterner than parading.

The soldiers did not share this let-down feeling and had no sympathy for the protests. Nor did they consider themselves inactive. Loving and trusting Little Mac, inspired by his presence when he rode his charger through their camps, they were content to leave military decisions to his superior judgment. "Marching Along," they sang on their conditioning hikes, back and forth across the "sacred soil" of their Virginia bridgehead:

> *"McClellan's our leader, he's gallant and strong;*
>
> *For God and our country we are marching along!"*

Prodded by the politicians, who kept pointing out that the weather was fair and the roads still firm, Lincoln hoped that the army would move southward before winter ended all chances for an advance. McClellan apparently having no such plan in mind, the President himself tried his hand at designing a frontal and flank attack on the Confederates at Manassas. This product of midnight fret and study was submitted December 1 to the young general-in-chief, who looked it over and replied ten days later that it was hardly feasible. "They could meet us in front with equal forces nearly," he objected.

Besides, he added as if by afterthought, "I have now my mind turned actively toward another plan of campaign that I do not think at all anticipated by the enemy nor by many of our own people." Thus Lincoln, who apparently was included under the general heading "our own people," received his first inkling of what came to be known as the Urbanna plan.

McClellan had never enjoyed the notion of a head-on tangle with Johnston on those plains where McDowell had gone down. Some day, given the odds, he might chance it; that was what he was building toward. But to attempt it while outnumbered, as he believed his army was, seemed to him downright folly. Then Buell's refusal to advance against and through Knoxville, which would have placed his army on Johnston's flank, in a position to coöperate with the Army of the Potomac, caused McClellan to abandon all intentions of a due south attack, present or future. Poring over headquarters maps he had evolved "another plan of campaign," one moreover enlisting the assistance of the navy, flushed with its three recent victories. He would load his soldiers aboard transports, steam down the Potomac into Chesapeake Bay, then south along the coast to the mouth of the Rappahannock, and up that river a short distance to Urbanna, a landing on the southern bank, less than fifty airline miles from Richmond, his objective. Without the loss of a man, he would have cut his marching distance in half and he would be in the rear of Johnston—who then would be forced to retreat and fight on grounds of McClellan's choosing. The more he thought about it, the better he liked it. It was not only beautifully simple. It was beautifully bloodless.

In the flush of first conception he planned to set out immediately. "I have no intention of putting the army into winter quarters," he declared. "I mean the campaign will be short, sharp, and decisive." But there were numerous details, including the assembling of transports for the 150,000 men he would take along, all of which had to be accomplished in great secrecy if Johnston was to be left holding the bag in northern Virginia. It was enough to overtax the energies of even so expert an organizer as McClellan. Presently he realized that it would probably be spring before he could get the campaign under way. Regretfully he wrote his wife, "I am doing all I can to get ready to move before winter sets in, but it now begins to look as if we were condemned to a winter of inactivity. If it is so," he added, flinching from the protest he knew must follow, "the fault will not be mine: there will be that consolation for my conscience, even if the world at large never knows it."

As if in confirmation, the rains came. The fields were turned to quagmires and the roads were axle deep in mud. At last he had a reason for not advancing which even the politicians could understand. Then, late in the month, he had an even better personal reason. He came down with a cold, which the doctors presently diagnosed as typhoid fever, and was confined to his bed for three weeks, into the new year.

His good friend Stanton, legal light of the War Department, came to his bedside, peering over his spectacles and murmuring, "They are counting on your death, and already are dividing among themselves your military goods and chattels." But when the President called — doing so for the first time since the snub McClellan had given him six weeks back — he was denied admittance. Lincoln was profoundly troubled. Not only was the general sick, but so was his chief of staff, Brigadier General R. B. Marcy, who was also his father-in-law. Subordinates might be able to administer the Army of the Potomac, which obviously was not going into action anyhow, but Lincoln wondered what was happening

McClellan made his headquarters in this house in Fairfax Courthouse, and here he planned his advance on the Virginian peninsula.

★

elsewhere, especially in the West, now that the guiding hand was paralyzed.

On the last day of the year he telegraphed Buell and Halleck, asking if they were acting by mutual arrangement. Buell replied that there were no provisions for concerted action; Halleck replied that he knew nothing of Buell's plans and that he was unable to coöperate in any case. "It is exceedingly discouraging. As everywhere else, nothing can be done," Lincoln wrote on the back of Halleck's letter, and wired for them to get in touch at once. That same day he went to the office of Quartermaster General M. C. Meigs. "General, what shall I do?" he groaned. "The people are impatient; Chase has no money, and tells me he can raise no more; the General of the Army has typhoid fever. The bottom is out of the tub. What shall I do?"

The question was rhetorical: Lincoln already knew what to do, and even how to do it. Midnight study of strategy texts, plus native common sense and conversation with professionals, had increased his understanding of the military problem. In language that was knotty and overpunctuated, showing thereby the extent to which he had labored to evolve it, he said in a letter to Buell at the time: "I state my general idea of this war to be that we have greater numbers, and the enemy has the greater facility of concentrating forces upon points of collision; that we must fail, unless we can find some way of making our advantage an over-match of his; and that this can be done by menacing him with superior forces at different points, at the same time; so that we can safely attack, one, or both, if he makes no change; and if he weakens one to strengthen the other, forbear to attack the strengthened one, but seize, and hold the weakened one, gaining so much."

However, the fact that he knew what to do, and could state it thus in one hard-breathing sentence — the awful hug of the anaconda becoming more awful still as it shifted its coils to exert more pressure where the bones would crack — only rendered more exasperating the fact that "nothing [could] be done." It was a question, Lincoln saw already, of finding the right man to do the job. Already he was looking for a general who would not only believe in his "idea of this war," but would follow it, inexorably, to the end. Meanwhile it was becoming increasingly evident that, for all his gifts, for all his soldiers' love of him, McClellan was not the man.

★ ★ ★ **The bottom was not really out of the tub.** That was only Lincoln's manner of speaking, designed perhaps to restore some measure of confidence when he got around to comparing the overstatement with the facts. He had known melancholy all his life, and this was one of his ways of working it off — just as sometimes, to clarify in his own mind a relationship with some individual, he would write the man a letter which he never intended to mail; Lincoln was his own psychiatrist. And yet the bottom had been almost out. Riding, or else tossed upon, the seethe and roil of popular opinion during the early weeks of what became known as The Trent Affair, public men on both sides of the ocean lost their heads, and England and the United States came closer to war than they had ever come without war following. Few doubted that it would come. Even fewer, apparently, did not welcome it in the heat of indignation, since in each case national honor seemed at stake.

Mason and Slidell had left Havana while the guns of Port Royal and Belmont were booming out accompaniments for victory and repulse. Next day, November 8, while Du Pont's sailors occupied Fort Beauregard and Grant was counting noses back at Cairo, the *Trent* and the *San Jacinto* met in the Bahama

> *"I state my general idea of this war to be that we have greater numbers, and the enemy has the greater facility of concentrating forces upon points of collision; that we must fail, unless we can find some way of making our advantage an over-match of his; and that this can be done by menacing him with superior forces at different points . . ."*
>
> — Abraham Lincoln

Passage, then wore apart, northward and northeastward over a glassy sea, the former having exchanged four passengers for a cargo of outrage explosive enough to blow the bottom out of any tub. In London on the 27th the captain gave the authorities the news.

Immediate and unrestrained, the reaction was in the nature of a shriek; Britannia had been touched where she was tender. "By Captain Wilkes let the Yankee breed be judged," the *Times* declared, and stigmatized both him and it: "Swagger and ferocity, built on a foundation of vulgarity and cowardice, these are his characteristics, and these are the most prominent marks by which his countrymen, generally speaking, are known all over the world." Entering a Cabinet meeting, the eighty-year-old Prime Minister, Lord Palmerston, flung his hat on the table and exploded: "You may stand for this but damned if I will!"

Accordingly, while the cry for war went up all over England, an army

In a Punch cartoon, Britain's Prime Minister, Lord Palmerston, considers whether or not to "recognize" Jefferson Davis and his Confederacy.

of 8000 boarded transports bound for Canada, where fortifications were ordered erected at strategic points along the border, and Royal Navy shipyards were thrown into a bustle of preparation beyond anything since the days when the first Napoleon was mustering all Europe for invasion. Lord John Russell was put to work drafting an ultimatum for presentation to the United States. Its terms were simple: either an abject apology, including surrender of the seized Confederate emissaries, or war.

The republic across the Atlantic had never been one to bow to ultimatums, least of all from its arch-enemy England, and especially not now, with its citizens engaged in a delirium of praise for the latest hero to twist the lion's tail. A week after taking his prisoners aboard, Captain Wilkes had put into Hampton Roads for coal, a tall, clean-shaven regular, romantic in appearance, with becoming streaks of gray in his wavy hair. From there, having informed his superiors of his action, he steamed north again, bound for Boston in accordance with instructions to deliver the rebel envoys at Fort Warren, where a congratulatory telegram awaited him from the Secretary of the Navy: "Your conduct in seizing these public enemies was marked by intelligence, ability, decision, and firmness, and has the emphatic approval of this Department." The Army Secretary was no less enthusiastic. When the news reached the War Department, that dignitary led in the giving of three cheers by a group which included the governor of Massachusetts.

From the press, from the pulpit, from the public at large came praise for the captain's forthright action. Congress rushed through a resolution thanking him for his "brave, adroit, and patriotic conduct in the arrest of the traitors," and voted a gold medal struck in his honor. He was wined and dined and paraded in Boston, and toasts to his boldness were drunk throughout the nation. For the Administration to submit to an ultimatum and apologize for the captain's action would be to disavow that action and repudiate the hero before the eyes of his adoring public. With the nation already split in half and one tremendous conflict already building toward a climax, no one could say for certain what the result would be if the people were forced to choose between their captain-hero and those who let him down.

Thus — as in 1812, with the roles reversed — the two nations were poised for a war that would surely come unless one, or both, backed down: which was plainly impossible, believing as they did the worst of each other. On one side of the water, the British assumed that the impressment had been performed under government sanction, probably in accordance with instructions. On the other, the Americans, already provoked by the granting of belligerency status to the Confederacy, saw only another instance of England's avowing her intention to further the rebellion and assist in the dismemberment of a rival in the scramble for world trade.

As if all this was not enough to make war seem inevitable, the British conception of what had fed the roots of the late outrage was reinforced by the aggressive diplomacy — the announced intention, even — of the American Secretary of State, who was known to favor war with England as a means of reuniting his divided countrymen. He had said so repeatedly, in interviews, in correspondence, and in after-dinner talk. If the North became embroiled with a foreign power, Seward believed, the South would drop its States Rights quarrel and hasten to close ranks against invasion: whereupon, with that war over, the two sections could sit down in a glow of mutual pride at having won it, and reconcile past differences without the need or desire for further bloodshed.

In this he was most likely much mistaken, for the main goal of Confederate diplomacy was to draw England into the conflict on the southern side. And yet he was not entirely wrong — at least so far as regarded human nature. Now that the hope seemed about to be fact, the reaction below the Potomac and the Ohio was not unmixed. Exultation was sobered there by the thought of Americans, under whatever flag, submitting to an old-world ultimatum. "As I read the Northern newspapers, the blood rushes to my head," one diarist wrote. "In the words of the fine fiction writers, my cheek is mantling with shame. Anyhow," she went on to predict, "down they must go to Old England, knuckle on their marrow bones, to keep her on their side — or barely neutral." Right or wrong, however, such was Seward's theory: a foreign war would still domestic strife. And now as if by the bounty of fate, without the slightest effort on his part, Captain Wilkes's action and England's reaction presented him with an all-out chance to test it.

Lincoln himself had his doubts about this theory, not only in general but in particular, as it applied to the case in point. He rather agreed with the southern diarist that there would have to be some knuckling done. "I fear the traitors will prove to be white elephants," he remarked when he received word of the seizure of Mason and Slidell. Unfamiliar with diplomacy, he was feeling his way. When a learned visitor explained to him that his blockade declaration had naturally gained for the Confederacy the rights of a belligerent in all the courts of Europe, since a nation did not blockade its own ports, Lincoln replied: "Yes, that's a fact. I see the point now, but I don't know anything about the Law of Nations and I thought it was all right.... I'm a good enough lawyer in a western law court, I suppose, but we don't practice the Law of Nations out there, and I supposed Seward knew all about it and I left it to him."

The words were passed along, laughter being added to amazement: "Mr Lincoln forgot it!" And then, perceptibly — whether because of the chilling effect of the laughter or because, as in certain diseases, the fever itself had cured the fit — the excitement ebbed.

He left it to Seward, but he did not let him go unsupervised. It was as if Lincoln said to him, as he had said to Herndon back in Springfield, "Billy, you're too rampant." Seward was called Billy, too — Billy Bowlegs, his enemies dubbed him: a bandy-legged, untidy man with a great deal of personal charm behind the bristling eyebrows, the constant cigar, and the nose of a macaw. Mrs Lincoln detested him outright. "He draws you around his little finger like a skein of thread," she warned her husband. But when other advisers urged that he drop the New Yorker from the cabinet, Lincoln said: "Seward knows that I am his master."

Seward knew no such thing, as yet, but he was learning. Though Lincoln liked him, enjoyed his stories, and respected his political astuteness, from Sumter on he watched him and rode herd on him, toning down his overseas dispatches, which in first draft rather demonstrated his theory that a war with Europe would solve the urgent problems here at home. It was characteristic of Seward that, having styled the coming civil war an "irrepressible conflict," he met it, when it came, with various efforts to repress it. Sumter at least had taught him that Lincoln was more than a prairie bumpkin, for the Secretary informed his wife in early June: "Executive skill and vigor are rare qualities. The President is the best of us, but" — he felt obliged to add — "he needs constant and assiduous coöperation." The *Trent* affair removed this final residue of doubt, and at the same time vindicated Lincoln's decision to keep Seward at his post, despite the clamor of his enemies and the trouble he had made.

Now that the war he thought he wanted was his for the asking — or, indeed, for the not-asking — Seward discovered, perhaps to his profound surprise, that he did not want it at all. He said so, in fact, as soon as the news arrived from Hampton Roads. In the cabinet, while all around them were wild-eyed with praise for the bold captain, only Seward and Montgomery Blair perceived that in turning his quarter-deck into a prize court Wilkes had not only been rash, he had been wrong, and by his illegal action had exposed his country to embarrassment. As Lincoln put it, "We must stick to American principles concerning the rights of neutrals. We fought Great Britain [in 1812] for insisting, by theory and practice, on the right to do precisely what Wilkes has done." Seward agreed. "One war at a time," Lincoln cautioned, and Seward agreed again.

However, these three alone, Lincoln and Seward and the practical-minded Blair, could not breast the popular current running full-tilt against them; they must wait. In his December 1 message to Congress, the President left the affair unmentioned. "Mr Lincoln forgot it!" someone remarked in shocked surprise at his thus ignoring the burning question of the day. The words were passed along, laughter being added to amazement: "Mr Lincoln forgot it!" And then, perceptibly — whether because of the chilling effect of the laughter or because, as in certain diseases, the fever itself had cured the fit — the excitement ebbed.

Cooler heads took over on both sides of the Atlantic. The British began to consider that Captain Wilkes might have acted without orders from his government, and responsible Americans began to see that the Confederate envoys locked up in Fort Warren — where Slidell was being given his chance to "conspire with the mice against the cat" and Mason was abiding by his oath (though in a manner not intended) never to visit that shore again "except as an ambassador" — were accomplishing more toward the fulfillment of their diplomatic mission than they would be doing if they had continued on their way to Europe.

The first official show of reason came from England. Prince Albert, closeted with the Queen in his last illness — he would be dead before the year was out — toned down Russell's ultimatum, modifying its phraseology until the demand for an apology became, in effect, a request for an explanation; so that, instead of finding it "dictatorial or menacing," as he had feared, Seward could pronounce it "courteous and friendly." It was still an ultimatum, requiring an apology for the insult to the British flag, as well as the surrender of the envoys, but at least it opened the door for a reply in the form of something except a declaration of war. That was much. As for the apology—the one thing Seward could not give—verbal additions to the message indicated that a statement to the effect that Wilkes had acted without instructions would render it superfluous, since a nation could hardly be expected to apologize for something it had not done. Seward already had in mind the terms of his reply, but before it could be sent he would have to win the approval of the rest of the cabinet. In the present state of public furor, with even Lincoln feeling that surrender of the captives was "a pretty bitter pill to swallow," nothing less than unanimous action would suffice.

For two days Seward remained shut away in his office, composing a reply to the British demand: a reply intended not only for the eyes of the Minister to whom it was addressed, but also for those of the American man-in-the-street, whose sensibilities were the ones considered most in this explanation of his government's being willing to give up the rebel envoys: so that, though in form and style the document was brilliantly legal, showing Seward at his sparkling best—this was one State Department dispatch Lincoln did not need to doctor—it was not so much designed to stand up under analysis by the Admiralty law lords, as it was to show the writer's countrymen that their leaders were by no means trembling at the roar of the British lion. Having complied with the basic demands of the ultimatum by 1) admitting that Wilkes had acted without orders and 2) offering to deliver the captives whenever and wherever they were wanted, Seward then wrote for his countrymen's eyes, with reasoning that was somewhat specious and language that was at times impertinent, what amounted to an indictment of the British point of view, past and present. In other words, under cover of an apology, he gave the lion's tail a final twist.

Down on the Virginian peninsula that summer, though by the rules of warfare he could not confiscate private property unless it was being used against him, Ben Butler had justified the receiving of slaves into his lines on grounds that their labor for the enemy made them contraband of war. "I'se contraband," they would say, smiling proudly as they crossed the freedom line, and Butler put them to work on his fortifications. Now Seward took a page from the squint-eyed general's book, affirming that the envoys and their secretaries were "contraband," liable to seizure. Wilkes therefore had done right to stop the ship and then to board and search her. His error lay in his leniency; for he should have brought not only the rebel envoys, but also the *Trent* and all her cargo into port for judgment; in which case, Seward was sure, the ship and everything aboard her, including the four Confederates, would have become the lawful property of the United States. However—and here was where the impertinence came in— the Secretary could appreciate his lordship's being taken aback, for in impressing passengers from a merchant vessel Wilkes had followed a British, not an American line of conduct. Seward saw the present ultimatum as an admission of past injuries inflicted by the mistress of the seas, and he congratulated Britannia on having come round to the point of view against which she had fought in 1812: "She could in no other way so effectually disavow any such injury, as we think she does, by assuming now as her own the ground upon which we then stood." Captain Wilkes had been mainly right, but the United States wanted no advantage gained by means of an action which was even partly wrong. Seward was frank to state, however, that if his nation's safety required it he would still detain the captives; but "the effectual check and waning proportions of the existing insurrection, as well as the comparative unimportance of the captured persons themselves, when dispassionately weighed, happily forbid me from resorting to that defense. . . . The four persons in question are now held in military custody at Fort Warren, in the State of Massachusetts. They will be cheerfully liberated. Your lordship will please indicate a time and place for receiving them."

Doubtless Seward had enjoyed those two days he spent locked away in his office, verbally building a straw man, straw by straw, then verbally demolishing him, handful by handful. When he emerged, however, prepared to receive

The appearance (left to right) of Lord Russell, Mason and Slidell, William Seward, and Jefferson Davis sums up The Trent Affair in this composite image.

★

the applause of his fellow cabinet members, he received instead cold looks and hot objections. They could appreciate the brilliance of his performance, but it did not obscure the fact that they were being asked to yield—which most of them had sworn not to do. It took him, in fact, as long to win their indorsement of the document as he had spent composing it, and the latter two days were far more hectic than the former.

Christmas morning the ministers assembled. When they adjourned that afternoon, to spend what was left of the holiday with their families, there had been no agreement. What Lincoln called "a pretty bitter pill" was for the cabinet, one member said, "downright gall and wormwood." The war was one year old that night, the anniversary of Anderson's removal of his eighty-odd men from Moultrie to Fort Sumter. Next morning the ministers reassembled; the discussion was resumed. It went hard, being asked to go down on their marrow bones against all their oaths and boasts, with only Seward's flimsy curtain of paradox and impertinence to hide them from the public and each other. In the end, however, as one of them wrote, "all yielded to the necessity, and unanimously concurred."

Mason and Slidell were handed over on New Year's Day to continue their roundabout journey, the latter being twenty days late for the appointment he had made with his wife when he told her on parting, "My dear, we shall meet in Paris in sixty days." The public reaction to the outcome of the crisis was considerably less violent than the cabinet members had feared. Though the anti-British press continued to fulminate according to tradition, in general there was a sigh of relief at having to fight only "one war at a time." When Captain Wilkes, still wearing his laurels, was sent about his business, to be supervised more closely in the future, the public did not even feel let down. Poker was not the national game for nothing; the people understood that their leaders had bowed, not to the British, but to expediency.

Only within one group was there despondency that the rebels had been freed. "Everybody here is satisfied with their surrender," Lincoln heard from a friend in Indiana, "except the secession sympathizers, who are wonderfully hurt at the idea that our national honor is tarnished."

★ ★ ★ On this diplomatic note, which opened shrill, then broke into falsetto, the first year of the conflict reached a close. Politically and militarily speaking, its laurels belonged to those who had established a nation within its span and defended that establishment successfully in battle, meeting and turning back attacks against both flanks of their thousand-mile frontier and staving off an advance against the center. McClellan's gains in western Virginia and the Federal navy's trident amphibious lunge did something to redress the defeats along Bull Run and Wilson's Creek, but when those checks were emphasized, east and west, by the rout at Ball's Bluff and the repulse at Belmont, there was a distinct public impression, North and South, at home and abroad, of failure by the Unionist government to deal with the Confederate bid for independence.

One side called this bid a revolution. The other insisted that it was a rebellion. Whichever it was, it was plainly a fact, and both sides saw clearly now that the contest between northern power and southern élan was not going to be the ninety-day affair they had predicted at the outset.

Realization that this was so had grown until it was unmistakable, at which point violent objections were sounded on both sides by the extremists who had been foremost in predicting that the conflict would be short and decisive. Southerners were all bluster and would not fight if their bluff was called, the abolitionists had declared, and when one fire-eater had offered to wipe up with his handkerchief all the blood that would be shed, a less squeamish colleague had backed him up by offering to drink it. Now that blood had dripped and flowed beyond their power to drink or wipe, they waxed bitterly accusative, North and South, against those who held the reins. Chagrined that the war they had done so much to bring about had been taken out of their hands when it arrived, the two groups still insisted that their prediction had turned out false only because their aims had been betrayed. It could still be rendered valid, they affirmed, provided the war was fought the way they wanted. Each favored an all-out invasion, with fire and sword and the hangman's noose, and each blamed its leader for an obvious lack of vigor in his thinking and in his actions.

"Jeff Davis is conceited, wrong-headed, wranglesome, obstinate — a traitor," Edmund Rhett declared, while back in Springfield the northern President's erstwhile law partner complained that Lincoln was attempting to "squelch out this huge rebellion by popguns filled with rose water. He ought to hang somebody and get up a name for will or decision — for character," Herndon wrote, and added scornfully: "Let him hang some child or woman if he has not the courage to hang a *man*."

Between these two extremes, while the anti-Davis and anti-Lincoln cliques were respectively consolidating their opposition and sharpening their barbs, the mass of men who would do the actual fighting, and the women who would wait for them at home, took what came with a general determination to measure up to what was expected of them. It was their good fortune, or else their misery, to belong to a generation in which every individual would be given a chance to discover and expose his worth, down to the final ounce of strength and nerve. For the most part, therefore, despite the clamor of extremists north and south of the new frontier, each side accepted its leader as a condition of the tour-

★

nament, and counted itself fortunate to have the man it had and not the other. Seen from opposite banks of the Ohio and the Potomac, both seemed creatures fit for frightening children into quick obedience. On the one hand there was Davis, "ambitious as Lucifer," with his baleful eyes and bloodless mouth, cerebral and lizard-cold, plotting malevolence into the small hours of the night. On the other there was Lincoln, "the original gorilla," with his shambling walk and sooty face, an ignorant rail-splitter catapulted by long-shot politics into an office for which he had neither the experience nor the dignity required.

What they seemed to each other was another matter. Lincoln had recognized his adversary's renowned capabilities from the start, but it was not until well after Sumter — if then — that Davis, like so many of the northern President's own associates, including even his Secretary of State, began to understand that he was having to deal with an opponent not below but beyond the run of men. Their official attitude toward one another gave a certain advantage to the Southerner, since he could arraign his rival before the bar of world opinion, addressing him as a tyrant and "exposing" his duplicity; whereas Lincoln, by refusing to admit that there was any such thing as the Confederate States of America, was obliged to pretend that Davis, too, was nonexistent. However, it was a knife that cut both ways. Lincoln was not only denied the chance to answer charges, he was also relieved of the necessity for replying to a man who wasn't there. Nor was that all. Constitutionally, the Illinois lawyer-politician was better equipped for accepting vilification than the Mississippi planter-statesman was for accepting what amounted to a cut; so that, in their personal duel, the advantages of a cloak of invisibility were canceled, at least in part, by the reaction of the man who had to wear it. Davis wore it, in fact, like an involuntary hair shirt.

Followed by the admiring glances of Richmond ladies in made-over bonnets and men in last year's winter suits, he continued to take his early morning and late evening constitutionals, to and from the office where he spent long hours on administrative details rather than on executive decisions. With the bottom gone out of the slave market and gold already selling at a premium of fifty percent, the croakers were saying that he expended his energies thus to keep from facing the larger issues. But that was to overlook the fact that, rightly or wrongly, those issues had been settled back in the spring, when he committed himself and his nation to the defensive. Now he was pursuing a policy which a later southern-born President would call "watchful waiting" — watching for another northern offensive and waiting for European intervention. His task was to turn back the former and welcome the latter. In the light of Manassas, which set the battle pattern, and the *Trent* affair, which strained British-U.S. relations even further, Davis considered both of these outcomes probable, either of which would validate for all time the existing fact of his country's independence. Waiting had already brought him much, and now that it seemed likely to bring more, he continued to watch and wait, going about his duties as he saw them.

Such duties involved an occasional social function and the daily hour which he reserved for his children. Of these there now were four, Mrs Davis having borne in mid-December the child christened William Howell for her ailing father. They were Davis' chief relaxation, for much as he enjoyed the social amenities, particularly an intimate evening spent with a few close friends, he mostly denied himself that pleasure in these times. He would drop in during his

Jefferson Davis' four children (above) had a relaxing influence on their father during his trying and tempestuous times in Richmond.

★

wife's receptions, spend an hour exercising his remarkable memory for names and faces, then dutifully, his invariable charm and courtesy masking whatever boredom he felt, take a cup of tea before retiring to his study and the paperwork that awaited him as a result of his unwillingness to delegate authority.

The lady guests might have their reservations about his wife — she was rather too "intellectual" for their taste; "pleasant, if not wholly genial," one Richmond matron called her — but the men, coming under the sway of those attractions which had drawn her husband, seventeen years and five children ago (Samuel, the first child, died in infancy), did not feel that the breadth of her mind obscured the charm of her person. All were agreed, however, as to the attractiveness of the husband and the dignity he brought to his high office. He was showing the strain, it was true; but that only served to emphasize the wonder at how well he bore up under it, after all. Whatever their opinion as to his policy in adopting a static defensive, they all agreed that as a figurehead for the ship of state he could hardly be improved on.

Ornamentally, Lincoln served less well — though in reply to complaints about his looks his followers could repeat what had been pointed out already: "We didn't get him for ballroom purposes." Even here, however, he was trying. At White House receptions he stood in line and pumped the hands of callers, performing the duty, one witness observed, "like a wood-chopper, at so much a cord." He was learning, too. Though his big hands split through several pairs of kid gloves on such evenings, now at least the gloves were white, not black as at the opera in New York ten months before. He had most of the problems Davis had, and some that Davis did not have. Office seekers still hemmed him in and placed a constant drain on his good humor. Finding him depressed one day, a friend asked in alarm, "What is the matter? Have you bad news from the army?" "No, it isn't the army," Lincoln said with a weary smile. "It is the post office in Brownsville, Missouri."

Unlike his opponent, he had no fixed policy to refer to: not even the negative one of a static defensive, which, whatever its faults, at least had the virtue of offering a position from which to judge almost any combination of events. This lack gave him the flexibility which lay at the core of his greatness, but he had to purchase it dearly in midnight care and day-long fret. Without practical experience on which to base his decisions, he must improvise as he went along, like a doctor developing a cure in the midst of an epidemic. His advisers were competent men in the main, but they were fiercely divided in their counsels; so that, to all his other tasks, Lincoln had added the role of mediator, placing himself as a buffer between factions, to absorb what he could of the violence they directed at each other. What with generals who balked and politicians who champed at the bit, it was no wonder if he sometimes voiced the wish that he were out of it, back home in Illinois. Asked how he enjoyed his office, he told of a tarred and feathered man out West, who, as he was being ridden out of town on a rail, heard one among the crowd call to him, asking how he liked it, high up there on his uncomfortable perch. "If it wasn't for the honor of the thing," the man replied, "I'd sooner walk."

In Richmond and in Washington, one hundred miles apart — the same distance as lay between Fairview and Hodgenville, their birthplaces in Kentucky — Davis and Lincoln toiled their long hours, kept their vigils, and sought solutions to problems that were mostly the same but seemed quite different because they saw them in reverse, from opposite directions. All men were to be weighed in this time, and especially these two. At the far ends of the north-south road connecting the two capitals they strained to see and understand each other, peering as if across a darkling plain. Soon now, that hundred miles of Virginia with its glittering rivers and dusty turnpikes, its fields of grain and rolling pastures, the peace of generations soft upon it like the softness in the voices of its people, would be obscured by the swirl and bank of cannon smoke, stitched by the fitful stabs of muzzle flashes, until at last, lurid as the floor of hell itself, it would seem to have been made for war as deliberately as a chessboard was designed for chess. Even the place-names on the map, which now were merely quaint, would take on the sound of crackling flame and distant thunder, the Biblical, Indian, Anglo-Saxon names of hamlets and creeks and crossroads, for the most part unimportant in themselves until the day when the armies came together, as often by accident as on purpose, to give the scattered names a permanence and settle what manner of life the future generations were to lead. The road ran straight, a glory road with split-rail fences like firewood ready stacked for the two armies, and many men would travel it wearing Union blue or Confederate gray. Blood had been shed along it once, and would be shed again; how many times?

Neither Lincoln nor Davis knew, but they intended to find out, and soon. The year just past had been in the nature of a prelude, whose close marked only the end of the beginning.

★　★　★

Shelby Foote

As the Federal gunboat flotilla attacks Fort Henry four abreast on February 6, 1862, the Essex (right) is hit in the boiler and put out of action.

EIGHT

The West:
Grant, Fort Henry

1862 ★ ★ ★ ★ ★ Albert Sidney Johnston, the ranking Confederate general in the field, was charged with maintaining the integrity of a line that stretched westward more than five hundred miles: from the barrens of eastern Kentucky, through the Bluegrass region, on across the Mississippi, and beyond the kaleidoscopic swirl of conflict in Missouri to Indian territory, where it ended, like a desert stream, as a trickle in dry sand. To accomplish the defense of this western-Europe-sized expanse, penetrated by rivers floating enemy fleets and menaced along its salient points by two Federal armies, each one larger than his own, he had a distinguished reputation, a nobility of looks and character, a high-flown official title — General Commanding the Western Department of the Army of the Confederate States of America — and all too little else. He was a big man, broad-shouldered and deep-chested, over six feet tall and just under two hundred pounds in weight. His wavy dark-brown hair touched with such gray as became his fifty-eight years, the Kentucky-born Texan gave at once an impression of strength and gentleness. No beard disguised his strong, regular features, but a heavy mustache offset somewhat the dominance of brow and width of jaw. Commanding in presence, grave in manner, he wore his dignity with natural charm and was not without the saving grace of humor. It was Johnston,

Albert Sidney Johnston (right) was, according to Jefferson Davis, "the greatest soldier, the ablest man, civil or military, Confederate or Federal."

for example, who remarked that there was "too much tail" to Frémont's kite.

In the thirty-five years since his graduation from West Point—where Jefferson Davis, looking up to him from two classes below, as at Transylvania earlier, contracted a severe and lifelong case of hero worship—he had distinguished himself in a colorful career: frontier officer, Texas revolutionist and Secretary of War in Sam Houston's cabinet, gentleman farmer, Mexican War colonel, U.S. Army paymaster, and commander of the famed 2d Cavalry, whose roster carried the names of four future full generals, including himself and R. E. Lee, one lieutenant general, and three major generals, all Confederate, as well as two of the leading Union major generals. Zachary Taylor was reported to have said that Johnston was the finest soldier he ever commanded, and Winfield Scott had called him "a Godsend to the Army and to the country."

While the national storm was heading up, he was a brevet brigadier in command of the Pacific Coast, with headquarters at Fort Alcatraz in San Francisco Bay; but when Texas seceded he declined an offer of high rank in the Union army, tendered his resignation, and led a group of thirty pro-Confederate officers and civilians eastward on horseback across the desert toward his adopted state, dodging Apaches and Federal garrisons on the way. From Galveston he came on to New Orleans, where he was greeted as if an additional army had flocked to the Stars and Bars. His route to Richmond, through a countryside still elated over the six-weeks-old Manassas victory, was blazed with fluttering handkerchiefs and tossed hats, the news of his coming having preceded him all

★

along the line. Davis was waiting, too, and handed him his lofty commission and the accompanying assignment to the far-flung Western Department.

"I hoped and expected that I had others who would prove generals," the southern leader afterwards declared; "but I knew I had *one*, and that was Sidney Johnston." Still later he put it even stronger, calling him "the greatest soldier, the ablest man, civil or military, Confederate or Federal, then living."

This high opinion was shared by the people of the region where the general's orders took him. From Richmond to Nashville, as from New Orleans to Richmond, the journey was one continuous ovation. Yet now that the new year had come in, with its hangover from the heady wine of Manassas and Wilson's Creek, all that seemed far away and long ago — as if it had occurred in another era, a dream world, even, divided from the present by an airtight door which slammed forever shut in mid-September when Johnston arrived and saw for himself, at unmistakable first hand, the magnitude of the task that lay before him and the paucity of the means with which he was expected to accomplish it. Politically the lines were already drawn; Kentucky and Missouri both had stars in the Confederate flag, though it was becoming increasingly clear that Lincoln had mostly won that fight, in spite of secessionist governors and Frémont. The problem now was military, and the line to be drawn lay not along the Ohio River, but along a zigzag course conforming to the mountains and rivers and railroads of Kentucky and the crazy-quilt pattern of Missouri. Such a line would be difficult to defend at best, but with the force at his disposal it was patently impossible. He had something under 50,000 men in all, scarcely amounting to more in effect than a 500-mile-long skirmish line, distributed about equally east and west of the big river that pierced his center.

In the Transmississippi the snarled military situation was aggravated by the rivalry of Price and McCulloch, whose victories had not brought them into accord. Since to elevate one would mean the probable loss of the other, along with many followers, Johnston proposed that the Richmond authorities assign to the region a field commander who would rank them both. Eventually this was done, and soon after the first of the year Major General Earl Van Dorn, West Pointer and Mississippian, a man of considerable fire and reputation, took over the job of welding the two commands into one army. Meanwhile, on his way from Richmond, Johnston stopped off at the far eastern end of his line and ordered Brigadier General Felix Zollicoffer, a former newspaper editor and Tennessee congressman, to take his little army of recruits through Cumberland Gap in order to post them where they could guard the passes giving down upon Knoxville and the Virginia & Tennessee Railroad.

Having provided thus for his flanks, Johnston looked to his center, the critical 150-mile sector extending roughly east-southeast from Columbus, Kentucky, to Nashville. Davis had empowered him to withdraw Polk from

Columbus, out of consideration for the state's political sensibilities, or to sustain the occupation. It was not a difficult decision; in fact, Johnston had already made it when he sent Zollicoffer forward. But now he did more. Finding Simon Buckner waiting for him in Nashville — the former head of the Kentucky State Guard was now a private citizen, offering the South his services — Johnston commissioned him a brigadier, assigned him several regiments, and set him in motion for Bowling Green, sixty miles to the north. Far from ordering Polk's withdrawal, the new department commander swung his central sector forward, gate-like, with Columbus as the hinge. The line now extended east-northeast, and within a week of his arrival he had thrown every available armed man northward across the Kentucky border to strengthen it.

It badly needed strengthening. At the outset Johnston had fewer than 20,000 troops to man the long line from the Mississippi to the mountains — 11,000 with Polk, 4000 each with Buckner and Zollicoffer — backed up by a few scattered camps of recruits in Tennessee, some without any weapons at all. But when Johnston appealed for arms and men to the governors of Alabama and Georgia, both were prompt in refusal. "Our own coast is threatened," the former replied, while the latter, if less explanatory, was more emphatic: "It is utterly impossible for me to comply with your request." Not all were so deaf to his pleas, however. More closely threatened, Tennessee coöperated better, putting fifty regiments into the field before the end of the year, and Kentucky volunteers continued to come in, some bringing their long rifles. Four regiments arrived from Mississippi before that state was shut off from him by governmental notification that the area was not properly within the limits of his command. Not that Richmond was unmindful of the danger. It sent what it felt it could afford, including 4650 Enfield rifles brought in by blockade runners, and transferred to the Army of Central Kentucky — so Johnston called it — several of the Confederacy's most distinguished brigadiers.

Georgia-born William J. Hardee, forty-six — not only a West Pointer and one-time commandant of cadets, but also the author of *Rifle and Light Infantry Tactics*, formerly an Academy text and now the official drill and tactics manual of both armies — brought his brigade from northeast Arkansas to Bowling Green, where he took over from Buckner and soon was promoted to major general, as befitted his wider experience and his position as commander of the vital center. Gideon Pillow, who had measured swords with Grant at Belmont, also was shifted eastward to bolster the advance. He too ranked Buckner, and for the present became second in command of the Army of the Center, under Hardee.

Three prominent Kentuckians, all in their forties, also were available for the defense of their state. The oldest was George B. Crittenden, forty-nine, West Pointer and regular army man, son of the senator whose compromise efforts had staved off war for a decade. Commissioned a major general he was sent to the Cumberland Mountains region, with headquarters at Knoxville. Lloyd Tilghman, forty-five, was also a West Pointer and a veteran of the Mexican War, but he had left the army for a career in civil engineering. Johnston soon had him busy designing and building fortifications. The youngest of the three, forty-year-old John C. Breckinridge, was also the most distinguished. Vice President under Buchanan, he had presided over the joint session of Congress which declared Abraham Lincoln elected President, the office for which Breckinridge himself had been runner-up in the electoral college. Since then, he had been elected to the Senate, where his opposition to the Administration's war policy resulted in an order for his arrest. When Buckner first got to Bowling Green, Breckinridge entered his lines as a fugitive. "To defend your birthright and mine," he told his fellow Kentuckians, "I exchange with proud satisfaction a term of six years in the Senate of the United States for the musket of a soldier." Rather than a musket Johnston gave him a brigade, despite his lack of military training.

In addition to these men of rank, all in the vigor of their prime, the army had two cavalrymen who had already contributed exploits to its legend: Captain John Hunt Morgan of Kentucky and Lieutenant Colonel Nathan Bedford Forrest of Tennessee. Though the former had fought in the Mexican War as a youth and later commanded his hometown militia company, neither man had had a military education. The latter, in fact, a Memphis slave dealer and a Mississippi planter, had had little formal schooling of any kind. By the end of the year, however, both had shown an aptitude for war. Morgan, who was thirty-six, took thirteen of his troopers on a reconnaissance completely around Buell's army and returned with thirty-three prisoners. In his first fight, northeast of Bowling Green, the forty-year-old Forrest improvised a double envelopment, combined it with a frontal assault — classic maneuvers which he could not identify by name and of which he had most likely never heard — and scattered the survivors of a larger enemy force. Standing in the stirrups, swinging his sword and roaring "Charge! Charge!" in a voice that rang like brass, the colonel personally accounted for three of the enemy officers, killing two and wounding one; he shot the first, sabered the second, and dislocated the shoulder of a third by knocking him off his horse. Ordinarily, infantrymen had small liking for any trooper, but these two lithe, violent six-footers caught their fancy, and soldiers of all arms predicted brilliant futures for them both — if they lived, which seemed unlikely.

Soon after New Year's the final brigadier arrived from West Virginia at the head of his command. John B. Floyd had had three months in which to recover from the rain-damped campaign under Lee in the Kanawha Valley, where he had been more successful against his Confederate rival, Henry Wise, than against the wily Rosecrans. Ranking Pillow, he now became second in command of the forces under Hardee north of Bowling Green, along the Green and Barren Rivers.

Johnston had to protect an awkward Confederate defensive line that arched from Columbus, to Bowling Green, and into eastern Kentucky.

Floyd's brigade completed the order-of-battle with which Johnston was expected to fend off Halleck and Buell, whose combined armies were about twice the size of his own. In the Transmississippi, a weird collection of 20,000 regulars, militiamen, and Indian braves awaited the arrival of Van Dorn to take the offensive against a well-organized command of 30,000 Union troops. East of the river, though Johnston had managed to double the number defending Kentucky, the odds were even longer. Between Columbus and Cumberland Gap, just over 50,000 Confederates opposed just under 90,000 Federals.

★

Polk on the left at Columbus had 17,000 men opposing Grant's 20,000 around Cairo; Hardee in the center at Bowling Green had 25,000 opposing Buell's 60,000 southwest of Louisville; Zollicoffer on the right had 4000 in front of Cumberland Gap, opposing 8000 under George Thomas north of Barbourville. Thus Johnston had drawn his line, badly outnumbered at the points of contact and in danger of being swamped by combinations. Fully aware of the risks he ran, he had no choice except to run them, making such use as he could of what he had and resorting to bluff whenever the danger seemed gravest, first at one point, then another. Also, a use had been found for Tilghman, who with 4500 men was stationed where geographical circumstances would give his engineering skill full scope.

The geographic factors were two rivers, the Tennessee and the Cumberland, whose existence threatened catastrophe for Johnston. Running parallel, and piercing as they did the critical center of his line, the two were like a double-barreled shotgun leveled at his heart. Despite the northern direction of their flow, they offered broad twin pathways of invasion for the steam-powered gunboats of the fleet which now controlled their mouths, twelve miles apart on the Ohio. Once into his rear, their paths diverged and they became separate threats, one deeper and the other more immediate, but both dire. Against its current, the Tennessee led down across both borders of the state whose name it bore, and then bent east and north, like a rusty hook plunged into the vitals of the South, touching northeast Mississippi on its way to Muscle Shoals in Alabama, beyond which it swung north, past Chattanooga, and finally on toward Knoxville and its source. The Cumberland, on the other hand, turned eastward soon after it crossed the northern border of Tennessee to curve back into Kentucky, across the front of Cumberland Gap and into the mountains that gave it both its waters and its name. Though the penetration was shallower, the consequences of an invasion along this line were no less stern; for during its dip into Tennessee the river ran past Clarksville and Nashville, the former being the site of the Cumberland Iron Works, second only to Richmond's Tredegar in output, and the latter, besides its importance as a manufacturing center, was the supply base for Johnston's entire army.

Those who were there before him had proposed to meet this two-pronged threat by constructing a fort to guard each river: Fort Henry, on the right bank of the Tennessee, and Fort Donelson on the left bank of the Cumberland. The first problem in each case had been location. Northward in Kentucky the rivers converged briefly to within three miles of each other, which would have allowed the forts to be mutually supporting; but since this was during the period of Bluegrass "neutrality," the chosen sites were necessarily south of the border, where the rivers were twelve miles apart—the same distance as at their mouths, fifty miles downstream—north of the two bridges over which the railroad, running northeast out of Memphis, brought food and munitions for the army. Work on the forts lagged badly from the outset, with much argument among the engineers. Yet enough had been done by the time of Johnston's arrival to cause him to leave them where they were, rather than change their location when he swung his long line outward, gate-like, with Bowling Green as the stop-post and Columbus as the hinge. Consequently, the gate was badly warped, swagged inward to include the forts commanded now by Tilghman, whom Johnston sent to strengthen and complete them.

The concave swag of the Columbus-Bowling Green sector violated the military principle requiring a defending general to operate on an interior line, so that in shifting troops from point to point, along the chord of the arc, he would be moving them a shorter distance than his opponent, outside the arc, would have to do. Between these salients the case was reversed: it was Johnston who was outside the arc, with the greater distance to travel from point to point. However, the textbook disadvantage was offset by the presence of the railroad running along the rear of his line, by which means he could shuttle his troops back and forth with far greater speed than an opponent, lacking such rapid transportation within the arc, could hope to match, despite any difference in distance. What was more, railroad and battle line were mutually supporting. So long as the line was held the road would continue its fast shifting of troops, and so long as the shuttle service went on, the line presumably could be held. The chink in the armor, Johnston knew, was where the railroad bridges spanned the rivers. Gunboats could reduce the trestles to kindling within five minutes of opening fire. They were only as safe as the forts downstream were strong. And that was why he kept urging Tilghman to exert all possible effort to get them finished.

Here as elsewhere, necessity being the mother of invention, Johnston broke or rewrote the rules whenever necessity demanded. Outnumbered severely all along his line, in each sector he improvised defenses which, in event of attack, called for reinforcements from less threatened points. His greatest advantage, indeed almost his only one, was that his army was united under a single leader, whereas the enemy forces were divided. So far, his opponents — Frémont and Anderson, then Hunter and Sherman, and finally Halleck and Buell — had failed to work in concert. What he would do if the latter pair mounted coördinated or even simultaneous offensives, from end to end of the long line or even against several points at once, he did not know and could not know, the odds being what they were. Meanwhile, he used the only means remaining: he used psychological warfare, including the dissemination of propaganda and misinformation. He used it with such skill, in fact, that it kept his shaky line intact throughout the fall and early winter and gave him time to shore it up with all the reinforcements he could find.

★

Throwing his troops forward he maneuvered them in a threatening manner, always as if on the verge of launching cut-and-slash attacks against the danger points. He announced to all within earshot that he had plenty of arms and plenty of men to use them; that, far from having any fears about being able to hold his ground, he was about to unleash an offensive that would roll to the Ohio, crunching the bones of whatever got in his way. The bluff had worked best against Sherman, who already had the horrors as a result of the insight which had told him just how bloody this war was likely to be. "I am convinced from many facts," he informed headquarters in a dispatch which his opponent might have dictated, "that A. Sidney Johnston is making herculean efforts to strike a great blow in Kentucky; that he designs to move from Bowling Green on Lexington, Louisville, and Cincinnati." Presently Sherman was on sick leave, restoring his Johnston-jangled nerves. If the bluff worked less dramatically on

Statements doubling and tripling his actual strength and hinting of an imminent offensive were printed in all the southern papers, in hopes that rival editors north of the defensive line would pick them up and spread them, which they did.

his successor, that was mainly because Buell had a less dramatic personality. At any rate, it caused him to enlarge upon the difficulties that lay between him and East Tennessee, where Lincoln so much wanted him to go. Halleck also felt its effects. They lay at the bottom of his reply that Buell's proposal for a joint advance on Nashville, up the Cumberland, "seems to me madness."

To confuse his enemies Johnston had first to mislead his friends, and this he did. Statements doubling and tripling his actual strength and hinting of an imminent offensive were printed in all the southern papers, in hopes that rival editors north of the defensive line would pick them up and spread them, which they did. Yet psychological warfare was a weapon that could boomerang, returning with a force in direct ratio to the success of its outward flight. While Halleck and Buell were counting themselves fortunate that the Confederates did not storm their lines, readers south of the border were also thoroughly taken in by Johnston, who thus compromised his reputation and risked his countrymen's morale by promising victories he knew he could never deliver with the present force at his command.

In a final effort to get more troops and supplies, on January 9, soon after the arrival of Floyd's brigade, which he had been warned would be the last, Johnston sent a personal messenger with a letter to his friend the President, reëmphasizing the gravity of the western situation. Within a week the messenger returned. He had found Davis in a "disturbed and careworn" frame of mind, but that was nothing compared to the state the Chief Executive was in by the time he had read the letter. "My God!" he cried. "Why did General Johnston send you to me for arms and reinforcements?...Where am I to get arms or men?" The question was rhetorical, but the messenger, who had been primed for it, answered that they might be spared from less immediately threatened points. Davis had heard this suggestion all too often of late, along with the conflicting clamor of governors whose states had Union gunboats off their shores. Petulantly he replied that it could not be done, and remarked in closing the interview, "Tell my friend General Johnston that I can do nothing for him, that he must rely on his own resources."

The slimness of those resources was known to only a handful of men within the limits of strict confidence. Others beyond those limits thought him amply equipped and bountifully supplied, about to launch an offensive. Johnston was therefore in the position of a financier who, to stave off ruin, had overextended his credit with both friends and enemies by putting his name to a sight draft that would come due on presentation. Now that he was in too far to turn back, the President's message reached him like a notice of proceedings in bankruptcy. Kentucky was the only theater in which there had been no major clash of arms. He must have known that reverses were coming, and he must have known, too, that when they came the people would not understand.

★ ★ ★   *They* came soon enough. In fact, they came immediately. Coincident with the return of the messenger, Johnston's right caved in, the troops there scattering headlong, demoralized and crying like their foes the year before: "We are betrayed!"

Primarily, though, he lost that wing of his army not because of a Federal advance, as he had feared, but because of Zollicoffer's rashness and military inexperience. After occupying Cumberland Gap, the Tennessean had been ordered to move seventy miles northwest to Mill Springs, on the south bank of the Cumberland River, from which position he could parry an enemy thrust either toward the Gap, where he had posted a guard, or toward Nashville, 150 miles southwest. However, when Crittenden reached Knoxville, assuming command of the region, he learned to his amazement that Zollicoffer had not been content to remain south of the river, but had crossed and set up a camp on the opposite bank. Here at Beech Grove, with a wide unfordable river to his rear, the Tennessean was defying a Union army twice his size and attempting to stir

Virginia-born George H. Thomas remained in the Federal army even after his native state seceded from the Union.

up the doubtfully loyal citizens with proclamations which boldly inquired, "How long will Kentuckians close their eyes to the contemplated ruin of their present structure of society?"

Despite this evidence of literary skill, Crittenden now began to doubt the former editor's military judgment, and at once dispatched a courier, peremptorily ordering him to recross the river. But when he went forward on inspection in early January, to his even greater dismay he found the citizen-soldier's army still on the north bank. Zollicoffer blandly explained that Beech Grove afforded a better campsite; he had stayed where he was, in hopes that they could talk it over when Crittenden arrived. Then too, he explained—to the West Pointer's mounting horror—there were reports that the Yankees were advancing, which made falling back seem a cowardly or at any rate not a manly sort of action.

Investigation proved that the reports were all too true. Not only were the Federals advancing, they had at their head the Union-loyal Virginian George H. Thomas. Whatever his fellow Southerners might think of his "treachery" in not going with his state, they knew him to be an experienced soldier, not the least of his recommendations being that he had been a major in Johnston's 2d Cavalry. Faced with this threat, Crittenden saw that to attempt to withdraw would be to risk being hamstrung while astride the river. So he assumed command and did what he could to brace his troops in their Beech Grove camp for the shock which he believed was imminent.

What came was not the Yankees but a week of pelting rain. Despite its chill discomfort he was thankful, for if it broadened the river to his rear, it also swelled the creeks to his front and transformed into troughs of mud the roads down which the Federals were approaching. "A continuous quagmire," Thomas called them as his army slogged in double column along the opposite watersheds of Fishing Creek, which emptied into the Cumberland just above the Confederate position. Within nine miles of the rebel outposts on the 17th, he went into camp near Logan's Crossroads to rest his men, dry out their equipment, and plan the assault against Beech Grove.

The rain continued all next day, affording Thomas little respite, but presenting Crittenden with what he believed was a chance to exchange probable defeat for possible victory. In its separate camps, the enemy force was still divided by Fishing Creek, which Crittenden figured was swollen now past fording.

They were launching a surprise attack against a man who could not be surprised, whose emotional make-up apparently excluded that kind of reaction to any event. Imperturbable, phlegmatic, his calm was as unruffled in a crisis as his humor was heavy-handed.

He would move his army out that night and strike the Union left in a dawn attack. Then, having destroyed or scattered it, he would turn and deal with the other wing, beyond the flooded creek. It was a gamble, even a desperate one, but after a week spent sitting in the rain, awaiting destruction while the river ran deeper and swifter at his back, it was a gamble he was glad to take. Zollicoffer approved as soon as he heard of the plan, and at midnight the two brigades — eight regiments of infantry, plus a six-gun battery and a cavalry battalion — set out on their march through mud and rain to fight the battle variously known as Mill Springs, Fishing Creek, and Logan's Crossroads.

They soon discovered the accuracy of the description the Federal commander had given of the roads. And after a nightmare march through shin-deep mud, with rain coming hard in their faces out of a darkness relieved only by the blinding glare of lightning as they hauled at the wheels of bogged-down cannon and wagons and the heads of foundered horses, they discovered something else about George Thomas. They were launching a surprise attack against

★

a man who could not be surprised, whose emotional make-up apparently excluded that kind of reaction to any event. Imperturbable, phlegmatic, his calm
was as unruffled in a crisis as his humor was heavy-handed. Lincoln had hesitated to make the forty-five-year-old Virginian a brigadier, having doubts about
his loyalty, but when he questioned Sherman and got the Ohioan's quick assurance that he personally knew Thomas to be loyal, he went ahead and signed the
commission. Coming away from the interview with the President, Sherman ran
into his friend on the street.

"Tom, you're a brigadier general!" he gaily announced. When
Thomas showed no elation at this, Sherman began to have doubts. "Where are
you going?" he asked, fearing he might be on his way to the War Department
with his resignation, like so many other Virginians.

"I'm going south," Thomas replied glumly.

"My God, Tom," Sherman groaned. "You've put me in an awful
position! I've just made myself responsible for your loyalty."

"Give yourself no trouble, Billy," Thomas said. "I'm going south at
the head of my troops."

That was where he was going now. After a night and a day and
another night spent in bivouac around Logan's Crossroads, straddling Fishing
Creek, he sent a cavalry patrol out into the stormy dawn of the 19th to explore
the roads leading south toward the Confederate camp. There was a spatter of
musketry beyond the curtain of rain, and presently the horsemen reappeared,
riding hard back up the puddled road, shouting that they had run into rebel
skirmishers in advance of a heavy column. The long roll sounded. Men came
stumbling big-eyed out of their tents, clutching weapons and clothes, and
formed their regimental lines as if for drill, despite the rain and the fact that it
was Sunday. All this while, beyond the steely glitter of the rain, an intermittent
banging warned that the pickets were engaged. It sounded more like range-
firing than a battle, but then the pickets came running in front of a double bank
of men in muddy gray.

Crittenden kept coming. The cavalry clash had cost him the advantage of complete surprise, but he knew his troops were in better shape for an
assault than for a retreat back down nine miles of churned-up road. Zollicoffer
launched the attack, and at first he met with some success; the Federals recoiled
from that first shock. But things went wrong in the Confederate ranks almost
from the beginning. The men were cold and hungry, exhausted from their all-
night march; the exhilaration of the charge burnt up what little energy they had
left. Also, their flintlocks would not fire when wet, and the regiments armed
with them had to be sent to the rear. Discouraged by all this, they saw the blue
troops massing thick and thicker as Thomas brought up reinforcements from
across the creek, whose flood stage Crittenden had mis-estimated.

★

The crowning blow, however, came when Zollicoffer lost his sense of direction in the rain. Conspicuous in a white rubber coat that made him an ideal target, he rode out between the lines, got turned around, and near-sightedly mistook a Federal colonel for one of his own officers. At this point his luck, which had been running strong, ran out. He was shouting an order when the colonel, a man who recognized an advantage when he saw one, leveled his revolver and put a bullet point-blank into Zollicoffer's breast.

A wail went up from the gray ranks; the Tennessean's men had loved him in spite of his rashness—if not, indeed, because of it. Their strength was mostly spent, and now this loss, occurring in plain view, cracked their spirit. They turned and made for the rear. "Betrayed!" they cried as they brushed past their officers. They ran and they kept on running, their panic infecting the other brigade, which also broke. It was Belmont in reverse, except that the Confederates had no gunboats to fall back on, or transports waiting to bear them away. Thomas replenished his ammunition and set out in pursuit, but his adversaries were well down the Beech Grove road by then. Under cover of darkness they

A Federal colonel shoots and kills Confederate General Zollicoffer in a fanciful engraving of the close-range fighting at Mill Springs.

★

crossed the Cumberland in relays on a rickety sternwheeler, which they burned against the southern bank. In the battle and the evacuation they lost more than 500 men, while the Federals, losing less than half as many, captured 12 guns, 1000 horses and mules, 150 wagons, and half a dozen regimental colors. By the time the pursuers could effect a crossing, there was scarcely anything left to pursue. Retreating through a region which so many of its men called home, Crittenden's army had practically ceased to exist.

Tactically complete as the Confederate defeat had been, it did not turn out to be strategically disastrous. Crossing the Cumberland, Thomas entered a region even more barren than the one he left, and though he put his men on half rations, intending to move on Knoxville, the rain continued and the roads were bottomless. He withdrew, and what was left of Crittenden's army finally called a halt at Chestnut Mound, about sixty miles from Nashville.

The respite was welcome, but it did not erase the fact that the Confederacy had suffered its first drubbing in the field. There had to be an explanation — or, failing that, a scapegoat — and Crittenden was the logical target for accusing fingers. "Betrayed!" the men had cried as they broke and fled. Investigation of what this meant turned up some strange answers, including testimony that the commanding general had been "in an almost beastly state of intoxication" throughout the battle. Remembering that his brother was a Union general, people began to suspect that his heart was not in the cause. There was even a rumor that one of his messengers had been captured bearing information to Thomas. The South had no Joint Committee, such as the North had after the Ball's Bluff fiasco; Crittenden was spared the fate of his Federal counterpart, General Stone, languishing now in a dungeon in New York harbor. But the South had other methods. Eventually a court of inquiry found the Kentuckian innocent of treason but guilty of intoxication. He was reduced to the rank of colonel, and presently he resigned to serve as a civilian on the staff of an obscure brigadier in the Transmississippi, the dustbin of the Confederate army.

That was still in the future, though, and Johnston had nothing to do with it. For the present, he wired Crittenden to regroup his men and offer whatever resistance he could if Thomas came on after him. The western commander had graver worries closer to Bowling Green, where he had set up his headquarters as the best location from which to survey his long, tenuous line. For while Buell was lunging at his right, Halleck was probing his left — particularly at the point of double danger, where the incompleted forts stood guarding the parallel rivers that pierced his front.

It was here that Johnston was most touchy, and with good cause. Arriving in late November, the engineering brigadier Tilghman had reported: "I have completed a thorough examination of Henry and Donelson and do not admire the aspect of things." He wanted more troops, muskets for his unarmed

Lloyd Tilghman, commander of Fort Henry, a Maryland-born aristocrat, graduated from West Point but was working as a railroad engineer when the war broke out.

men, and "more heavy guns for both places at once." The report had a gloomy, determined ending: "I feel for the first time discouraged, but will not give up."

Tilghman's gloom was warranted. Neither of the forts was in anything resembling a condition for offering stiff resistance to amphibious attacks. To make matters worse, Fort Henry was located on low ground, dominated by heights across the river and subject to flooding when the river rose. He later declared outright, "The history of military engineering records no parallel to this case."

One solution was to relocate the forts. Another was to fortify the opposite heights. Pondering which was preferable, he did neither. Johnston meanwhile sent him what he could, so that by mid-January Tilghman had 5700 troops: 3400 at Henry and 2300 at Donelson. Then came Buell's lunge and Halleck's probe. Both withdrew, Buell because of the rain and lack of rations, Halleck because he had only intended a feint; but Johnston knew they would be back soon enough. Three days after the Mill Springs rout, announcing the death

★

of Zollicoffer and predicting a Federal strike against the forts, he made a final appeal to the Adjutant General: "The country must now be roused to make the greatest effort that it will be called upon to make during the war. No matter what the sacrifice may be, it must be made, and without loss of time ... All the resources of the Confederacy are now needed for the defense of Tennessee."

Now as before, Johnston did what he could with what he had. He sent Pillow to Clarksville, sixty miles down the railroad, within supporting distance of the forts. Floyd and Buckner were sent with their brigades to Russellville, midway between Pillow and himself, within reach of both. Then, as January wore to a close, he learned to his dismay that Tilghman at Fort Henry was still pondering whether to fortify the high ground across the river. "It is most extraordinary," Johnston exclaimed. "I ordered General Polk four months ago to at once construct those works. And now, with the enemy on us, nothing of importance has been done. It is most extraordinary."

Mastering his alarm as best he could, he wired Tilghman: "Occupy and intrench the heights opposite Fort Henry. Do not lose a moment. Work all night."

★ ★ ★   Johnston was not the only commander alarmed by the success of Buell's lieutenant in East Kentucky. On the day after the battle, still not having heard the news, Henry Halleck returned to his desk after a four-day bout with the measles. During his time in bed he had reconsidered the suggested move against Nashville by means of a two-pronged advance up the Cumberland and the Tennessee. He no longer considered the operation "madness." In fact, he wrote McClellan that Monday morning, such an advance would follow "the great central line of the Western theater of war." However, he was quick to add, the movement should not be launched without a force of at least 60,000 effectives. As for Buell's proposed simultaneous advance upon the Tennessee capital, he considered it neither wise nor necessary. It was "bad strategy," he wrote, "because it requires a double force to accomplish a single object." Halleck wanted a one-man show, with Halleck as the man.

Having dispatched his letter to the General-in-Chief, the convalescent author of the *Elements of Military Art and Science* sat back and scratched his elbows. It was then that the news of Fishing Creek arrived, and the effect was as if a bomb had been exploded under his desk. What Thomas had done for Buell in eastern Kentucky was comparable to what Rosecrans had done for McClellan in western Virginia the year before. McClellan's elevation had followed swiftly after Philippi: so might Buell's after Fishing Creek—especially considering the fact that the advance had opened the way to East Tennessee, which everyone knew was Lincoln's pet concern. In the glare of that bomb-burst, Halleck saw his worst fears outlined stark before him: Buell might get the West.

That changed everything. Before he could consider what to do, however, he must somehow recover from the paralyzing shock which was his first reaction to the news. U. S. Grant returned to Cairo on the same day Halleck got up from the measles; his demonstration to immobilize Polk had not only been successful, it had given him ideas. "A fine reconnaissance," he called it, and requested permission to visit St Louis for a discussion with the commanding general. Halleck by now had the news from East Kentucky. "You have permission to visit headquarters," he replied, as if in a daze, and by Friday Grant was there. He found Halleck vague and noncommittal, still suffering from the shock of his rival's success. Consequently, the interview fell flat. "I was received with so little cordiality," Grant later declared, "that I perhaps stated the object of my visit with less clearness than I might have done, and I had not uttered many sentences before I was cut short as if my plan was preposterous." He returned to Cairo "very much crestfallen."

He was not crestfallen long. On his return he found a dispatch from Brigadier General C. F. Smith, who had demonstrated up the Tennessee while Grant had been pretending to threaten Columbus. Smith was sixty, with a ramrod stiffness, a habit of profanity, and a white walrus mustache. He had been commandant of cadets when Grant was at West Point, but now, as was often the case with old line officers who had stayed in the service, he was outranked by the volunteer commander and came under his authority. His advance had taken him down near the Tennessee line, within three miles of the fort on the east bank of the river, and in his report to Grant he stated flatly, "I think two ironclad gunboats would make short work of Fort Henry."

On his visit with Halleck in St Louis the week before, Grant had proposed a general forward movement. Now here was something specific. Returning to the charge, he promptly wired:

Cairo, January 28

Maj. Gen. H. W. Halleck

Saint Louis, Mo.:

With permission, I will take Fort Henry on the

Tennessee, and establish and hold a large camp there.

U. S. Grant

Brigadier General.

★

Halleck was just emerging from his state of shock. Perhaps by now he was even beginning to hear the words Grant had spoken three days ago, before he cut him short. At any rate, he saw that he must accomplish something to counterbalance the success his rival had scored at the opposite end of the line, and on second thought this looked like just the something. A week back, he had told McClellan that the advance up the rivers should not be undertaken by a force of less than 60,000 effectives. Grant had barely one-third that many men, including Smith's. However, leery as Halleck was of the wild man of Belmont, he knew that when Grant said plainly, "I will take Fort Henry," it meant an all-out effort and quick movement by field-hardened troops. There was the risk that Polk might move forward from Columbus, threatening the line of the Ohio while Grant was on his way southward up the Tennessee, but Halleck thought this unlikely, considering the success of the recent feint in that direction.

He was still pondering his decision when a telegram arrived from McClellan, reporting that a rebel deserter had just informed him that Beauregard was leaving Manassas to go to Kentucky with fifteen regiments of Confederate infantry. That resolved Halleck's final doubt. He would strike before Beauregard arrived. Next morning, Thursday the 30th, he wired Grant: "Make your preparations to take and hold Fort Henry. I will send you written instructions by mail."

Fort Henry being in Tennessee, he availed himself of the opportunity to request an enlargement of the area of his command, wiring McClellan: "I respectfully suggest that that state be added to this department." One thing remained to be done: inform Buell. With his campaign launched beyond any possibility of his rival's being able to claim a hand in its inception — but not too late to call on him for help if help was needed — Halleck telegraphed him curtly: "I have ordered an advance of our troops on Fort Henry and Dover. It will be made immediately." Now it was Buell's turn to be shocked at rival progress. "I protest against such prompt proceedings," he wrote McClellan, "as though I had nothing to do but command 'Commence firing' when he starts off."

The written instructions Halleck had promised his lieutenant were short and to the point, giving the latest intelligence on the strength of the fort, repeating McClellan's warning that Beauregard was on the way with reinforcements, and including the sentence, "You will move with the least delay possible." Knowing his man, Halleck knew that such words were as apt to produce results as a yank on the lanyard of a well-primed cannon. Grant's reply, from Paducah during the daylight hours of February 3, was the briefest yet: "Will be off up the Tennessee at 6 o'clock. Command, twenty-three regiments in all." And so it was. In the gathering dusk the transports slipped their moorings. The campaign to take Fort Henry was under way.

Connecticut Yankee Andrew Foote (right) commanded the Federal flotilla of Eads-built gunboats, two of which are seen (below) under construction at the Carondolet shipyards near St Louis.

*I*n the lead were four ironclad gunboats, unlike any ever seen before on this or any river. They were the invention, the product—and at this stage the property—of James B. Eads, who had built them in one hundred days on an army contract let to him in August, when they were intended, along with three others, to constitute the hard core of the column that would accomplish Frémont's lopping descent of the Mississippi. The Pathfinder was gone now, along with his plan, but the gunboats remained. Designed for river fighting, they were 175 feet long and a bit over 50 feet in the beam. Two and one-half inch overlapping plates of armor were bolted to the bows to give protection from head-on fire, and the sides were sloped at 35° to deflect shots taken broadside. For armament they mounted thirteen guns apiece, three at the bow, two at the stern, and four on each side. Despite the weight of all this metal, they were surprisingly maneuverable and drew only six feet of water: which meant, in river parlance, that they could "run on a heavy dew."

Eads, a native of Indiana and a man of industry, was one of those included in the southern sneer at the North as "a race of pasty-faced mechanics." When he arrived in St Louis to start work on his contract, the trees from which he would hew timbers were still standing in the forests. Within two weeks he had 4000 men at work around the clock, Sundays not excepted. When he ran out of money he used his own, and when that gave out he borrowed more from friends. By the end of November he had launched eight gunboats, a formidable squadron aggregating 5000 tons, with a cruising speed of nine knots an hour and an armament of 107 guns. The government was less prompt in payment, though, than Eads was in delivery. He still had not been reimbursed when the fleet set out for Henry: so that, technically, the ironclads were still his own.

The turtle-back steamers were not a navy project; the admirals left such harebrained notions to the army. For the most part, even the sailors aboard the boats were soldiers, volunteers from Grant's command who had answered a call for river- and seafaring men to transfer for gunboat service. Once the fleet was launched and manned, however, the navy saw its potential and was willing to furnish captains for its quarterdecks. Having made the offer, which was quickly accepted, the admirals did not hold back, but sent some of their most promising officers westward for service on the rivers. None among them was more distinguished, more experienced—or tougher—than the man assigned to flag command.

Commodore Andrew H. Foote was a Connecticut Yankee, a small man with burning eyes, a jutting gray chin-beard, and a long, naked upper lip. A veteran who had fought the Chinese at Canton and chased slavers in the South Atlantic, he was deeply, puritanically religious, and conducted a Bible school for his crew every Sunday, afloat or ashore. Twenty years before, he had had the first temperance ship in the U.S. Navy, and before the present year was out he would realize a lifelong ambition by seeing the alcohol ration abolished throughout the service. At fifty-six he had spent forty years as a career officer fighting the two things he hated most, slavery and whiskey. It was perhaps a quirk of fate to have placed him thus alongside Grant, who could scarcely be said to have shown an aversion for either. But if fate had juxtaposed them so, in hopes that they would strike antagonistic sparks, then fate was disappointed. Foote, like Grant, believed in combined operations, and had joined with him in bombarding Halleck with telegrams urging the undertaking of this one. Army and Navy, the commodore said, "were like blades of shears—united, invincible; separated, almost useless."

So built, so manned and led, the fleet put out in the rainy, early February darkness, southward up the swollen Tennessee: four ironclads and three wooden gunboats escorting nine transports with their cargo of blue-clad soldiers, the first of Grant's two divisions, which together totaled 15,000 men. Having landed the first, the transports would return downriver to bring the second forward; then the two would move together against the fort, the gunboats meanwhile taking it under bombardment. The initial problem was to locate a landing place as near the objective as possible and yet beyond the range of its big guns. One complication was Panther Creek, which flowed westward into the river, a little over three miles north of the fort. A landing north of the creek would mean that the troops would have to cross or go around it. That was undesirable, involving problematical delay. Yet a landing south of the creek might bring the transports under the rebel guns, with resultant havoc and probable disaster. Grant must first determine their range. He did so, characteristically, in the quickest, simplest way: by personal reconnaissance. Halting the fleet in the cold predawn darkness, eight miles short of the fort, he ordered three of the ironclads forward to draw the fire of the guns, and boarded one of them, the *Essex,* to go along and find out for himself.

He found out soon enough. The ironclads steamed past the creek mouth and opened fire within two miles of the fort. The answering shells fell short until a 6-inch rifle came into action, splashing its first shot not only beyond the gunboats, but beyond the mouth of the creek as well. Grant now had the information he wanted; no landing could be made south of the creek without bringing the transports under fire. But then the rifle's gunner made the information even more emphatic by demonstrating the kind of marksmanship the gunboats would encounter in an attack against Fort Henry. Shortening the range, he put the next shot squarely into the *Essex.* Having secured the information they sought, and more, the ironclads turned and went back down the river, the wounded *Essex* bringing up the rear with a 6-inch shell in her steerage and a wiser troop commander on her bridge.

Now that he knew how to do what must be done, Grant went back

An 1862 map prepared by the U.S. Topographical Engineers shows the terrain around Fort Henry, including Confederate fortifications and the point where Grant's troops landed.

to get the movement started. The fleet proceeded southward, landing the First division north of the creek, and while the empty transports set out downriver on their hundred-mile round trip to bring the Second division forward, he completed the details of his attack plan. The key to the position, he saw — Belmont having taught him just how briefly troops could hold an objective which came under the plunging fire of enemy guns — was the high ground on the west bank, dominating the low-lying fort across the river. Reconnaissance had drawn no fire from there and Grant had been able to spot no guns through his glasses.

But that was inconclusive. Intelligence had warned him that the Confederates were at work there; the batteries might be masked, under orders to hold their fire until a target worth their powder hove in view. Therefore he assigned the Second division the task of seizing the left-bank heights, planting artillery there, while the First division moved against the fort itself, angling around the head of Panther Creek to come in from the east and thus prevent the escape of the garrison in case it tried to retreat from under the fleet bombardment.

How large that garrison was he did not know. There was no way of telling how many reinforcements might have arrived overland from Donelson, twelve miles away, or by rail from Bowling Green or Memphis, since the defenders first learned of the task force moving up the Tennessee. In any case, the right-bank attack would be the main effort, and he detached one brigade from the Second division, which had three, ordering it to land on the eastern bank and support the First division, which had two. One more detachment from the Second division, a rifle company to act as sharpshooters on the warships, and Grant's attack plan was complete. If Fort Henry could be taken by 15,000 men and seven gunboats, he was going to take it.

There were other problems: the fact that the river was mined, for instance, which meant that at any minute any vessel, ironclad or transport, was apt to go sky-high in smoke and flame, the attacking force reduced to that extent by quick subtraction. Contact mines, or "torpedoes" as they were called, were a new and formidable weapon, a fiendish example of rebel ingenuity. Anchored to the river-bottom by cables that held them upright underwater, they were equipped with pronged rods extending upward to just below the surface, ready to trip the detonators on contact. The rising river had reduced their effectiveness, some being submerged by now beyond scraping distance and others floating around loose, torn from their moorings; but there was still a good deal of conjecture and concern about them.

On the afternoon of the 5th, while in conference with Foote and the two division commanders aboard the flagship, Grant got a chance to make a firsthand inspection of one of these new implements of war. A gunboat tied up alongside and her captain sent word that he had fished a torpedo out of the river. He had it there on deck, he said, in case the commodore and the generals wanted to see it. They did indeed want to see it, if only as a diversion. The conference was about finished anyhow; little remained to be done except to await the arrival of the Second division, still being brought in relays from Paducah. Crossing over to the gunboat, the commodore and his aides and the generals and their staffs clustered on the fantail and stood in a semicircle looking down at the torpedo.

It appeared to be quite as dangerous as they had feared. A metal cylinder five feet long and a foot and a half in diameter, the thing was made especially venomous-looking by the pronged rod extending from its head. Grant wanted more than a look, however. He wanted to know how it worked. So the ship's armorer came with his wrenches and chisels, and while he tinkered the interested officers watched. Suddenly, as he was loosening a nut, the device emitted an ominous hissing sound, which seemed to be mounting swiftly toward a climax. The reaction of the watchers was immediate. Some ran, exploding outward from the semicircular cluster, while others threw themselves facedownward on the deck. Rank had no precedent; it was each man for himself.

Foote sprang for the ship's ladder, and Grant, perhaps reasoning that in naval matters the commodore knew best, was right behind him. If he lacked the seaman's agility in climbing a rope ladder, he made up for it with what one witness called "commendable enthusiasm." At the top, the commodore looked back over his shoulder and found Grant closing rapidly upon him. The hissing had stopped. Whatever danger there had been was past. Foote smiled.

"General, why this haste?" he asked, and his words, though calmly spoken, were loud against the silence.

"That the navy may not get ahead of us," Grant replied.

───────── ⚬⚬⚬ ─────────

★ ★ ★ *L*loyd Tilghman was slim and dark-skinned, with a heavy, carefully barbered mustache and chin-beard, an erect, soldierly bearing, and piercing black eyes intensifying what one observer called "a resolute, intelligent expression of countenance." His resolution had not waned, but after two days of watching the Federal build-up to his front, he was beginning to realize that the fate of the fort was scarcely less predictable than that of a shoe-nail about to be driven by a very large sledge-hammer lustily swung.

His 3400 men were miserably armed with hunting rifles, shotguns, and 1812-style flintlocks, and his cannon were scarcely better. Two out of a shipment cast from what looked like pot-metal had burst in target practice, and several others had been condemned, a British observer pronouncing them less dangerous to the enemy than to the men who served them. Tilghman was threatened, in fact, by more than the gunboats and the blue-clad infantry, and weakened by more than the shortage of serviceable arms. In one week, back in mid-January when the rains came, the river had risen fourteen feet, demonstrating graphically the unwisdom of the engineers who had sited Fort Henry at this particular bend of the Tennessee. Only nine of the fifteen guns bearing riverward remained above water in early February, and now while the river continued to rise, lapping at last at the magazine, it had become a question of which would get there first, flood crest or the Yankees.

In spite of all this, the Kentucky brigadier did not despair when his lookout, peering downriver through the rainy dawn of the 4th, announced the approach of gunboats and behind them the coal-smoke plumes of the transports winding northward out of sight. Determined to fight, he wired Polk for reinforcements from Columbus, and the following day, having turned back the ironclad reconnaissance and seen that the Federals were landing in force, three miles north of the fort, he wired Johnston at Bowling Green: "If you can reinforce strongly and quickly we have a glorious chance to overwhelm the enemy." Accordingly, he sent his troops with their squirrel guns and fowling pieces to man the rifle pits blocking the landward approaches. If no help came, he would fight with what he had.

However, as the day wore on and the transports returned with further relays of northern troops, he began to realize the full length of the odds — particularly on the opposite bank, where the Union brigades were landing and preparing to move against the unfinished, unmanned works on the high ground which dominated the shipwrecked fort on this side. Without losing his resolution to give battle, he saw clearly that whoever stood on this nailhead, under the swing of that sledge, was going to be destroyed; and he saw, too, that, whatever his personal inclination, his military duty was to save what he could of a command whose doom was all but sealed.

At a council of war, called that night in the fort — the enemy buildup continued, seemingly endless, three miles downriver, on both banks — he announced his decision. While a sacrifice garrison manned whatever guns were yet above water, discouraging pursuit, the infantry would be evacuated, marching overland to join the troops at Donelson. Next morning a company of Tennessee artillery, two officers and 54 men, took their posts at the guns, awaiting the attack they knew was coming, while the foot soldiers filed out of the rifle pits and the fort, taking the road eastward.

Tilghman went a certain distance to see them on their way, and then, still resolute, turned back to join the forlorn hope. It was noon by now. As he drew near, the sound of guns came booming across water.

★ ★ ★ Two-thirds by land, one-third by water, Grant's triple-pronged upriver attack, designed as a simultaneous advance by the two divisions, one along each bank while the gunboats took the middle, was slated to get under way at 11 o'clock, by which time the final relay of troops had arrived from Paducah. Both infantry columns went forward on schedule, but Foote, on his own initiative, held back until almost noon, allowing the landsmen at least a measure of the head start they needed. The rain had stopped; the sun came through, defining the target clearly, and there was even a light breeze to clear away the battle smoke and permit the rapid and accurate fire the commodore expected of his gunners. For almost an hour the crews stood by — converted soldiers and fresh-water sailors bracing themselves for their first all-out action, with "just enough men-of-war's men," as one skipper said, "to leaven the lump with naval discipline" — until the attack pennant was hoisted and the squadron moved upstream, the ironclads steaming four abreast in the lead and the three wooden gunboats bringing up the rear.

"The flagship will, of course, open the fire," Foote had ordered, and at 1700 yards she did so. The others joined the chorus, firing as many of their 54 guns as could be brought to bear on the fort, whose nine gun-crews stood to their pieces and replied at once in kind, loosing what one of the defenders proudly called "as pretty and as simultaneous a 'broadside' as I ever saw flash from the sides of a frigate." This continued. Preceded by "one broad and leaping sheet of flame," as the same defender said, the ironclads deliberately closed the range to

---

Aboard the warships, men were deafened by the din of solid shot pounding and breaking the iron plates and splintering heavy timbers, while shells screamed and whistled in the rigging, bursting, raining fragments.

---

600 yards while the more vulnerable wooden vessels hugged the western bank, adding the weight of their metal to the pressure on the earthworks.

Based as it was on predetermined ranges, fire from the fort was accurate and fast. For a time at least, the Tennessee artillerists seemed to be inflicting the greater damage. Aboard the warships, men were deafened by the din of solid shot pounding and breaking the iron plates and splintering heavy timbers, while shells screamed and whistled in the rigging, bursting, raining fragments. Foote's flagship, the prime target, was struck thirty-two times in the course of the action, two of her guns disabled and her stacks, boats, and after-cabin riddled. The captain of the ironclad on her left, which took thirty hits, said of one shot which he saw strike the flagship, "It had the effect, apparently, of a thunderbolt, ripping her side timbers and scattering the splinters over the vessel. She did not slacken her speed, but moved on as though nothing special had happened." Not so the luckless *Essex*. Patched up from the hurt she had received two days ago, she took another now through her boiler: an unlucky shot which left her powerless in a cloud of escaping steam, with twenty-eight scalded men aboard, some dead and

*The six-inch gun in Fort Henry explodes
during the Federal attack, killing a sergeant
and wounding the rest of the crew.*

others dying. Out of control, she swung broadside to the current, then careened, leaving a gap in the line of battle, and drifted downstream, out of the fight.

　　　　Encouraged by this proof that the turtle-back monsters could be hurt, the defenders cheered and redoubled their efforts. But they had done their worst—in fact, their all: for now there followed a series of accidents and mishaps which abolished whatever chance they had had for victory at the outset.

★

Only two of their guns could really damage the ironclads, the high-velocity 6-inch rifle, which had already proved its effectiveness, and a giant columbiad which made up for its lack of range by the heft of its 128-pound projectile. The rest, low-sited as they were, with their muzzles near the water, could do no more than bounce their 32- and 42-pound shells off the armored prows of the attackers. First to go was the rifle, which burst in firing, disabling not only its own crew, but also those of the flanking pieces. Next, the big columbiad was spiked by a broken priming wire and thus put out of action, despite the efforts of a blacksmith who attempted to repair it under fire. Of the seven cannon left, which could only dent the armor and shiver the timbers of the gunboats, one had to be abandoned for lack of ammunition and two were wrecked almost at once by enemy shells. That left four guns to face the fire of the attackers, the range now being closed, almost point-blank, and even those four were served by skeleton crews, scraped together from among the survivors.

These included Tilghman. The fort commander had returned from seeing the infantry off, and was serving as a cannoneer at one of the four pieces. He had asked the artillerists to hold out for an hour, affording the garrison that much of a head start on its march to Donelson. Now that they had held out two, with the long odds growing longer all the time, the tactical considerations had been satisfied twice over, and those of honor as well. He ordered the flag struck. It was done and the firing ceased.

★ ★ ★ "That the navy may not get ahead of us," Grant had said, and it was as if he spoke from prescience. In the combined attack, as in the scramble up the ladder, Foote came out on top. The navy fired not only the first shot and the last, but also all the shots between, and suffered all the casualties as well: 12 killed and missing and 27 wounded, compared to the fort's 10 killed and missing and 11 wounded. In fact, the navy's closest rival was not the army, but the river. Another few hours would have put

the remaining cannon under water. As it was, the cutter bearing the naval officers to receive the formal surrender pulled right in through the sally port.

Tilghman was waiting for them. He had already earned their respect
by his bravery as an opponent, and now, by the dignity of his bearing as a prisoner, he won their sympathy as well. However, his reception of the copy-hungry
northern correspondents, who were soon on hand to question him, was less
congenial. As a southern gentleman he believed there were only three events in
a man's life which warranted the printing of his name without permission: his
birth, his marriage, and his death. So that when a Chicago reporter asked him
how he spelled his name, he replied in measured terms: "Sir, I do not desire to
have my name appear in this matter, in any newspaper connection whatever. If
General Grant sees fit to use it in his official dispatches, I have no objection, sir;
but I do not wish to have it in the newspapers."

"I merely asked it to mention as one among the prisoners captured," the correspondent said. But the Confederate either did not catch the
dig or else ignored it.

"You will oblige me, sir," he repeated, as if this put an end to the
matter, "by not giving my name in any newspaper connection whatever."

Grant arrived at 3 o'clock, by which time the Stars and Stripes had
been flying over the fort for nearly an hour. His two divisions were still toiling
through the mud on opposite banks of the river, one bogged down in the back-
water sloughs of Panther Creek and the other slogging toward the empty western heights. Who won the race meant less to him, however, than the winning —

★

An engraving published in Leslie's Illustrated depicts Federal troops occupying the flooded earthworks of Fort Henry the morning after its capture.

and neither meant so much, apparently, as the fact that more remained to be accomplished. He had his mind on the railroad bridge fifteen miles upriver, over which Johnston could speed reinforcements from flank to flank of his line. The three wooden gunboats were dispatched at once to attend to it: which they did in fine style that same day. Nor was that all. Continuing on to Muscle Shoals, the head of navigation, they destroyed or captured six Confederate vessels, including a fast, 280-foot Mississippi steamboat being converted into an ironclad. Intended as an answer to the fleet of the invaders, she became instead a member of that fleet and saw much service.

This 150-mile gunboat thrust, all the way down past Mississippi and into Alabama, was dramatic proof of the fruits resulting from control of the Tennessee. A highway of invasion had been cleared. Yet Grant had his eye on another goal already, another fort on another river a dozen miles from the one he had just taken: as was shown by his wire to the theater commander on the day of his success. "Fort Henry is ours," the dispatch began, and ended with a forecast: "I shall take and destroy Fort Donelson on the 8th and return to Fort Henry."

Halleck passed the word along as promptly to McClellan, repeating Grant's first sentence and adding two of his own: "Fort Henry is ours. The flag of the Union is reëstablished on the soil of Tennessee. It will never be removed."

★ ★ ★

Epilogue

en months into the war, Lincoln and Davis — so similar and yet so different — sat in White Houses barely one hundred miles apart and pondered the future of their nations. Territorially the lines were drawn close to where they would remain for the duration of the war. Soon after Fort Sumter was surrendered, Virginia, Tennessee, North Carolina, and Arkansas had swelled the original Confederate ranks from seven to eleven states. Judicious Federal political and military maneuvers were in the process of holding Delaware, Maryland, and Kentucky in the Union camp, where Missouri would presently join them.

Both sides had hoped for an easy, three-month conflict, ending in one winner-take-all battle. But that hope had faded in the light of bloody fighting, East and West. Each side could claim victories. Among them, the South had Fort Sumter, Big Bethel, Wilson's Creek, Manassas, and Belmont, while the North had Rich and Cheat Mountains, Hatteras Inlet, Ship Island, Port Royal Sound, and Fort Henry. However, at this time, neither could claim a real advantage over the other.

Strategically, Davis and Lincoln had the same goal. Each man had pledged to protect the sovereignty of his respective nation. Lincoln, elected President of all of the United States, chose to attack, and thus drag the seceded states back into the Union. Davis, on the other hand, chosen to lead the Confederacy out of that Union, opted for a static defense, to let the Yankees come and try to take away his country's recently declared independence. He also sought the political and material backing of foreign nations. Southern attempts to gain European recognition had led to The Trent Affair, and the North had only narrowly averted going to war with Great Britain through some adroit diplomatic maneuvering. Davis' plans had been thwarted. The nations across the Atlantic remained reluctant to offer open aid to the new Confederacy.

As they fought each other, the warring nations were plagued by internal squabbles that, at times, appeared to doom their cause. Each looked for the right combination of political leaders, men who could work peaceably together toward the common goal of destroying the enemy. Both presidents had to wrestle with, and shuffle around, their fractious cabinets.

Militarily, both sides seemed to have plenty of potential associates, many of them West Point trained and Mexican War blooded. The Confederate roster had Albert Sidney Johnston, P. G. T. Beauregard, Joseph E. Johnston, Robert E. Lee, and Thomas J. Jackson. The Federal list included Winfield Scott, Henry W. Halleck, Irvin McDowell, George B. McClellan, Don Carlos Buell, and Ulysses S. Grant. But, like their political counterparts, they too argued, almost childishly at times. All had looked promising at the outset. A few seemed initially to meet or exceed their nations' expectations, while many had thus far been disappointments. All would show their true colors in the months to come.

Looking back, Lincoln realized that, although Scott's Anaconda Plan had been ridiculed at first, Federal gains on the southern coast, in western Virginia, in the border states, and down the western rivers seemed to prove that the serpent was alive and well. While that northern serpent ruffled at the fringes of the Confederacy, Davis could see that the southern heartland, including Richmond, seemed secure behind defensive lines, especially following the drubbings given to the Yankees at Manassas, Wilson's Creek, Ball's Bluff, and Belmont. Apparently it would remain safe for a good long time. Neither man could foresee, however, that during the next few months, even though Federals planned an end run up the York-James peninsula toward Richmond, and Confederates would enliven things in the Shenandoah Valley, west of Washington, all would remain fairly quiet in the East. Nor could they envision that there would soon be important battles in the West. The serpent's coils would seem to draw a bit tighter about the rebel domain after the upcoming clashes at Fort Donelson, Shiloh, New Orleans, Corinth, and Memphis. In the remote Far West, the so-called Transmississippi Department, the battle at Pea Ridge, Arkansas, would determine Missouri's fate, and New Mexico Territory would be fought for at places like Valverde and Glorieta Pass.

As the two presidents, Janus-like, contemplated the past and present states of their nations, neither could guess the outcome of the war. They both knew, however, that recent events were but a prologue, marking the end of the beginning. There was much to be done.

★   ★   ★

Picture Credits

Dust jacket: front, Valentine Museum, Richmond; rear, Library of Congress, Neg. No. B8184-10006; flap, photo by Larry Shirkey.

12-14: Courtesy Meserve-Kunhardt Collection. 16: Library of Congress. 19: Kentucky Historical Society, Frankfort. 22, 23: Courtesy of Mississippi Department of Archives and History, Jackson. 23: Museum of the Confederacy, Richmond. 26: Library of Congress, Neg. No. Z62-5962. 29: Dartmouth College Library; Hanover, NH; Collection of the New-York Historical Society. 31: Collection of The New-York Historical Society. 35: Library of Congress, Neg. No. Z62-7992. 38: Courtesy Meserve-Kunhardt Collection. 39: Brown University Library, Providence. 42: Library of Congress, Neg. No. Z62-12457; Library of Congress, Neg. No. Z62-12458. 45: Courtesy Meserve-Kunhardt Collection. 49: Library of Congress. 52: Kansas State Historical Society, Topeka-Courtesy of the B & O Railroad Museum, Inc., Baltimore. 55: Chicago Historical Society, Neg. No. ICHi-22208. 56: Courtesy Meserve-Kunhardt Collection. 58-60: Library of Congress/Photri-Microstock. 63: Courtesy Museum of Fine Arts, Boston. 65: Library of Congress. 66: Chicago Historical Society, Neg. No. ICHi-12644. 68: The National Archives. 72: Valentine Museum , Richmond. 75: from *The Genesis of the Civil War*, by Samuel Wylie Crawford, published by Charles L. Webster & Company, New York, 1867. 79: National Archives, Neg. No. 111BA-1226. 80: Courtesy National Park Service, photographed by Mike Wiltshire—William Clements Library, University of Michigan, Ann Arbor. 85: Collection of The New-York Historical Society. 88: Courtesy of the Atwater Kent Museum, Philadelphia. 90-92: Collection of The New-York Historical Society. 94: Massachusetts Commandery Military Order of the Loyal Legion and the U.S. Army History Institute, Carlisle Barracks, Pa. MASS-MOLLUS/USAMHI. 96: Library of Congress, Neg. No. T38171 7542. 99: Museum of the Confederacy, Richmond, photographed by Henry Beville. 100: Courtesy, Georgia Department of Archives and History, Atlanta. 106, 107: Courtesy of the Boston Athenaeum. 109: Library of Congress—collection of The New-York Historical Society. 111: Library of Congress, Waud #738. 114-116: Courtesy Larry Freeman, American Life Foundation, photographed by Lon Mattoon. 118: Library of Congress, Neg. No. B8184-4099. 121: Map by

Walter Roberts. 123: Courtesy South Caroliniana Library, University of South Carolina, Columbia. 125: Courtesy of Stonewall Jackson Foundation, Lexington, Va.—Virginia Military Institute Museum, Virginia Military Institute, Lexington, Va., photographed by Larry Sherer. 128, 129: M. and M. Karolik Collection, courtesy Museum of Fine Arts, Boston. 134-136: Library of Congress. 138: Courtesy Meserve-Kunhardt Collection. 143: State Historical Society of Missouri, Columbia. 146: Prints Division, The New York Public Library, Astor, Lenox and Tilden Foundations. 152, 153: Library of Congress. 155: National Archives, Neg. No. 111-B-4385. 160: National Archives, Neg. No. 111-B-3804. 163: John M. Nielson Collection. 165: Library of Congress, Neg. No. BH8301-1732. 168-170: The Western Reserve Historical Society, Cleveland. 172: MASS-MOLLUS/USAMHI, copied by Robert Walch. 176: The New Jersey Historical Society, copied by Henry Groskinsky. 180, 181: U.S. Naval Academy/Beverley R. Robinson Collection. 184-186: National Archives, Neg. No. 111-B-6332. 191: Library of Congress, Neg. No. USZ62-10731—USAMHI, copied by A. Pierce Bounds. 193: Library of Congress, Neg. No. B8184-10658. 194: Cook Collection, Valentine Museum, Richmond. 197: Courtesy Frank & Marie-Thérèse Wood Print Collections, Alexandria, Va. 199: Painting by William Edward West, Washington/ Custis/Lee Collection W & L University, Lexington, Va., photographed by Thomas C. Bradshaw. 203: MASS-MOLLUS/ USAMHI. 205: Library of Congress Neg. No. BH82 4613. 206: Collection of The New-York Historical Society. 210: Courtesy National Archives/ Photo Assist, Inc., Washington, D.C. 216: From *The Spy of the Rebellion* by Allan Pinkerton, published by G.W. Dillingham, New York, 1883. 217, 219, 223: Library of Congress. 224, 225: From *The American Soldier in the Civil War*, published by Stanley Bradley Co., New York, (c)1865, courtesy Library of Congress. 231: MASS-MOLLUS/USAMHI. 234: Library of Congress. 239: Courtesy Meserve-Kunhardt Collection. 243: Library of Congress, Neg. No. B8184 10296. 246-248: U.S. Naval Academy, Beverley R. Robinson Collection, Annapolis. 250: Jessie Ball duPont Library, University of the South, Sewanee, Tenn. 254: Map by Peter McGinn. 259, 262: Library of Congress. 264: USAMHI, copied by A. Pierce Bounds. 268: Library of Congress— National Archives, Neg. No. 165-C-702. 271: Library of Congress. 276-278: Courtesy Frank & Marie-Thérèse Wood Print Collections, Alexandria, Va.

★

Index

SHELBY FOOTE, THE CIVIL WAR,
A NARRATIVE
VOLUME 1 SECESSION TO FORT HENRY

Library of Congress Cataloging-in-Publication Data
Foote, Shelby.
  [Civil War, a narrative]
  Shelby Foote, the Civil War, a narrative / by Shelby
Foote and the editors of Time-Life Books.— 40th
Anniversary ed.
      p. cm.
  Originally published: The Civil War, a narrative.
New York : Random House, 1958-1974, in 3 v.
  Includes bibliographical references and indexes.
  Contents: v. 1. Secession to Fort Henry
  ISBN 0-7835-0100-5
  1.United States—History—Civil War, 1861-1865.
I. Time-Life Books. II. Title.
E468.F7 1999   99-13486
973.7—dc21   CIP

For information on and a full description of any
of the Time-Life Books series listed at right,
please call 1-800-621-7026 or write:
Reader Information
Time-Life Customer Service
P.O. Box C-32068
Richmond, Virginia 23261-2068

Time-Life Books is a
division of Time Life Inc.

TIME LIFE INC.
PRESIDENT and CEO: George Artandi

TIME-LIFE BOOKS
PUBLISHER/MANAGING EDITOR: Neil Kagan
VICE PRESIDENT, MARKETING: Joseph A. Kuna
VICE PRESIDENT, NEW PRODUCT
DEVELOPMENT: Amy Golden

PROJECT EDITOR: Philip Brandt George
DIRECTOR, NEW PRODUCT
DEVELOPMENT: Elizabeth D. Ward
DIRECTOR OF MARKETING: Pamela R. Farrell
Design Director: Tina Taylor
Art Director: Ellen L. Pattisall
Marketing Manager: Peter Tardif
Copyeditor: Christine Stephenson
Picture Coordinator: Susan L. Finken
Editorial Assistant: Christine Higgins

Special Contributors: Jane Martin/PhotoAssist,
Beth Levin (research); Melanie Byas, John Drum-
mond, Kimberly Grandcolas, Janet Dell Russell
Johnson, Monika Lynde, Kathleen Mallow, Alan
Pitts, Don Schaaf and Friends, Inc. (design and
production); Roy Nanovic (index).

Correspondent: Christina Lieberman (New York).

Director of Finance: Christopher Hearing
Directors of Book Production: Marjann Caldwell,
Patricia Pascale
Director of Publishing Technology: Betsi McGrath
Director of Photography and Research:
John Conrad Weiser
Director of Editorial Administration: Barbara Levitt
Manager, Technical Services: Anne Topp
Senior Production Manager: Ken Sabol
Quality Assurance Manager: James King
Chief Librarian: Louise D. Forstall

OTHER TIME-LIFE HISTORY PUBLICATIONS

Our American Century
World War II
What Life Was Like
The American Story
Voices of the Civil War
The American Indians
Lost Civilizations
Time Frame
The Civil War
Cultural Atlas
Echoes of Glory